P9-CQP-927

A PASSION FOR Birds

A PASSION FOR

Birds

Dedicated to the

ROYAL SOCIETY FOR THE PROTECTION OF BIRDS

on its centenary

Edited and compiled by

TONY SOPER

DAVID & CHARLES

Newton Abbot · London · North Pomfret (Vt)

FRONTISPIECE: *Gannet/David Hosking*
CONTENTS PAGE: *Tawny Owl/Eric Hosking*

British Library Cataloguing in Publication Data

A Passion for Birds
  1. Birds
  I. Soper, Tony
598

  ISBN 0-7153-9229-8

© 1988 Tony Soper (except where otherwise stated)

All rights reserved. No part of this
publication may be reproduced, stored
in a retrieval system, or transmitted, in
any form or by any means, electronic,
mechanical, photocopying, recording or
otherwise, without the prior permission
of David & Charles Publishers plc

Typeset by Character Graphics,
Taunton, Somerset
and printed in The Netherlands by
Royal Smeets Offset Weert
for David & Charles Publishers plc
Brunel House Newton Abbot Devon

Published in the United States of
America by David & Charles Inc
North Pomfret Vermont 05053 USA

Contents

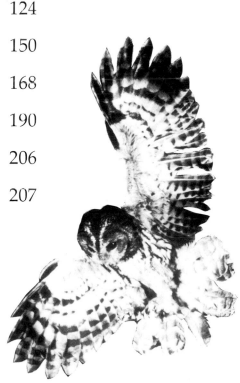

Introduction

It is not easy to define exactly what it is that makes birds so fascinating. Yet although bugs have their admirers and most of us enjoy a warmth for badgers, hedgehogs and even toads, our interests are more firmly held by the astonishing variety of birds. Unlike badgers, they are not even closely related to us, yet it is easier to feel a sense of neighbourliness with them. The mammals which are our close relations tend to be creatures of the night, whose smell is their most important sense. Most birds are active in the daylight hours and make great use of sight and sound, thus tending to live lives which seem more familiar to us. And, best of all, it is not too difficult to *see* them. Their comings and goings, their songs and dances, have parallels in our own lives which make it only too easy to see them as honorary people, and to interpret their behaviour in ways which seem familiar to us. But, of course, the more we learn about them, the more we dimly perceive the complexities of another world.

Birds are not unique in their power of flight. Insects and bats fly with aplomb, we can even do it ourselves with the aid of expensive and extravagant use of resources. But only birds have feathers, and the feather is their secret weapon. Not only does it give them the freedom of the skies but it keeps them warm and it serves as a medium for display in achieving a home and a partner. And the colourful plumage

Grey heron fishing in a reed swamp

J. Watkins/FLPA

Eric & David Hosking

Mute Swans with cygnets

ot birds is one of the delights which gives us so much pleasure. Bird-song is another. Arguably the garden Blackbird
has one of the most musical of all bird-songs, yet we enjoy
it from the comfort of our own home in the season of the
year.

The seasonal comings and goings and changes in bird
activities also provide much of the rich enjoyment of
birdwatching. The song and dance of spring courtship followed by the quiet time of incubation and the frantically
busy time of feeding insatiable gaping chicks. Then the
grand dispersal of autumn followed by the influx of northern
and continental birds which winter with us. And in many
ways winter is the time of greatest activity for birdwatchers.

The distinction between a birdwatcher and an ornithologist becomes ever more difficult to define. Relatively
few people earn a living as professional ornithologists, but
their work is underpinned by a veritable army of amateurs
who collect the nuts and bolts of information which translate
into science. From the moment when you cease simply to
take pleasure in the colour and movement of birds and start
asking questions about their lives, you are in serious danger
of becoming an ornithologist and you will never be bored
again.

Tony Soper

Robin Prytherch

Birdwatching sounds like an idle sort of hobby, and indeed I meet many people who clearly think that most of
my life is spent reclining in a deckchair with a pair of binoculars casually raised occasionally to identify some passing
rarity. Yet, in reality, and quite apart from the fact that I
more often than not have some difficulty in identifying the
passing bird, birding involves a great deal of exertion.
Through the years I have spent long hours tramping moorland, climbing cliffs and mountains, sailing small boats
round islands and headlands, and generally acting like
someone looking for a Duke of Edinburgh's Award. I have

Eric Hosking

Starlings may not be everyone's favourite but they improve on acquaintance!

camped for glorious weeks on uninhabited islands and on tiny cliff ledges on bird cliffs, been nearly frozen and, as doubtless many of my friends would like to say, half baked. But all of it has been hugely enjoyable, if sometimes only in retrospect.

The fact is that while birds are indeed fascinating, bird places are a great part of the attraction. City centres and public parks offer real challenges and pleasures, but think of all the other bird-rich habitats that we visit again and again . . . the glorious mud and saltings of estuaries, with waders and herons to decorate them; streams and valley woodlands with Dippers and Buzzards; open heathland, sadly so rare and extra precious, with its Nightjars and Hobbies; honest farmland with productive insect-rich head-lands to the fields and hedgerows, rushy ponds for Moorhens and the occasional copse for finches and thrushes, the sort of farmland which farmers, so long brain-washed to the concept of 'improving' land with artificial fertilisers, are slowly returning. Good luck to them, and long may we all enjoy the varied birding of our tiny island. In truth, the British Isles may well be only a big island surrounded by a lot of little ones, but we enjoy as varied a range of habitats as you will find anywhere in the world. And that makes it a good place for a birder to live!

This book seeks to remember some of the great pleasures I have had in reading bird books through the years. I acknowledge gratefully the enjoyment I have had from sampling the words of a great number of nature writers, from my first chance discovery of Henry Williamson in the Penzance Public Library, leading to an inevitable discovery of Richard Jefferies and the sea-shore books of Philip Henry Gosse and the incomparable island books of Ronald Lockley. In preparing this offering I have trawled through material published both in book form and in the excellent birdwatching magazines, selecting choice morsels from a variety of sources and attempting to present them as a balanced meal. There are titbits which aim to stimulate the appetite, an array of hors d'oeuvres, some dishes of the day, some more substantial dishes and there are sugary confections for pudding.

The RSPB has reached its centenary year and must now look forward to another century of representing all that is most admirable in the pursuit of the understanding of the birds' place in the scheme of things and the help they need from us. The Society was formed by people who were appalled at the way birds were killed simply in pursuit of fine feathers for fashion-conscious women indifferent to the sufferings inflicted in their name. Through the years the RSPB has grown and aimed its canon in other directions, always in defence of the rights of birds to play their proper part in society. The problems may be different ones today, but we can all be sure that the RSPB will serve us well in fighting the good fight. They have to succeed, for life would be distinctly drabber without the company of birds.

The elegant Avocet is the symbol of the Royal Society for the Protection of Birds

Discovering Birds

What was the first bird you remember seeing? I can't be sure of mine, but I suppose it was most likely a pigeon in the park. Or perhaps it was a Mallard on the pond, seen from the pram. A few years later there were little boats on a park lake that we used to visit on holidays. They were propelled by paddle wheels worked on a pedal system. It was hard work but you could steam in amongst the ducks and the enormous Mute Swans. And those were precious hours which sealed for ever my twin passions for boats and birds. Like birds, all boats are beautiful though again like birds some are more beautiful than others. And a great deal

Feeding Canada Geese in St James's Park, London . . .

Eric & David Hosking

10

of fun lies in finding out why their designs are so different.

I can remember being taken on a 'nature walk' by the parents of one of my school friends. Though I was reluctant to go, it turned out to be a fascinating trip. And I soon realised that it wasn't good enough just to watch for birds; you have to listen as well. They knew a Chaffinch was about, long before they saw it, because they heard the tell-tale 'pink, pink'.

Then a few years more, and one of my jobs was to take my father's lunchbox to him at the wharfside in Plymouth. He worked in the offices, but my best friend there was a docker who came to work in a sturdy punt which he pulled across the Cattewater. Not only did he lend me his boat, but he knew all about Cormorants and Curlews and different kinds of seagulls and he was perfectly happy to talk about them. Later still, I had the good fortune to work for Desmond Hawkins at the BBC in Bristol, when the natural history programmes on radio and television were on the verge of a boom. And so I met people like Peter Scott and James Fisher, Maxwell Knight and Ronald Lockley. All of them were generous with time and knowledge, none of them more so than Ronald Lockley, with whom I have enjoyed glorious weeks sailing and birding the Pembrokeshire coast.

So there's no doubt in my mind that it is the succession

. . . and at Leeds Castle in Kent

Eric & David Hosking

of bird-teachers who are kind enough to give their time and effort to encouraging youngsters to start birdwatching who deserve all the encouragement they can get. And the organisation which most effectively channels this work is the junior branch of the Royal Society for the Protection of Birds. The Young Ornithologists Club publishes one of the liveliest of children's magazines and organises a constant stream of field trips and outings. School groups are an important mainstay of the club, and this anonymous writer is clearly on the brink of forming a new branch – or is she? . .

This is a true story – only one name has been omitted to protect the innocent which I certainly was. Are you sitting comfortably? Then I'll begin.

'Catch them young,' the man from the RSPB headquarters at Sandy had advised, so with missionary zeal and misplaced enthusiasm I embarked upon a 'Feathered Flight' project with my class of socially disadvantaged six-year-olds. We made and erected four bird-tables in all. Three vanished overnight, only to reappear in various gardens on the estate. The fourth fanned the flames of an impromptu Guy Fawkes night – in mid-April. I tried a bird count. The area revealed eighty-four sparrows, three racing pigeons, and one gull, two Rooks and a blue feral Budgerigar which seemed to belong to everyone's gran.

'Why not take them to the country park?' suggested the headmaster. 'There are lots of ducks and swans there.' He declined our invitation to accompany us so, aided by the Welfare Assistant and three mums dressed to kill in white stilettos and Ra Ra skirts, we clambered off the bus.

'Miss! Darren's left his lunch on the bus.' 'Please Miss. That big white duck's gone and eaten my jam and banana butties.' 'It's a swan,' I said crossly as I redistributed the sandwiches, ignoring murmurs of 'I don't like sardines' and 'Me mam gave me Jaffa Cakes not them old Rich Tea rubbish.' 'Miss! Danny's put his foot in something nasty.' And the man from the RSPB had made it all sound so easy . . .

We moved off and an uneasy peace ensued as miniature Mallards tickled little fingers as they took the brown breadcrumbs offered. The whole class stood mercifully still, their faces full of wonder as a grebe sailed majestically by with three babies on its back.

'Miss, Perry is trying to put a duckling in his pocket.' 'Perry! Put that duckling down.' 'Ha has, Miss. You made a joke. Dukling down. D'you get it?' I began to sound rather like Joyce Grenfell tinged with hysteria. The mums have disappeared into the bushes for a quick smoke. We stop for lunch, an indigestible mixture of bloater paste butties, custard creams, cheese and onion crisps and a rather peculiar cake which Louise later informs me was sent by her mother for the birds. I begin to wonder how many will be sick on the bus home.

Suitably refreshed, we carry on and successfully identify a Canada Goose which eyes us warily and beats a hasty retreat into the pond. We all converge on a friendly fisher-

The nature walk

When schoolchildren were first taken out on nature studies, a master from a London school took his class out onto a nearby common. One boy who was not interested in the plants and insects wandered on ahead. He had not gone far when he put up a Skylark; the bird gained height and when it reached the peak of its climb, it hovered and sang. The boy watched for some minutes, spellbound. He then ran back to the master and said 'Hey, Mister, come and look at this sparra. It can't get up and it can't come down and it ain't 'arf 'ollering!'

man who is only too pleased to open his box of seething maggots for our inspection. 'No, Russell, they would not make nice pets. Tell the kind gentleman "No thank you".' We straggle back to the car park where they use their spending money on yet more food and fold my carefully devised fact sheeets into paper boats and paper hats to keep off the rain which has now set in. I don't care – just let me get them all back home in one piece. Count them onto the coach. Perry comes running up last, breathlessly handing me a stick of rock, 'For you, Miss'. I spend the journey back to school guiltily pondering all the malevolent thoughts I have been harbouring against him. My musings are interrupted by giggles and scuffles from the back seat. 'Perry. Just what have you got in that kit-bag?'

I wonder if the man from Sandy has ever had to steal a stolen Mallard back into its duck pond under cover of darkness. It isn't easy.

Some YOC groups are created in response to a demand from birdwatching youngsters but there is usually at least one teacher in every school who is keen to become involved . . .

When I started out on my teaching career, I innocently thought that my birdwatching activities would virtually cease between the hours of nine and four, but it was not long before I became aware that there was a definite ornithology of school playgrounds and properties – indeed a whole unexplored realm of bird study worthy of the attentions of some future PhD student.

To begin with, many birds love school, which is more than can be said for some of the pupils. The birds appear like magic each interval, swooping down as soon as the bell rings and the playground clears, to a positive feast of unconsidered trifles. Dropped potato crisps in assorted flavours, and an astonishing variety of related products, whose names escape me for the moment, are all eagerly devoured by the birds as their benefactors shuffle unwillingly back to their

Howlers

Q. Which bird is always out of breath?
A. The Puffin.

Q. Why did the Owl Owl?
A. Because the Woodpecker Woodpecker.

Q. What do you call a man with a Seagull on his head?
A. Cliff.

Why the songster gets the bird

Why do so many of our song birds spend more time singing at dawn than at any other time of day? There are a number of plausible explanations for the 'dawn chorus'. Mortality is highest at night, and so dawn is a good time for a bird without a territory to search for a newly vacant one. It is therefore important for a bird to advertise that he is alive and well and ready to defend his territory at this time.

Also, sound carries best early in the morning when the air is still. Poor light at this time means that insect-eating birds will probably benefit if they do their singing now and hunt for prey later in the day.

But Ruth Mace of the Edward Grey Institute of Field Ornithology, Oxford, has come up with another possible reason for the dawn chorus, after studying the way in which the behaviour of female Great Tits influences the duration of the all-male chorus.

In March, the males sing throughout the day, but in April and early May, when breeding activity is at its height, Mace noticed that the males started singing as soon as they awoke continuing for about twenty-five minutes but ceasing abruptly when their partners (who roost separately) emerged from their roost holes. Mating would then take place.

To discover whether it was the appearance of the females which stopped the males singing, rather than both events being governed by some environmental cue such as light intensity, Mace devised a simple experiment: after the females had gone to roost, she plugged each roost hole with a piece of foam attached to a string leading from the hide. She was then able to prevent the females from emerging the next ▶

Making friends in Trafalgar Square

W. Broadhurst/FLPA

desks. The exact flavours don't seem to matter much, but in this day of scientific accuracy I must confess that without recourse to slide rules, statistics and computers, I am unable to vouch for the total accuracy of this statement. What I can definitely say, however, is that the species involved most commonly are House Sparrow, Starling, feral pigeon, Pied Wagtail, Herring and Black-headed Gulls.

The same individuals come back time after time, like one particular sparrow with a white head. Either it was a good example of partial albinism, or else an awful warning to the other sparrows as to what an excessive dose of crisps might do. They seem so attuned to scavenging for the remnants of this ritual feasting that I can picture them on Saturdays and Sundays hanging around the playground looking thoroughly miserable, waiting for a bell that never rings. In my last school the sparrows fed their young great quantities of this unorthodox chick food and one pair duly rewarded the pupils for their generosity by stopping up the outside bell with a solid mass of nesting material so that it could no longer summon the unfaithful back to work.

Unsolicited gifts of injured birds are an occupational hazard for a teacher misguided enough to reveal his interest in birds. 'Please sir, my mother was wondering if you could call in after four o'clock and have a look at a sick Blackbird . . .' Sometimes the dreaded parcels arrive on my desk bearing live – or dead – occupants.

Sometimes whole lessons may be interrupted by important ornithological events. Pupils know instinctively the weakness of every teacher, and shamelessly exploit it at every opportunity. Only a few weeks ago in the middle of a lesson on France came the exciting news: 'Please sir, that seagull's just killed a Blackbird.' As usual, I give a composed look and try to pass the matter off quietly, while having a quick look out of the window myself, but it's no use. The gull has ulterior motives in making the kill. *'Please*, sir,' (the voice is more insistent this time) . . . 'he's *eating* it!'

The Paris Basin is forgotten for a moment as all eyes turn to the window. The attention of even the most lethargic pupil with the least possible interest in such dull things as birds is riveted on the gory scene. At last only the two legs remain in sight until these too finally disappear down the gull's gullet to a chorus of 'Ughs!' and 'Yuchs!' Finally, the murderer flies off, and peace returns to the classroom and to the Champagne Humide . . . or was it the Champagne Pouilleuse? . . . I'd better start again!

For some time I taught on lower Deeside, overlooking the valley which was a flyway for birds. One day the telephone rang at the other end of the corridor. In a few moments a colleague arrives breathless at my classroom door. 'It's the headmaster – urgent!'

I panic. What heinous crime have I committed? Or is it some sin of omission he wants to see me about so urgently? Did I forget to hand in my register on Friday? It must be something big or he would not have phoned in the middle of a lesson. I take a deep breath, lift the dangling receiver and prepare myself for the worst. A distant, gruff voice booms across the line: 'Huge flock of geese passing west up the valley . . . Should be over your side now.' I race back to my room to relax and appreciate this terrific spectacle: huge skeins of Greylags in great 'Vs' against a cloudless blue sky, and with the corries of Lochnagar sparkling white in the distance.

School playing fields attract birds like magnets – thrushes, Blackbirds, Redwings and Fieldfares all probe for worms in the well-tended turf. Gulls love to roost on the flat sward, and thereby hangs another tale. Across from the school and its playing-fields there was the local rubbish dump. Now, being a high-class neighbourhood, there were doubtless plenty of high-class pickings in the dustbins, for there was never any shortage of gulls round the tip. After each newly dumped load had been noisily picked over, the gulls would retire to the playing-field replete and ready to regurgitate not only pellets, which as gulls they have every right to do, but a range of indigestible objects from chicken bones to margarine wrappers and all sorts of unmentionable leavings. In addition, there were also the vast amounts of the more usual offerings commonly associated with a congregation of gulls.

Hockey matches became a nightmare. Fast tackles became rapid slides and grass stains took second place to more nasty and smelly evidence of contact with the ground. It was all a bit much, but afforded hours of interest from my classroom window, and some pupils were able to make an interesting little study out of it which went to a YOC display in Edinburgh. In course of time it became clear that pupil players were not the only ones being affected by the gulls' anti-social roosting habits. In the area favoured by the gulls the grass grew ever more green and long, till in summer the

morning until fifteen minutes after their normal time. The males carried on singing beyond this time for a significant period averaging seven and a half minutes.

The following day, the birds returned to their normal routine. This seemed to confirm that it really was the emergence of the females which brought the male chorus to an end. But what did this behaviour signify?

Many songbirds lay their eggs at dawn, and females of some species are known to be at their most fertile in the first hour after laying. So mating during this one hour may result in more successful fertilisations.

poor groundsman was forced to tear up and down on his motor mower like a thing demented, in an effort to check the super-grass which grew with such abandon.

When I moved north it was to new surroundings and new school birds. Now I look across to the rounded shapes of the distant Monadhliath Mountains and out over the waters of the Firth. Last year from my window I watched Skuas passing in the autumn and Whooper Swans in the winter . . . Whoever said that classrooms were dull?

If all goes well, young ornithologists eventually grow up and become enthusiastic members of the local bird society, which offers bird news, gossip and the stimulus of field trips. But a really successful outing depends on the expertise of the leader, who needs to be a master of fact as well as a mine of information. John Burton has had years of experience . . .

HABITAT IS EVERYWHERE

There was no intention that it should be a busman's holiday. The idea was to get a complete change of intellectual scene – a rapid roving around those famous (some infamous) historical places of the Ancient World which, since youth, one had found so enthralling, yet had never entertained much hope of seeing at first hand. I would look at birds, of course, if they should come my way – otherwise, heigh-ho for the hieroglyphs, tumbledown temples and time-hallowed tombs.

But habitat is everywhere, and you can't get away with it as easily as that. Ephesus was impressive – I had no idea it was so vast, in time and space; and the whole area resounded with the songs and challenges of Rock Nuthatches, their bell-like voices splintering among the grey stones. One, with a fine sense of high drama, performed in the great theatre, and sounded ten times larger than life. At the top of the Street of the Couretes, beyond the Odeon , they thinned out – but the Isabelline Wheatears hopped in, and sabotaged my concentration on Corinthian columns.

Of course, there were Rock Nuthatches elsewhere – at Xanthos, Fethiye, Delphi – and one railed at us from the Lion Gate at Mycenae, most fabulous and fascinating of all Greek sites. But at Ephesus they were so concentrated as to create the character of the place. The dead island-city of Delos, on the other hand, belonged to the larks, both Crested and Short-toed, whose songs and calls shimmered in the heat-haze all that hot afternoon. Olympia I shall recall for its Rock Sparrows and Sardinian Warblers; Corinth Canal had Lesser Kestrels; and the courtyard of the Palace of the Grand Master at Rhodes had been taken over by Crag Martins. An Eleonora's Falcon swept past the ship and added the final touch of sublimety to the Acropolis at Lindos, while at the opposite end of the scale all that the Valley of the Kings could offer was a wrangling of House Sparrows (*P.d. niloticus*, no doubt) outside Tutankhamun's Tomb. The Nile at Luxor was enlivened with Pied Kingfishers, and Little Egrets littered the fields like pieces of blown paper all the way to the airport. The Sacred Lake at Karnak was a-flutter with those beautiful red-bellied Egyptian Swallows *Hirundo rustica savignii*, and the gloomy columns in the Court of Amenophis III echoed the hoarse timeless voice of Brown-necked Ravens.

At odd moments Bulbuls, Bee-eaters and brown Palm Doves distracted my attention from the matter in hand; Hoopoes hopped on Cephren's Pyramid; White Storks wandered over the flood-plain of the River Xanthos (no wonder there are so many children in the Turkish villages); and Black Kites soared effortlessly over the minarets and main streets of Old Cairo. Now that it is all over the memories crowd in, a sort of archaeological patchwork quilt indelibly embroidered with the sight and sounds of birds. Habitat is everywhere, and the birds are loath to let you forget it!

Kenneth Williamson

'Mr Burton, we've ony seen 16 species so far'

Jan van de Kam

Since my natural history interests range over the fields of both ornithology and entomology I have had the 'privilege' of leading the field meetings of my local natural history society in both subjects. I feel justified therefore in making a few comparisons between them.

Experience taught me to be very careful in the choice of a locality for a forthcoming birdwatching field outing. At first, I always chose my favourite local haunts, forgetting that although I might be quite happy with a poor total of species seen, others might not. Thus I shall not easily forget one of the first I ever led which was haunted by a tall, bespectacled, middle-aged woman who plagued me through most of the afternoon with the persistent complaint 'Mr Burton, we've only seen sixteen species so far,' varying the total as each new one was painfully added to the list. Even when, by diligent observation, we raised the total to twenty-four, she still grumbled about that. To cap it all, I cannot recollect her helping one iota to scrape even that meagre total together, although when we did see a bird she almost fell over herself in the rush.

Following that and a later, hardly more successful experience, I decided to lead all future bird trips on some coastal marshes where birds were rather more conspicuous and where one could be reasonably certain of seeing a good total of species. However, even marshland field meetings had their drawbacks. People would often come unsuitably dresed and shod. On one such occasion, as I struggled across a swollen, muddy ditch with a gumbootless lady of striking proportions on my back, I heard another lady clad in a scarlet wind-cheater say to a companion in a sky-blue one 'When Mr Burton says marshes he certainly means *marshes*.'

These marshland field meetings were often very well attended – sometimes up to thirty or more people came. Apart from the unsuitably dressed ones, there were always those without field-glasses or others who strove to see waders at hundreds of yards range with opera glasses. Of course,

In a city

What a biological desert the centre of a city would be without the clapping wings, the graceful flight and seductive cooing of pigeons. How much more loneliness would there be if people couldn't feed the odd crust to a seagull or a gang of sparrows. They make a mess, it's true. But at least it's a straightforward dollop of nitrogen-rich manure, much welcomed by plants

*Island field meetings offer good
photography opportunities*

there was also a strong element of 'experts' equipped with enormous binoculars and festooned with telescopes. The more generous would usually lend their glasses to less fortunate companions and help them to find the birds with them, but generally such experts were a problem.

The usual practice during field meetings on salt marshes is to keep mainly to the sea-wall, gazing seawards for waders, ducks, etc on the mud-flats and landward for the birds of the dyke-dissected reclaimed marshes. The biggest disadvantage of this procedure is that your party can become strung out along half a mile of sea-wall with the young and energetic grouped around a bunch of 'experts' at the fore, while dawdling in the rear straggle the 'beginners' and opera-glass fraternity. Somewhere around the middle of the line you try to restrain the 'experts' from putting up all the best birds before your beginners get to them, and at the same time endeavour to help the rearguard to see something, even if it is only a Meadow Pipit.

Entomological field meetings are, perhaps, rather easier to lead. Given a warm, sunny day and providing you choose your locality carefully, you may be pretty sure of finding enough insects to satisfy the usual motley collection of butterfly, moth, beetle and fly specialists. If the weather is bad, nobody will blame you for the inevitable scarcity of insects. Moreover, most entomologists are fairly resourceful and keep themselves happy enough – one rarely seems to encounter 'beginners' (at least in the helpless ornithologial sense) in the same way that you do on bird trips. Possibly this is because only the keenest 'nature-lovers' take up entomology.

The attendances at entomological trips also tend to be smaller than on their ornithological counterparts: I have rarely had more than ten on mine, sometimes only three or four. Normally you are blessed with a small group of butterfly and moth collectors, this being the most popular order of insects to study, plus a couple of coleopterists (beetle watchers), an hymenopterist (student of bees, wasps, sawflies, etc), and a dipterist (two-winged fly expert) or two.

Unlike the average bird-watcher, they do not cling to you tenaciously, but, like cats, go their own ways. All you have to do is to lead them to promising localities. They will then potter about cheerfully, the butterfly collectors careering wildly after their swift-flying prey, the moth collectors swiping away at branches and bushes in search of caterpillars and the beetle experts quietly turning over rotten logs and cow pats, or critically examining flower heads along with the dipterists or the hymenopterists. The last two often have large, stoutly constructed sweep nets which they frequently put right over their heads when they think they have caught something. The only way to find it is to get right in with it! Sometimes they suck away at flowers or tree-trunks with a pooter, a bottle-like contraption, managing somehow to avoid consuming the desired insects, which they suck into it.

The pace at which a bug-hunting field meeting moves is noticeably different from a bird one. None of the latter's mad jockeying for position takes place; it is altogether a more leisurely affair. It may, for example, take all day to cover a few fields and half a wood.

If a leader of an entomological field meeting desires to impress his flock, there is a simple deception which he can employ with advantage. All he has to do is to arrange the start of his meeting sufficiently late to allow him to go over the proposed route beforehand and note the positions of all the moths he can find resting motionless on tree-trunks. He can even plant specimens collected the previous day, knowing full well that they will remain just where he puts them. Later, when the party comes along, he can remark

> ### Flight of birds
>
> I have read somewhere that in the old days coasting sailors occasionally took pigeons with them, and when they lost their bearings they let one fly, which it did at once to the land.
>
> Francis Galton's *Art of Travel* (1872)

Roger Tidman/FLPA

A party of twitchers bags a rarity

19

The birdsman in society

One of three questions is inevitably asked of the birdsman following the stock introduction by his hostess: 'Oh, Mabel, I do want you to meet Mr Er; he's a great authority on birds.'

(a) 'Oh, how interesting, do tell me, is this a good place for birds?'

Provided the questioner is not outstandingly pretty, and it is not desired to prolong the conversation for other reasons, the correct answer here is a flat, 'No place is bad for birds, you know.' Unless Mabel is a real trier, there will be no come-back to this and an escape can quickly be made.

(b) 'Oh, how interesting, do tell me, do you know Peter Scott?' Answer: 'Well, I saw him when I was at the New Grounds the other day.' This is what C. E. Montague called paying truth the homage of equivocation, since it does not stress the fact that you were one of a coach party from your local natural history society and that all you saw of the director was the top of his head as he talked to two admirals and a bishop at the far end of the Rushy Pen.

From this it should be easy to lead on to an account of your own observations on wildfowl, which should play out time successfully.

(c) 'Oh, how interesting, do let me tell you about my Robin!' This is superficially the easiest of the three to meet, since it initially requires from you only a listening role, but as the inevitable anecdote (the bird is sometimes a Blackbird, occasionally a Chaffinch or 'a little brown bird, definitely not a Sparrow' and it always does one of three things: taps on the window, builds two nests on top of each other, or seems *really* to recognize her) winds to its end, you realise that some fitting comment is needed. ▶

casually 'I think we should find a *nebulosa* or two on those trees over there; it looks the right sort of place,' and can then bask in the admiring glances of the more impressionable of the members of the party when his words come true. (Very important, if there is one of those rare organisms present – a young and pretty female entomologist.)

An important event characteristic of all natural history field meetings which should never be forgotten by the leader is – tea. When I led my first one, I didn't even bother: it just never entered my head. Consequently the subsequent reproachful remarks and glances of my companions were a source of surprise to me. At that time I was still a schoolboy and was quite happy to spend a day in the field, subsisting on nothing more than a bottle of pop and a couple of fish-paste sandwiches.

In some remote spots far from civilisation, members do not mind bringing their own tea (a notice beforehand in the society's bulletin stating this should not be overlooked). On one such occasion in 1959, I was taking birdwatchers around some desolate salt marshes in north Kent. We spent the lunch period happily collecting on some tidal saltings, followed by a pleasant afternoon pottering along the sea-wall. Around 4pm, I suggested that we should all sit down and partake of tea with our backs to the sea-wall where we could watch the flight of terns and gulls as we ate. Everyone removed their rucksacks from their backs and sat down eagerly. I felt for mine in vain, then realised that I had left it 2 miles away on the saltings. When I got back there, having left my munching colleagues, I found that a high tide had risen in the meantime and covered the saltings. Eventually, after a considerable amount of wading about, I retrieved my sodden rucksack. I knew that I need not look inside to know the worst – there was no tea for me that day.

There is no doubt that afternoon tea in a nice 'olde tea shoppe' in a pleasant village amid the scene of the day's excursion is looked forward to by entomologist and ornithologist alike as a perfect ending to a successful day. It is wise therefore never to ignore this fact and to ensure that some café near the end of the road awaits your weary companions' arrival.

John Burton is an authority on recorded bird-song (for many years he was librarian of the BBC's Wildlife Record Library). In that capacity he advised countless drama producers, making sure that they used the right 'atmospheric' backgrounds to their outdoor scenes, avoiding Cuckoos in a Home Counties' December, wild geese calling over a Scottish loch in midsummer and so on. But quite apart from his professional interests, he is a true field naturalist with an enquiring mind and a feel for wild places . . .

Apart from watching a television version a year or so ago, I have never read Paul Gallico's charming little story of *The Snow Goose*. Then quite recently Spike Milligan telephoned to ask if I could help him choose the natural effects for an adaptation he proposes to make of the story. So I sent my secretary out to buy a paperback edition, and read the whole story through soon after she placed it in my hands.

To my surprise I was far more moved by the written word than by the television play. Then I realised that this was because the latter concentrated on the action between the main characters and failed to convey adequately the setting in which the story unfolds: the lonely salt marshes of the Essex coast.

For me it was the simple evocative descriptions of the desolate, yet beautiful surroundings of the old lighthouse in which the young hunchback artist/naturalist Philip Rhayader lives in solitude, shunned by the outside world except for Fritha, a young girl from the nearest village who finds and brings the injured Snow Goose to him, that made it so moving. As readers of the book – or viewers of the play – will know, through their mutual concern for the recovery of this bird, Fritha discovers his true, gentle disposition, and, despite his grotesque appearance, grows in time to love him. Unfortunately Philip is killed while rescuing British troops from the Dunkirk beaches in his small boat; the now recovered Snow Goose, which had followed him out there, returning alone to the marsh to tell the waiting, watching Fritha that he would never come back again.

Ever since my schooldays, when I used to spend much of my spare time roaming over the North Kent Marshes from Plumstead to the Isle of Sheppey, either alone or with birdwatching friends, I have been fascinated by flat, desolate marshlands and their wildlife inhabitants. The average person, I believe, finds little in them to enthuse about. Indeed, they are regarded, in general, as wasteland fit only for the disposal of refuse, or development as coastal industrial sites.

But to those who know them well, salt marshes have a very special appeal of their own: a romantic beauty which is, perhaps a little difficult to convey to the unconverted. A magical blending of land, sky and water, one into the other. Above all, as John Constable demonstrated so well, it is a landscape which, because of its very flatness, is dominated by the sky – ever-changing skies which, with varying degrees of light and darkness, bestow upon the mixture of marsh, mud and water a greater diversity of moods than is

▶ By far the best is: 'Most interesting: of course, there's something just like it in the Dutch literature.' The beauty of this is that your questioner probably does not know the specialised meaning of 'literature', and will credit you with uncanny omniscience; in any case the fact that many Dutch papers have English summaries or are abstracted in *The Ibis* will almost certainly be unknown to her.

Bruce Campbell

Early observations

That the Woodcock conveys its young from the woods to the marshes and other feeding grounds has been frequently proved by observation.
Sir Ralph Payne-Galway (1909)

The Goshawk today killed four rabbits and the tiercels killed a Partridge. One of them flew a Kingfisher which dived under the bank.
George Lodge's *Hawking Diary* (1888)

Woodcock have been often collected together by decayed apples . . . in Dorsetshire they are called 'ditch owls'.
Col Peter Hawker

encountered in almost any other kind of country.

Moreover, the cries of the wild birds that inhabit such places seem to fit perfectly their changing moods and one's own too. If you feel sad and lonely, and perhaps full of self-pity, then the sweet melancholy whistles of the Grey Plovers drifting in from the sombre mud-flats will identify with your emotions, and so too will the wild, lilting calls of the Curlews and Redshanks. If, on the other hand, your spirits are high then you will hear not sorrow in their cries, but an exhilarating joyousness that stirs and inspires. And if the day is bright, and Sky Larks rise to sing over the pastures of the reclaimed marsh, then the sheer uninhibited exuberance of their sustained melody will bring a lightness to your heart and a springiness to your feet which is glorious to feel.

Yet to become susceptible to the spell-binding atmosphere of the salt marshes, there is no necessity to be in an emotional state already. Has any birdwatcher or wildfowler crouched either at dusk or dawn, and waited for a flood-tide to bring in the wild geese, ducks and waders from the distant mud-flats to his close proximity, and remained unexhilarated and unmoved while the setting or rising sun has reflected a dozen or more changing colour patterns across the expanses of smooth, silky mud and the shimmering, rising tide; until in the half-light he has tensed to the sight and sound of wave after wave of dark, winged shapes speeding towards him over the dark saltings – a thousand or more wild, echoing voices?

From my youth I have been deeply impressed by such experiences, even then trying from time to time to write them down so that I might never forget them. For instance, when contemplating this article, I came upon an account in my log-book for 27 January 1952, when I was not quite twenty-one, of a visit with my friend Denis Owen to the Hoo Marshes in north Kent (made famous by Dickens in *Great Expectations*).

It was a bitterly cold day with bright sunshine and two inches of snow all over these marshes which lie on the south shore of the Thames estuary. All the fleets, ditches and pools were frozen over with quite thick ice. Along the Thames the tide came in fast that day carrying a good deal of melting ice before it, which piled up along the shore like a miniature sea-wall.

Around 4pm, as dusk approached, the mood of the marshes changed and I recorded this in my field notebook before I left for home from Cliffe Railway Station:

By then the light was fading, for it was late afternoon, and the blue snow clouds were rolling up from the western horizon, preceded by a light mist. Through it the sun glowed, a flaming red orb casting an orange glow upon the snow. At one spot, as we tramped along the top of the river-wall, I turned my gaze from the river and its abundant wildfowl to look upon one of the wildest and most beautiful scenes I have ever observed. It was Cliffe

Eric Hosking

Fleet frozen as far as the eye could see. The sun had transformed the grey ice into a fiery orange expanse from which the legions of dead, black reeds rose in contrast, swaying rhythmically in the northerly wind. If only one could have captured the wild scene in some way; with a camera or, perhaps, with paint and brush. But I could not. It is days and scenes like this that maintain the spell that salt marshes weave around their admirers, like some lovely captivating girl.

Soon the sun disappeared altogether behind the now dark snow clouds. It was really eerie out on the marshes in these conditions and the scores of marshland sheep seemed as phantoms in the mist. As we tramped across the damp pastures to Cliffe village, disturbing hares here and there from their 'forms' in the rushy tussocks, flocks of Starlings which had been feeding out on the marsh blundered past us in and out of the mist to their roost in a distant chalk quarry.

I first discovered the marshes of the Thames estuary in the early spring of 1945 when I was thirteen years of age and the war was almost over. At last, with the unnerving threat of the V2 rockets a thing of the recent past, I felt free to explore farther afield from my home in Greenwich. So one bright morning that March found me arriving at the edge of the Plumstead Marshes. Before me stretched 5 miles of mostly lush green levels intersected by reedy ditches.

One of these ditches barred my further progress. It had steep muddy sides which, as a result of heavy rain during

Waders congregating at high water – mostly Knot, Dunlin, Redshank, Turnstone and Oystercatcher

A week to remember

Little did I know what was in store for the Napoleonic Fort Café when Nick Ward walked in on Easter Monday and said that he had just spotted a Gyr Falcon.

Having lived in my beautiful fort guard house for nine years, I'm used to a gentle start to the season. I was just not prepared for what was to follow.

Tuesday morning brought the first sighting of the enthusiastic birdwatchers. What looked like a hundred people were standing on the battlements, looking across to the quarry, happy that they had seen the falcon take to the sky for his morning flight, finding that Berry Head Jackdaws made a very tasty breakfast.

Wednesday came and went in a flurry of activity; whilst the birders watched the falcon feed, I fed the very hungry birders. By Saturday the word had reached the length and breadth of Britain. They came from Scotland, Wales, London, Birmingham, Derby, Kent, Southampton – the list seemed endless. Gentle, quiet, patient people, all recalling interesting stories of their overnight journeys.

The sight that greeted me on Saturday morning at 5.30 is something I shall never forget. Quietly waiting for dawn to break were about 500 people, lining the fort walls four-deep. Their enthusiasm was contagious: by the following Tuesday morning I too was watching from the battlements for that first morning flight. I thank the Gyr Falcon for the extra business. I thank you, my birder customers, for such a memorable week at the Berry Head Fort Café.

Mrs. J. A. Parr
Brixham, Devon

the previous week, were very wet and slippery. Undaunted, I took a flying leap across the muddy water, landed halfway up on the opposite bank, lost my foothold and fell spreadeagled on my face in the wet mud, then slipped slowly down into the water. When I eventually scrambled out of the ditch my new school raincoat was generously covered with mud. I shuddered at the thought of the inevitable reaction from my mother, but 'in for a penny, in for pound', so I pressed ahead across a large ploughed field, collecting notable amounts of thick mud on my wellingtons as I did so.

But I was in a new world. Lapwings rose in front of me from the lumps of earth among which they had been so well camouflaged, at first in twos and threes, then in larger numbers, until a couple of hundred were wheeling above my head, calling plaintively. A large covey of Partridges sped away low over the dark soil, occasional Snipe rocketed skywards from pools among the furrows, while high above me several Sky Larks were in full song.

Beyond the ploughed field I came upon yet another ditch which this time I crossed by a small plank bridge, and thus gained access to a large area of very marshy pasture land. Near the middle, where the ground dipped gently and the rushes grew more and more thickly until they merged with sedges, reeds and great water dock to form a small swamp, I heard the sound for which I had been hoping. A Redshank rose in yodelling song-flight, circled the marsh a couple of times and then planed down to land on an old fencepost.

In those days I could not afford binoculars, but my eyesight was a good deal keener than it is now, so I relied instead upon stalking. As my raincoat was already heavily mud-stained I was past caring about parental recrimination, so I edged forward on my stomach until I was close enough to see the bird clearly. It remained perched there for at least ten minutes. I was able to admire its elegant build, its mottled plumage, and especially the long diagnostic red legs and red bill tipped with black – my first full view of a Redshank and within 10 miles of central London! Although I have seen many thousands of Redshanks since then, indeed, can see them whenever I choose to walk along the shore near my Clevedon home, to this day I can picture that bird perched on that post in London's last salt march, the giant pylons which carry the national grid across the Thames soaring up behind it. Today that little swamp is no more, the Redshanks and Snipe which nested there have gone too. In its place is a boating lake surrounded by the stark, futuristic blocks of flats of Thamesmead, London's newest garden city.

From that now distant day in 1945, like many other ornithologists, I have been hooked on salt marshes and the kinds of wild birds that inhabit them. In my teens and twenties I cycled many miles almost every weekend to my favourite haunts in the lonely marshes of the Thames and Medway. How in those days I would have envied my present location:

Jan van de Kam

Turnstone feeding at the tide's edge

only five minutes walk away from the fresh marshes and the saltings of the Somerset coast where Shelduck and waders of several species abound.

Ideally I would dearly love to live at the end of some secluded lane, bordered by pollarded willows and quiet rhynes of stagnant water, in a farmhouse of character, its stone walls mellowed with age and yellow lichens, and with views across the levels to the distant sea-wall. And where at the highest tides I could watch the long lines of waders and wild duck flighting in over the sea-wall from the saltings to roost in the wide green pastures.

Instead I live with my family in a modern house on a modern Clevedon estate built on what long ago was once a salt marsh, and which, to my great satisfaction, is at least called 'The Saltings'. And at night, when the tide is high, I can sometimes hear the sound of the sea along the shore and hear the clear calls of Curlews, Whimbrels, Redshanks and Oystercatchers wafting to me on the wind from the mud-flats and saltings of Clevedon Pill.

Curiously enough, another of the BBC's stalwart ornithologists, Eric Simms, recently moved from one major
habitat to another having lived in, and immortalised in print,
his surburban retreat in north London . . .

When, some two years ago, I announced to birdwatching
friends that I was about to leave Dollis Hill in north-west
London, some of them held up their hands in horror! How
could I possibly give up research into the birds of a region
which after twenty-nine years (according to one writer) I
had made my *Selborne*? However, I was to embark on a new
adventure. A new life in a small village in south Lincolnshire
would enable me to compare the birds and their behaviour
with those of suburban London.

House Martin at the nest

Eric Hosking

Peggy Heard/FLPA

Jay cheerfully making use of a bird-bath

Some differences between the birdlife of the two regions were immediately obvious: Swallows (only passing migrants in Dollis Hill) now nested in the barns next door and sang from the powerline alongside the garden. House Martins built their nests on old buildings and new bungalows alike, while Swifts bred in holes in the masonry of the twelfth-century church. Redpolls 'buzzed' the garden regularly, Linnets twittered overhead and Sky Larks soared and sang in the sky. Not since 1954, when a group of allotments were cleared for building development, had larks raised their joyful song above my London home. Collared Doves were common in the village and the surrounding woodlands, and from my bedroom I could hear Woodpigeons, Stock Doves and Turtle Doves. At Dollis Hill Stock Doves were unknown, Collared Doves scarce and Turtle Doves extremely rare visitors.

There is a small rookery of five nests on the edge of the village and a few Jackdaws nest in the chimneys of some of the older and larger houses, but in north-west London these species were rarely seen. By contrast, Greenfinches seem to be much scarcer in Lincolnshire and the Goldfinch also appears to be very rare.

The village itself consists of some 125 houses spread over a rectangle of land about 700x350yd. There are rather few trees – principally ash, sycamore and horse chestnut – but they grow well along a disused railway line on the outskirts of the village. All round lie fields of cereal, beet and rape, bounded by low hawthorn hedges, too many of which are being destroyed by indiscriminate stubble burning. The roads have wide grassy verges rich in limestone flowers, and the village gardens tend to be rather small, many adjoining arable land.

Soon after my arrival, it was clear that thrushes were very scarce with only two male Blackbirds and single Mistle and Song Thrushes audible in territorial song from my house. In Dollis Hill, before the advent of the Magpie, I could listen each spring to no fewer than thirteen Blackbirds and three Song Thrushes. After all, suburbia was the most favourable habitat for these birds. Unfortunately, it seems that heavy predation by Magpies has seriously reduced thrush num-

DESERT ISLAND BIRDS

Although several surveys have established the Robin as the national bird, it is not necessarily the most popular species among those whose interests range further afield than the kitchen window. In an attempt to find the most popular species among Beech Grove (headquarters of the British Trust for Ornithology) staff, a majority were asked the following question: 'If you were cast away on a deserted island, which ten British birds would you most like to take with you, and which five would you most like to leave behind?' The results proved quite interesting, and you might like to consider the question yourself before reading on.

Although one greedy member of staff wanted to take ten habitats instead, the other replies showed some agreement, especially over those species to be left behind. Indeed, only six species accounted for over one-half of the 'unpopular' vote. Pheasant topped the poll, followed by House Sparrow, Woodpigeon, Starling, Collared Dove and Canada Goose, with Carrion Crow and Herring Gull not far behind. The more popular species were a complete surprise, with Swallow first and Nightjar second. There was a multiple tie for third place between Black-throated Diver, Wigeon, Curlew, Roseate Tern, Tawny Owl, Kingfisher, Stonechat, Nightingale, Lesser Whitethroat and Willow Warbler. Neither the Robin nor the poor old BTO Gannet got a single vote. Although the Swallow was clearly the most popular, it only received 3.6 per cent of the votes cast, compared with 11.4 per cent for Pheasant. No less than ninety species received one or more 'popular' votes, so there was clearly little agreement between staff, although rare species generally did very badly. This suggests that the choice of bird reserves should be based on diversity and the absence of unpopular species, rather than the presence of a few rare species.

That entry in *BTO News* flushed a prompt reply from another stronghold of professional ornithology at Tring, home of the British Museum (Natural History) Bird Room . . .

Dear Editor,
A cursory survey among the staff of an ornithological establishment not a hundred miles from the BTO revealed that the ten birds they would *most like to take if cast away on a desert island*, assuming that the obvious euphemism is ruled out, were – carrier pigeon, domestic fowl, Kori Bustard, Turkey, domestic goose, domestic duck, Pheasant, Guinea Fowl, Eider Duck and Woodpigeon. Can't think what you were going to do with all those others!

Yours ever,
Anon

bers in Dollis Hill. Magpies first appeared there in 1969 and since then these buccaneering but handsome birds have systematically visited suburban gardens, especially in the early morning, to look for the eggs and nestlings of songbirds. Their usual technique was to fly low and practically hover over likely nesting sites in trees and shrubs until an unfortunate, sitting hen Blackbird or thrush would lose her nerve and fly off with a loud alarm call. Now knowing that a nest would be their guaranteed reward they would then work steadily down into the bush. In the two years that I have lived in south Lincolnshire I have had only sixteen sight records of Magpies within 6 miles of the village: it is a very scarce bird in my part of England!

In winter, several Blackbirds and Song Thrushes come regularly into my garden with a single territory-holding Robin and two Hedge Sparrows but when March comes, they depart for the copses, woods and hedgerows outside the village. I have heard no Robin or Hedge Sparrow song in the village in two full summers. The Blackbirds are very much birds of the summer hedgerows, staking out 100yd lengths of roadside territory and singing from the hedgetops and telegraph poles and in some cases sharing their domains with Yellowhammers, Reed Buntings and even Sedge Warblers. Unlike the shrubby gardens of suburbia, the village offers few nest sites for thrushes. Two pairs of Great Tits hold territories in the village and Blue Tits raise their young in a nestbox in my garden. House Sparrows are the commonest birds, nesting in many roofs to which they gain access through small gaps under the eaves or between the red curved tiles which are so characteristic of this part of the world. I watched a cock sparrow this last summer with a beakful of dry grass spend twenty minutes fruitlessly trying to squeeze through too small a space under a tile! Starlings also nest in the barn roofs, entering them in exactly the same way as the sparrows.

It was clear soon after I moved into my new home that no one was in the habit of feeding the birds in winter or providing them with water. In the autumn of 1980 I put up plastic bags of peanuts, spiral tit-feeders also full of nuts and one of the clear plastic globes that the RSPB sell, filled with Swoop. It was fascinating to compare the learning abilities of the Lincolnshire sparrows with those of London. Take, for example, the simple plastic nut bags normally put out for tits. In my London garden the first sparrow had learned how to alight on one of these bags after only thirty-five minutes. (Incidentally, I knew at the time that no one was using any bird-feeding equipment other than open bird-tables in my neighbourhood so the sparrows were undergoing a new experience.) However, it was three weeks before the first village sparrow could land on a bag. In London, the spiral feeder was mastered by sparrows within three days whereas the Lincolnshire birds took six weeks. As for the plastic globe, that was a tough proposition for even the adaptable London sparrows and it was two months before

Eric Hosking

Male Blackbird feeding ravenous young

Roger Wilmshurst/FLPA

In hard weather Starlings shelter behind a Snipe which in turn shelters behind a Lapwing

the first one was able to project itself through the hole, then extricate part of itself, clasp the lower rim of the hole with its feet, grasp a millet seed and either manage to swallow it and continue feeding, or fall backwards, twist round and then gain flying speed before it crashed into the ground. In my new garden one whole winter and two months of the succeeding one were to pass before the first sparrow solved the problem, although the tits had been extracting nuts from inside almost from the beginning.

Why should there be such a striking difference in performance between the town and country birds? When the weather becomes very severe in the winter the village sparrows fly into the surrounding countryside and forage near the grain dryers and stackyards. It was not unusual to see up to a thousand sparrows or more in a flock. The London sparrows in bad weather had no such food resource to fall back on and so it would seem not unreasonable to believe that with stronger pressures upon them the London birds, in order to survive had to learn faster and indeed proved more adaptable. I have also found it much harder to tame the village sparrows than those in London.

One other great difference is the frequency with which birds in this limestone area come to drink at the bowl in the garden. Blackbirds will visit it half a dozen times a day, taking up to ten or more deep draughts in their bill. Song Thrushes, Starlings, Robins and sparrows seem to drink much more frequently in my garden than birds in London.

Over twenty-nine years in north-west London I used to watch autumn migrants passing over, often when north-west winds were blowing as birds crossed over the English Channel. On some mornings I counted over 2,000 Swallows passing through, 2,500 Fieldfare, 7,500 Chaffinches and 10,000 Starlings. Now I watch Lesser Black-backed and Black-headed Gulls, Common and occasional Herring Gulls, Swallows, House Martins, Redwings, Grey Wagtails, Sky Larks, Chaffinches and Starlings all flying to the south-west.

When autumn comes huge flocks of Lapwings are swept in by the easterly winds and hundreds of Golden Plover move on to the higher ground. For a few weeks in October or November hundreds of Redwings and Fieldfares come to the haws from the hedges and then pass on to reappear in the following March. Only in recent years has the Redwing overwintered in many city parks including St James's and Gladstone Park in London.

After the noise and bustle of London, I enjoy the peace of this Lincolnshire village. Although in the village there are in fact fewer birds, both in species and in number than in Dollis Hill, there are nearby woodlands rich in orchids and warblers, copses full of Turtle Doves and hedges with Lesser Whitethroats and wild roses. Rutland Water with its waders and wildfowl lies across just 6 miles of open countryside. The area has its own special charm and beauty. My long study of suburban birds has helped me to understand a little better the way in which the same species may behave in different habitats and I look forward to discovering more about the birds near my new home!

Most birdwatchers enjoy recording the comings and goings of residents and visitors in their gardens and the immediate vicinity. But the lure of distant places and the never-ending puzzle of bird movements soon engages their attention. Then they become embroiled in one of the monitoring and census operations of the British Trust for Ornithology. Many of the surveys are concerned with questions which seem superficially easy to answer. For instance, 'What is the commonest breeding bird?' The problem is that the answer may vary from year to year . . .

For a small island, Britain supports a phenomenal number of birds, somewhere in the region of 120 million. Of the 430 or so species which regularly visit and could be called 'British', sixteen of them represent populations of more than a million. It is possible that the Wren is the commonest

The Wren is one of our commonest birds

Peter Reynolds/FLPA

A loony species

Rich White and Jackie Tonge have sent us an article which appeared in the *Guardian* on 23 February 1987, reporting on the then forthcoming European Birdwatch Day, 24 May 1987. It indicated that Red-coated Divers might appear in Orkney. Rich and Jackie suggest that, if this proves to be a new species for the world, a suitable scientific name might be *Gavia butlinicus*. We wondered whether its call note is distinctive? 'Hi de hi' perhaps?

British Birds

breeding bird we have, found anywhere that offers a scrap of cover. One estimate is that there could be 3,000 pairs in every 6 mile square, resulting in a total population of 10 million pairs. That figure would be seriously reduced after an icy winter. Starlings are serious contenders, but Blackbirds and Chaffinches are nearly as numerous with some 7 million breeding pairs. Robins, Blue Tits and House Sparrows have populations of some 5 million pairs apiece. There may be more than a million and a half waders on our estuaries just after Christmas, a quarter of this number in the Morecambe Bay area alone. There must be well over 150,000 pairs of Gannets nesting round the British Isles, a number which is increasing all the time and which has benefitted from the changes in public attitudes over the last 100 years; instead of being over-exploited for food and 'sport', the species is now held in high regard and carefully protected.

Counting birds is something of a sport in itself, much indulged in by the majority of birdwatchers, yet it is much more than a sport; it is a useful exercise that reveals a great deal of information about the general health of an environment. It was the catastrophic breeding failure of our birds of prey in the late 1950s that highlighted the dangers of toxic agricultural pesticides and led to their control.

Over the years, various techniques for estimating populations have been devised and these are the subject of continuing study, mainly by the British Trust for Ornithology. The longest running species census involves the Grey Heron, whose easily mapped and conspicuous breeding places were first counted in 1928 and are still carefully monitored every year. The observers are careful not to risk any disturbance of the colony until well into the breeding season. It is relatively easy to get a fairly accurate idea of the number of nests and young in a heronry but counting serried ranks of Guillemots or Kittiwakes on cliff ledges from a wildly moving boat is a different kettle of fish. Trying to count the seemingly endless crowd at a gannetry is not easy either. The most effective way seems to be to take a photograph from the air, more or less directly above the colony, and then laboriously to prick the white spots (each one a bird) on an enlargement, counting as you go. This method serves very well with a colony such as the one at Grassholm, in Dyfed, where the birds nest on a comparatively level island top but on the much steeper faces of, for instance, the Bass Rock, it is less easy to count the Gannets.

From the counts on photographs taken at Grassholm, it has been shown that the colony has increased its numbers greatly since the birds first came to the island more than 100 years ago. In 1913, there were about 275 pairs occupying nests. By 1939, this had risen to nearly 6,000 pairs. Ten years later, the number was nearly 10,000. Another ten years saw another 5,000 pairs on the island. During the great seabird census of 1969/70, Operation Seafarer, the figure was estimated at 16,128. By 1978, the figure was more than 20,000.

David T. Grewcock/FLPA

The story is one of continual and dramatic increase, a consequence of reduced exploitation and an abundance of pelagic fish in the Celtic Sea. It will be interesting to see what will happen if the current overfishing of mackerel continues. There is also the as yet uncalculated effect on breeding success of the recent explosion in the use of synthetic ropes, which often end up in gaily coloured pieces in Gannet's nests, there to ensnare both adults and young.

Great Crested Grebes and Rooks have also been the subject of large-scale census work. In the case of the Rook, the study was grant-aided by the government, who wanted to know the economic significance of Rooks on farmland. Wintering wildfowl populations have been studied since 1947, co-ordinated by the Wildfowl Trust and with the long-term object of conserving the stocks of this valuable resource. The other important continuing census is the BTO's Common Birds Census, started in 1962 and providing an annual account of status and distribution which is invaluable to conservationists and all who are concerned with the maintenance of a healthy and diverse wildlife population.

Gannets are increasing in numbers – well over 15,000 pairs breed round the British Isles

33

Ticking and Twitching

'Wrens normally sculpt in bramble and ferns'

The Times
13 April 1987

When you can tell a Robin from a Blue Tit and a Rook from a Carrion Crow, you can't help beginning to compile a bird list, even if it's only in your head. There are the birds you can see in your garden, the ones you see on the way to work, the ones you can see at work, on train journeys, on holidays and so on and so on. Different seasons, different places all offer a different spectrum of bird sightings. You soon start to sort out the difference between residents, summer or winter visitors, spring and autumn passage migrants.

Bird listing can become an obsession. Your family house and garden list, your personal life list, your year list, holiday list – there is ample opportunity. Perhaps the ultimate for a lister is to get a new bird accepted for the British List but there are plenty of second bests, like getting one of your records accepted for a county list. And, while this may begin to sound like a feeble kind of sport, the fact is that there is plenty of solid worth in lists and the tally-ho of rarity-hunting.

Over the last few years a form of sport has developed in which birdwatchers try to set up a record for the number of species seen in a single day. This stems from an American phenomenon known as the Christmas Bird Count, when members of the Audubon Societies all over the USA go out on a pre-determined day to count the birds of their local patch. John Jones organised a Big Day in his home county of Devon . . .

What, you may ask, is a Big Day? Quite simply, it is an attempt to see as many species of birds as possible in a period of twenty-four hours, starting at midnight, within a defined geographical area. As far as I know, the present Big Day record in Devon stands at 111 species. The next question you might want to ask is, 'Why a Big Day?' What is the point of rushing around seeing all these birds? The most sensible answer I can give is that when you combine it with fund raising by being sponsored, then a Big Day is an excellent way of getting in the cash! There are obviously three ways of raising more money by such sponsorship: 1 get a few rich sponsors, 2 get a lot of poor sponsors or 3 get people to sponsor you for a small amount per species and then go out and see a lot of them. Ask a non-birdwatcher about how many types of birds you might be able to see in a Big Day and you can see how well method 3 works! My mother for instance, thought I would see about twenty. She now knows better!

Our Big Day was 3 May 1986. As part of the society's sponsored birdwatch in Spring 1986, Tony John, Bob Jones, Humphrey Sitters and myself decided to see how close we could get to the above record, raising as much cash as we could at the same time. To make a Big Day succeed there must be careful planning. My wife was not convinced that the Friday nights spent in a local pub were all connected with this planning, but they were. Honest! Bob volunteered to drive, a timetable was agreed and then all that was left was to cross our fingers for good weather on the day.

Saturday 3 May arrived. We met, bacon sandwiches and tea on hand, at 4.15am at my house in Dousland, so that by 4.50am we could be at Burrator ready for the dawn chorus. One of the rules of a Big Day is that you can identify the birds by sight or sound. Even before we left the house, we had our first bird – a Tawny Owl calling at 4.46. We obviously had an idea of what birds we would like to see at each of the fourteen locations we planned to stop at. As usual, however, the best laid plans did not work out exactly. My nestboxes at Burrator failed to produce Pied Flycatchers and the Siskins and Redpolls I had seen only days before would not appear. There were bonuses, though. Goosanders were still present and Humphrey located a pair of Willow Tits, unusual in the area. It was while watching and listening to the tits that an event which later proved quite significant

The excitement of a 'first' attracts a twitch of birdwatchers

Eric & David Hosking

TWITCHING

In recent years there has been a tremendous increase in the number of people enjoying the hobby of birdwatching. It is an interest which can take many forms and many of the most enthusiastic birdwatchers soon become dedicated 'twitchers'.

A 'twitcher' is a birdwatcher who is fascinated by the variety of bird species that evolution has produced. He is prepared to travel extensively to try to see for himself as many different species as possible. He is a scientist, a sportsman and a conservationist, but above all he is a bird fanatic. He 'collects' sightings of different birds by ticking them off on his list and cares deeply about the birds and their conservation – he wants to continue seeing as many different species as possible.

Twitchers keep lists of the birds they have seen, indeed in America they are known as 'listers'. For example, they keep life lists (of birds they have seen anywhere, ever), county lists (birds seen in a particular county) and British lists (birds seen in Britain). One of the most popularly kept lists is the British Year List – just a handful of the most dedicated twitchers have achieved the magic number of 300 species seen in Britain in a single year.

The RSPB has pioneered the provision of public birdwatching hides

To see 200 bird species in a year in Britain is not too difficult, but to see 300 requires dedication – and the help of many other birdwatchers. The extra hundred species are made up of the rare visitors, some of which annually occur in Britain. Many of these birds appear just briefly at unpredictable and out-of-the-way places, so the twitcher must hear about them quickly, and then move fast before they have disappeared. Some of the rarest birds may appear in Britain just once and perhaps never again, so it is especially important to try not to miss seeing them. It may literally be a chance of a lifetime.

Most of these rare birds are relatively common species in other parts of the world, and they normally undergo long migrations. They are sometimes off course by thousands of miles when they appear in Britain. For example, it is not unknown for a bird which normally summers in Alaska and winters in South America to take a 'wrong turn' on the way and appear in Cornwall.

Twitchers cannot exist without the goodwill of the birdwatchers who are the lucky finders of the more exciting birds. It is these generous and unselfish birdwatchers who start the telephone 'grapevine' working, so that other people can come and enjoy their finds.

Eric Hosking

occurred. It is a rule of the Big Day that a team of four is needed and that each member of the team agrees on the identification of each species – ie each person must hear or see the bird and agree with everyone else that the identification is correct. Bob and I heard a Great Spotted Woodpecker in the distance; the other two hadn't heard it, but we had the rest of the day to pick up another one and you would have thought it easy to find one, but we didn't!

We returned to Dousland to try to find a Siskin, but failed and at 7.30am set off for Cadover Bridge with fifty-five species under our belts. I had three different sites where I expected Little Owls, but again failure. It was still cold and a little windy on the moors and the owls were keeping their heads down. On the way to Wembury we made a quick stop on the Plym. Wembury gave us the promised Cirl Buntings as well as Gannet offshore. By noon we had called in at Start Point and were on our way to Slapton. This gave us several bonus birds – Ruddy Duck, Gadwall and, unusual

A certain amount of attack has been levelled at twitching on occasions, mainly from people who do not really understand it. It is sometimes something of a shock for a birdwatcher to find his usually quiet local spot invaded by crowds, but when the rare bird disappears so do the twitchers and the sighting has given a great deal of pleasure to many birdwatchers. Problems occasionally arise when an unusual number of birdwatchers descend on a site which has become temporary host to an extreme rarity, but very seldom is actual harm done, either to the bird or the habitat. Neither, generally, do twitchers disturb rare breeding birds. Most have a sound ornithological knowledge and therefore know how to watch even shy breeding birds without disturbing them.

A few more sedentary birdwatchers accuse twitchers of mindless competition and 'tick' collecting, and the fact that a certain amount of jargon is used tends to alienate some people. But it must be stressed that – 'tick' collecting and jargon apart – twitchers do fully appreciate the aesthetic quality of the birds. The keenest are undoubtedly bird-enthusiasts first and 'tick-hunters' second. They include amongst their ranks some of the best field ornithologists in the country. Lists are a way to catalogue some of the enjoyment of birdwatching and to provide personal achievement as well as friendly competition. A bird is more than a 'tick'; it is a living wild creature that presents the birdwatcher with an absorbing and wonderful experience. If it is a species he has never seen before then the experience is all the more exciting.

31 August, NW3 mainly sunny
Drift Reservoir, Cornwall 06.15–08.00
At least six Common and 3+ Green Sandpipers feeding in muddy bays, also 1 Oystercatcher, 3 Greenshanks, 2 Dunlin and 1 very tame Curlew Sandpiper seen along edge of reservoir.

One Lesser Yellowlegs located on grassy shoreline. Scoped at about 40yd and seen to resemble a slim, elegant Redshank, but rather smaller, with very long, slender legs and straight fine bill. Plumage basically dark grey above, liberally speckled with white and some darker feather-centres, striated grey on head, neck and breast, with pale supercilium and eye-ring, white below. Bill and eye black, legs yellow (though perhaps not as bright as some), the latter extending beyond the tail in flight, when square white rump, finely barred tail and unmarked wings also noticeable.

Called several times – 'hu hu hu', rather similar to Greenshank but lacking the strength or ringing quality, and occasionally only as a double note.

Richard Millington

Eric Hosking

A conveniently sited vantage point for a keen group of ornithologists

Cretzschmar's Bunting would be a megatick on any Big Day

Tony Soper

for May, a Long-tailed Duck. Another instance of controversy occurred here. Certainly a Reed Warbler sang, but we could not agree on a single burst of song, we didn't count it, but was it a Sedge Warbler? Still, the sun was out and we enjoyed a restful lunch, still in the field by the way!

At 3.45pm we arrived at Dawlish with ninety-three species up. This again gave us some bonus birds: a Mediterranean Gull, a single late Brent Goose and Red-breasted Mergansers flying out of the estuary to sea. We also saw several police cars chasing over the golf course, plus a police helicopter swooping low over the hide. Not the calmest of times to birdwatch! Some youths had caused trouble and were duly apprehended. We searched for Arctic or Roseate Terns among the Common Terns but found none. At nearly 7pm we finally found a Siskin on Haldon. One hundred and eight species now. Could we reach the total of 111 and could we pass it? At 7.30pm Nightingales sang as we arrived at Chudleigh.

The sky was now grey and rain threatened. It arrived along with us at Warren House Inn. We searched vainly in failing light for some moorland species. We had hoped for Whinchat, Redpoll and Ring Ouzel. We eventually found our Ouzel, it called, sad notes in the rain, but it gave hope to us. 8.45pm. We had planned to finish our day at the inn, but with only two species to go it was too good a chance to miss. After an excellent meal produced by Carol, Bob's wife, we decided to try once more for Little Owl and chance

David Hosking

an encounter with a Barn Owl. I will tell you that listening for calling Little Owls in the wind and rain on Dartmoor at 11.30pm is not a pleasant experience. However, they didn't let us down. We had half an hour left and spent it driving around Dartmoor in the hope that one of the few Barn Owls left might be out feeding, but no luck. We had seen 111 species and were content with that. In all we raised nearly £400 between us.

In 1986 the sponsored birdwatch was aimed at raising money for 'pocket conservation' – buying small areas of land such as marshes and woodlands as sites for birds. This year we need a lot more for the purchase of South Milton Ley. We hope to repeat our Big Day with the aim of making more money for the society. I understand a group from south Devon is attempting to break the Devon Big Day record and we wish them well. I would urge everyone to get involved with our sponsored birdwatch this year. It acts as a focus for non-birdwatchers, they just think that anyone who chases around watching birds is eccentric, and we know how we all love eccentrics. If a Big Day causes more people to sponsor more money and so enable more land to be bought, it cannot be a bad thing. You don't have to go quite so far, however; any birdwatching activity for which you can be sponsored will help. If everyone in the society was able to raise a few pounds by sponsorship, the total money raised would provide a good fund with which to purchase, as the RSPB calls it, 'a place for birds'.

Common Terns – here the male brings the female a choice morsel during courtship

At the other end of England, Dave Webb and his son Adrian enjoyed their Big Day in Suffolk . . .

It's 00.20 hours on 12 May 1985 and we're about to enter Walberswick's giant reed-bed. There's total darkness, no moon, no stars, and the wind is blowing. Surprisingly, I'm feeling very relaxed: at last it's all about to happen.

The last few months have been spent organising this year's birdwatch, with the main task being to contact as many people as possible to raise money for the RSPB. This year my son Adrian, a YOC member, and I were determined to raise £1,000. To be sure of reaching our target we would have to see well over the 110 species we managed in 1984, but where were we going to find them all? Then it came to me – Wales! We could whip round Suffolk picking up as many species as possible until about 9am, and then rush across to Wales where there is a whole new range to be found, such as Pied Flycatcher, Dipper and Grey Wagtail, Buzzard and Red Kite, Guillemot, Razorbill and Puffin.

Next I had to select the best sites in each area. The obvious choice for Suffolk was Minsmere, so we went to see Trevor Charlton, the assistant warden, and he agreed to join us for the early part of the day. The following Sunday we were off again, this time to Wales to work out our travelling times and sites to visit. Our first stop was Lake Vyrnwy, where we met Paul Hill, the summer warden, who was also keen to help. As well as Lake Vyrnwy, we decided we would go to Stackpole Head in Pembrokeshire for the seabirds, and

Dippers like to perch on a convenient rock in the stream

Eric Hosking

Eric Hosking

arranged to meet warden Bob Haycock on the day. We would also call in at Ynys-hir for Red-breasted Merganser, and Tregaron Bog for Red Kite.

My next job was to recruit another team member, a co-driver with a knowledge of birds who could possibly help with sponsors. Bob Graves, a local birdwatcher, agreed to join us.

We left home on Saturday at 9.45pm and about two hours later reached Trevor's house at Minsmere. Here a Nightingale was in full song, but this one would not count at it was only 11.55pm. Trevor hurried out and ten minutes later we were at Walberswick. As we made our way to the reed-bed there were faint indistinguishable sounds in the distance, but the wind was making it difficult to hear anything. Then a Greylag Goose honked, followed by the sudden burst of a Nightingale. Our Big Day had finally started.

We managed ten species at Walberswick, including Water Rail, which was very pleasing, but missed Savi's Warbler, which was not. We drove back to Island Mere at Minsmere and from the bushes beside the path came the rich, unmistakable song of a Cetti's Warbler. We went to the Mere Hide and stumbled upstairs in the dark, opening the viewing hatch just in time to hear the hoot of a Tawny Owl. Forty-five minutes and only two more species later, we made a dash for the West Hide by the Scrape: 4.05 and the weather had deteriorated beyond belief – bitterly cold and windy. Nevertheless, we did muster another twenty-six species,

Tricky identifications . . . Greenland (top) and Common Wheatears

R. Tidman/FLPA

'We sped off to find a Parrot Crossbill'

including Marsh Harrier, to bring our score to forty-one. Driving down to the sea we added Mute Swan. It was now 5.39 and in the next eleven minutes we recorded another eight species, including a Greenshank, calling as it flew over. A short sea watch turned up a Little Tern busily fishing. 'Fulmar,' called Trevor, 'coming out of the mist.' There is was, about 50yd from the shore and, just below it, a Kittiwake. Although both common in Wales, they are real ego-boosters if you happen to be in East Anglia. Just one more species here, a Meadow Pipit, then it was time to go to the woods.

All of a sudden everything became urgent – it was 6.35 and there was much to do before nine o'clock. Goldfinch, Blackcap, Song Thrush, and then Cormorant, all in the same minute. Cuckoo, House Sparrow and, luckily, Black Redstart, our reason for stopping at this point. In the next half-hour we ticked off another twenty-two species, making eighty-four in all. One final look in at Island Mere produced seven more, including three feral species. Eastbridge was our next stop as Trevor knew a good site here for Tree Sparrow and Grey Partridge. Sure enough, there they were, together with other common species we hadn't yet seen.

We sped off to find Parrot Crossbill, which we saw along with three other species before returning to Minsmere. A Whinchat had been seen behind the information centre less than half an hour earlier, and a quick look round proved well worthwhile, producing not only Whinchat but also Wheatear, Wryneck and a late Fieldfare.

The time was 9.30am, the number of species 106, but it hadn't gone at all to plan because of the weather. We had wanted 120 before leaving, as well as time to visit one or two other sites on the journey to Wales.

We finally left Minsmere at 10am, an hour behind schedule, arriving at Lake Vyrnwy five hours later, having only added another four species on the journey. We met up with Paul Hill in the car park, where we soon had Siskin and Firecrest on the list before visiting a Pied Flycatcher sit. Up of the moors we saw a Peregrine being harrassed by a Carrion Crow. Back at the information centre, Paul gave a shout of excitement, pointing towards the sky. Wheeling high above us was a Red Kite; what a lucky break, as this was only the seventh all-time record for the area. On our way to Ynys-hir we saw a Dipper, Red-breasted Mergansers when we arrived on the reserve itself, and then a Spotted Flycatcher as we were leaving.

At last we were on the final leg of our journey. We had 100 miles to go and only fifty-seven minutes to do it in if we were going to meet Bob Haycock at 7.30pm as arranged. If anyone needed a jet plane, it was us. We did manage to arrive in daylight and Bob was there waiting patiently for us. We piled into his van and bumped our way to the cliff-top. It wasn't long before we had added Guillemot and Razorbill, but the light was fading fast and with it any chance of seeing much else. We saw a Chough flying round the

Eric & David Hosking

Rose-ringed Parakeets – here in courtship display – are establishing a foothold in the South-East

Eric Hosking

headland and a Rock Pipit calling as it passed by. We looked for Raven and Puffin, but the darkness had beaten us.

Our Big Day was over and we had seen 129 species in twenty-one hours. It looked as if our target of £1,000 would be achieved.

A mixed bag of shorebirds – Oystercatcher, Redshank, Turnstone and Knot

Dave Webb raised £1,116.40 for the RSPB's funds and the sponsored Big Day seems destined to run for ever.

But while the day list has its charms, the life list has to be the biggest one, and many birdwatchers go to inordinate lengths to tick off rarities to boost their personal achievement. Sometimes these are solo efforts, but very often the news has travelled fast on the grapevine, and the rarity is surrounded by an army of 'twitchers'. Peter Goodfellow joined a typical pilgrimage . . .

There were certainly over a thousand of us, but we were not all sitting still, watching. From the car park at Cley village to the principal viewing point, half a mile away across the Blakeney water-meadows, a continuous straggle of people moved to and fro. Almost everyone was armed: binoculars and cameras and lenses and telescopes and tripods. The troops were a thin khaki line from base to the Front. For several hours (from dawn so we heard – we didn't arrive till just after eleven), reinforcements and replacements had been purposefully plodding towards the action, ticking it off, and returning to 'Lucy's' for refreshment and the display of campaign medals.

'I was at Marazion yesterday'. (So I overheard.) 'Any good?' 'Two Pec Sands and a Killdeer.'

'Yeh? There's a Pallas's Grasshopper in Northumberland.' 'Seen it.' 'Jammy swine! I tried for six hours – hopeless. Got an Ortolan, though, on Holy Island.'

'Hang on. There it is. Just come out into the open by those

Parrots in the car park

For a second year, visitors to Wells-next-the-Sea in Norfolk could watch Parrot Crossbills from the comfort of their cars in the public car park, just behind the beach. These nesting birds were protected by a warden – whose caravan was parked next to the ice-cream van! With plenty of food in the pine trees where they were nesting and water in puddles in the car park, the pair successfully raised two broods. Four, or possibly five, young fledged on 4 April and a probable two more on 17 May.

As another pair also nested for the second year at an undisclosed site in Suffolk, it is hoped that these Scandinavian birds may become a regular East Anglian breeding species.

COMIC TURNS

While he was still working for the BBC's Natural Mystery Unit and before he extended his range to the RSPB, Jeffrey Boswall offered this revision of the British List to readers of *BTO News*, the newsletter of the British Trust for Ornithology, asking for further suggestions . . .

Slowly Wol, Arctic Stuka, Glucose Gull, Common Sandpaper (or Emery Birds), Grape Lover, Lady Chatterley's Plover, Evening Jar, Backchat, Temminck's Stink, Wee Tear, Would Lark, Spotted-fly Catcher, Hipfinch and Wide Pagtail (or 'Chisick' Flyover).

Practically by return of post an army of word botchers offered more . . .

Sighting by Barry L. Evans occurred after several Evening Jars and included the Laserbill, Caper-gaily (or Scots-turn). Bar-tailed Oddwit, Carryon Crew, Harsh Marrier, Torn Yowl and Red-backed Strike. In urban Edinburgh Lennox Campbel finds the Common Scooter *Melanitta lambretta* a frequent passage migrant, and in the larger stores, both Y-fronted *Anser cumfifrons* and Lesser Y-fronted Geese *Anser indecenta* are for sale.

Robert Gillmor invites you to Keep your Heron when making a Right Hand Tern, By Gadwall; and at the garage we are urged to fill up with a Cutprice Petrel (per C. B. Lax) and Lesser Castrol (per Denis Taylor). More upright than using Siphoned (or Collared) Petrel (per Norman Gammon). Besides Johnson's Backchat, we now have the Ceaseless Chat *Nagsicloa perpetuum*. Tea-time Chit Chat, and the Rock Talk (or Stonechat).

Ardeola ralloides is renamed Squaw Coheren (by Norman Gammon) and Stucco Heron by Norman Kirkman whose masterly list also includes the Neverwort *Alauda shelleyi*, the Little Creep *Crepulus minor*, the Dapper *Cinclus sinartus* and Arctic Bedroll *Carduelis dormiendus*. The Flied Piecatcher and Warden Garbler have been widely observed; so, curiously, has the Once Bittern.

All in all then, a few Miserable Bustards and many Comic Turns.

In spite of an editorial plea to 'cool it', the entries poured in . . .

Perched on television aerials in Reading, Robert Gillmor has seen the Kojakdaw and the Pot Blackbird.

Closely related species-pairs include the Bumbling and the Shuffeler differentiated by Peter G. Swain, and the Waste Knot and Want Knot often found in one another's company

by Molly Hill. The Two-toned Tit Wobbler and the Double-breasted Pushover apparently breed sympatrically in Shetland, home too of the Cream-coloured Corset (per Bobby Tirrick).

By Kudwig Loch, G. Cuthbert identified a Seagle, no doubt a hybrid and in Kent Major David Counsell tells us the Rock Bun Ting is not uncommon and that he frequently sees the Fried Pie Catcher.

Various vagrants include the Tittle Tattler (per K. G. Spencer); the Bronxie and the Dollared Cove, spotted by Peter and Rosemary Banks; and the Corsican Nutcase (or Bonaparte's Gall) and the Ob Skua from Western Siberia. The latter was identified by a Stoned Curlew calling himself 'Predacious of Newtonmore' who asked whether Lady Amherst's Peasant might have been a neighbour of Lady Chatterley's Plover, and who urges that on humanitarian grounds one should destroy badly distressed birds like the Sorer Rail and ignore supercilious ones like the Snob Bunting in favour of kindly and entertaining ones like the Good Wit; but I must stop before I get Bittern with the subject.

The prize for sheer deviousness goes to Marion Shimeld whose list includes Pint Ale, Moor Wren, Night Talk, Grey Tweed Warbler, Grey Twite Egret and Bloody Hell Duck. Ernest C. Sterne suggests a Sure Lark is preferable to my Would Lark. It would take a Bearded Twit to disagree with that.

David Chatfield of Swansea complains of Whooping Chough and Hacking Chough, but is taking a Cox's Orange Pipit a day washed down with expensive Angostura Bitterns. Let's hope his Bank Tanager won't object.

In the new selection the tribe *Somateriini* is well to the foreshore in the Plain Ida (per Malcolm Ogilvie) and the Four Eider or Spectacled Eider (per Ken Osborne). No doubt Devon's Eider (per Charles Lax) and Bulmer's Eider are con-specifies.

In a *tour de force* to be compared only with Norman Kirkman's brilliant selection published earlier, L. J. Davenport with M. J. Watts as ammanuensis offer their own Aida, and suggest that any *Charadrius alexandrinus* seen east of the Medway should be dubbed Plovers of Kent. They christen also: Daylight Robin, Wombel, Tottenham Longspur, Black Velvet Soaker, Semi-frustrated Sandpiper, and Richard's Poppet (also known as Payne's Pipit). And perhaps cleverest of all: Black-wellied Dipper.

Eric Hosking

Winter visitors; Waxwings if you're lucky

Jackdaws.' A ripple of movement ran along the ranks, telescopes swung, tripods were readjusted, range and focus were checked.

'Great! That really is a megatick. Probably never see another, unless I get sent to Siberia! Damn, those Jackdaws have scared it! It's off, east. Look, moving high over those Friesians back towards Cley coastguard hut. Come on.' The orderly retreat began, but not before I had photographed a battery of telescopes, several ranks of watchers at the favourite viewpoint, and the patient crocodile of troops returning to base.

Peter and I moved off to join our families and we all headed for a pot of tea at 'Lucy's'. By the time we arrived it was not busy, presumably everyone was still busy twitching. We did 'tick off' Bryan Bland, birdwatcher extraordinary and leader of expeditions. We were soon in this twitcher-world even more deeply when the café's phone rang. A lad from a neighbouring table answered it. ('But he's a visitor like us, not café staff!') He jabbered away about local news. Clearly, phoning in was a regular pastime, an essential part of twitching. A few minutes after the lad had left, the phone rang again, and Peter answered it. He was astonished to learn (and take down on a pad provided by the phone) that a Reef Heron was reported on the River Exe. Here we were in Norfolk hearing about what was worth seeing back home in Devon! It was supposed to be a good record because Griff had seen it. Before we left I had my turn, and had to tell an enquiring voice the latest: 'Yes, the bird's still here; and a Bonaparte's on the pool by the Norfolk Naturalists' Trust hide . . . a Bonaparte's Sandpiper . . . sorry, I saw one in 1955, it *was* a Bonaparte's then, now it's a White-rumped.

And there's a Reef Heron on the Exe. Griff's seen it . . . No, I don't know exactly where . . . Cheerio.'

And we had seen It, too. But our 'It' had been *Numenius minutus*, the Little Whimbrel, only the second ever to be seen in Europe, in August 1985, and it should have been in Australia, misguided bird. Adrift perhaps, but it had given us all great pleasure. 'Little' by name, but 'great' by reputation and effect: a minute part of the bird world, but a big entry in my log-book, a megatick!

Brian Unwin is a newspaper reporter working for the Sunderland *Journal*. He is a keen birder, always on the look-out for a rarity, especially if he can write it up for his regular 'Wildlife Watch' column . . .

As a birdwatching Sunderland football supporter, I have an astonishing stranger-than-fiction tale to tell today.

Many fellow red- and white-eyed fans cannot understand why our team ended up with their fourth defeat in a row last Monday. One explanation, which I can reveal exclusively, is strictly ornithological.

Certainly the bank holiday drubbing from Oldham came as no surprise to me. In fact I predicted the exact 0–3 score five hours before the kick-off, as I watched a rare Wilson's Phalarope, freshly flown in from America, at Teesmouth.

You see on 1 September 1979, I was about to set off to watch Sunderland play at Oldham when I heard two Wilson's Phalaropes had turned up at Teesmouth. So I called to look at the birds before driving to Greater Manchester – see Sunderland comprehensively beaten 3–0.

Wilson's Phalaropes are still very unusual visitors to Britain – there have been fewer than 170 records in the space of 200 years – so the occurrence of another coinciding with last Monday's Sunderland–Oldham fixture just had to mean history repeating itself, I considered.

Well, I was proved right, wasn't I? The next time Sunderland are due to play Oldham I suggest manager Lawrie McMenemy seeks a postponement if there happens to be a Wilson's Phalarope around at the time.

If he gives me a call I will be only too happy to inform him whether this bird of apparent ill-omen has dropped in. Meanwhile, the least Oldham could do is to include this attractive wader in the club crest.

Apart from any unfortunate effect it may have had on Sunderland's performance, the appearance of the phalarope was certainly welcomed by birdwatchers who travelled widely to see the bird thousands of miles east of its normal migratory route between the North American prairie regions and its wintering haunts, the Andean lakes of South America.

One of the ways phalaropes differ from other members of the wader group is their feeding action. Although they do catch insects while wading in shallows or walking on mud, they are best known for their habit of swimming in deeper water and spinning their bodies around, then seizing

The Collared Dove

Some megaticks settle to become everyday birds. The Collared Dove first showed itself in Britain in 1953 as a twitcher's dream, a 'first', but now it has colonised the whole of Britain and many call it a pest.

Frank Gribble

Cormorants preening and wing-drying

the minute life disturbed in the process.

Unlike my football team, the Teesmouth bird with its soft grey and white plumage was in cracking form, pirouetting almost non–stop on the murky water of the Reclamation Pond and constantly striking out with its long, needle-like bill to pluck insects from the air.

Brian Unwin reports the local soccer matches on the sports page of his newspaper, but then doubles his wordage for the day by writing up the same match for his bird column on the feature page! . .

Although theoretically on the terraces to watch activites on the pitch, I always keep glancing skyward but rarely have I seen anything more than flocks of gulls or Starlings, or parties of Cormorants returning to roost on Marsden Rock after a day's fishing on the Wear.

So I was quite amazed to see a tiny Blue Tit fly the length of the pitch during the second-half of the Sunderland v Leeds match a fortnight ago.

Leeds had just narrowed the score to 3–2 and along with thousands of other Wearsiders I was beginning to fear the worst, but this unusual avian visitor to the ground completely took my attention away from the nail-biting soccer drama.

The bird actually landed on the crossbar of the Leeds goal, quite unconcerned by the presence of keeper Day directly below or the thousands of roaring fans in the Fulwell End.

Whether the Blue Tit had anything to do with it is a matter for speculation, but seconds later Sunderland were awarded the penalty that brought their 4–2 victory.

Maybe luck flew in with the bird – and on that score I can recall a precedent, way back on 16 October 1965 when another struggling Sunderland side was losing 2–1 against Nottingham Forest at half-time.

During the interval I glanced to the heavens for a sign and, as if on cue, a skein of Pink-footed Geese – always an uncommon sight in the North-East – flew over. Within half an hour Sunderland had notched two goals to win the match.

Such a coincidental ornithological blessing would not come amiss at this afternoon's FA Cup-tie against Manchester United at Roker Park.

The sight of something even as humble as a Kestrel hovering over the United goalmouth would, I reckon, guarantee a place for Sunderland in the next round.

A world away from the rousing camaraderie of the football terraces William Condry also writes of the pleasure of his birdwatching while engaged on his professional duties. But he is the RSPB's warden at Ynys-hir in Dyfed. He combines work with enjoyment in a way which naturalists very often achieve. Here he checks on his estuary at the turn of the tide . . .

The tide is flooding. Looking seawards down the estuary with the evening sun in my eyes, I catch the gleam of white water pouring in over the bar 4 miles away. But for a while yet the estuary will remain an almost dry plain, a loneliness of empty creeks and sand, and spartina grass which lies like a golden cornfield, beautiful but unloved by naturalists because each year it chokes more and more precious acres of mud-flats – the estuary birds' feeding grounds.

I walk along the railway with the sea breeze softening the warmth of the autumn sun. For a week it has been grey and wet off the Atlantic. But today the heat of summer has come back and with it a summer smell – the reek of tar melting out of the railway sleepers. So I am glad to leave the embankment for the sweeter air of the marshes.

A Wheatear hops quickly ahead of me across turf where it is hard to find a grass leaf 2in high, so cleanly is everywhere

Kestrel.

nibbled by the sheep. But that's how Wheatears like it, this close-cut, sea-enriched sward, the envy of gardeners and the food of our winter Wigeon – sweet grass in a world of salt. For a quarter of a mile I walk this immaculate pasture. More Wheatears flit before me, so brown and drab when I think of the clear colours – black, grey, white and pink – of those I watched on these same saltings in May.

I come to where the grassland ends in a line of wave-broken clay cliffs a yard high. Here two worlds meet: the world of the upper saltings which the sea reaches only a few days a month and the world of the lower saltings where all tides flow. I find a cavity to crouch in – shake the sea wind from my ears to hear the calls of approaching birds. I settle down to watch the coming of the great tide. A creek beyond the yellow prairie of the spartina is filling fast. Only moments ago it was a thin pale line – now it is a broad bar of tremulous, silvery water. Quickly, other creeks begin to fill and widen. Everywhere through my binoculars I see grey water over-spilling from a maze of winding runnels and advancing across the wide muds and through the spartina meads.

With it come the birds. When I arrived all I could hear was the frenzied piping of unseen Oystercatchers, the sad notes of Redshanks and the yodellings of Curlews, all very far away. But now, retreating before this quick tide, they are quite suddenly my neighbours. Two hundred Curlews have flown in unusual silence to gather along a sandback just in front of me. But in a tide like this, with all the Irish sea behind it, they cannot stay there for long. Minute by minute the estuary is becoming more and more an arm of the sea and the dazzle of light increases. The fields of spartina have shrunk to spiky islands which are vanishing fast. Already the long-legged Curlews are up to their bellies in seawater and now they raise a querulous chorus; a strange, tremulous, deep-voiced bubbling they reserve for such tide-harassed moments. Then with one resolve they all rise and fly off in a long, calling procession to settle on the turf of the higher saltings. I watch them landing – many immediately swing round their curved beaks, bury them amongst their back feathers and apparently go straight to sleep.

I turn away only for a few minutes to look inland where distant flocks of Dunlin and Ringed Plovers are weaving restlessly about the sky seeking somewhere to rest through the high-tide hour. And when I turn again seawards the scene has changed already. Shallows that had been lively with wading Godwits, Whimbrel and Knot have been swept by deep water and all the birds have taken to the air. I picked them up as they are patterning the sky above the rough line of the dunes. Then they sweep across the estuary mouth and I lose them against the dark shape of the northern hills until they swing round to let white underwings take the sunlight. Now they throw themselves down the sky towards me, sweep low with a rush of wings and excited voices, then off they go racing inland.

A probing question

Why do Curlews have decurved bills? This is the question which Nick Davidson, Dave Townshend, Mike Pienkowski and John Speakman set out to answer in their papers in *Bird Study* (Vol 33 Part 2).

The shape and size of a bird's bill is closely correlated with its feeding habits. However: it can be difficult to identify the purpose for which the bill form is chiefly adapted, especially in species which occupy several habitats and take different foods at different times of the year. In setting out their stall the authors argue that decurvature is an adaptation for probing along complex pathways and to aid extraction of worms without breaking them; also that the very long, decurved bill of the Common Curlew is chiefly an adaptation for probing along such pathways deep into mud-flats.

Comparison is made of prey capture techniques of Curlews and Bar-tailed Godwits on mud-flats eg both species can detect prey by sight and sound, but while the Godwit plunges its bill rapidly and, on most occasions, vertically into deep sediment, occasionally pivoting around the hole with the bill still deep in the mud, the Curlew probes more slowly, moving its bill along a complex route both in line with and perpendicular to the axis of the bill, and seldom pivoting round the probe site.

BTO News

An assortment of other waders make their way up the estuary. Most are just voices in the upper air. Greenshanks, two or three together, call their distinctive 'tew-tew-tew' as they pass. And far off the 'chew–it' of a Spotted Redshank and the mournful 'tee-loo-ee' of Grey Plovers. Then pack after hastening pack of common Redshanks, scurrying like children late for school.

Hissing and bubbling and edged with white foam the water is now round my gumboots and like the waders I am forced into speedy retreat across the saltings, just in time to ford the last filling creek. Seconds later it is 3ft deep in muddy water, so forceful is the final leap of the tide. I find a hard perch on the rocks of the railway bank amid a bright-yellow gaiety of Oxford ragwort. In no time the last of the green saltings are awash and the estuary, the familiar estuary of mud and sand and spartina, has entirely vanished, replaced by a fjord 6 miles long, 2 miles across.

This is the cue for the final actors. From the open sea the long-winged, graceful terns come in lightly on the breeze, diving here and there into the green streaming tide and coming out with little bright fish. For half an hour I watch them – how fleeting the moment; for they are rare, these surges of ocean life into our estuary. They happen only in the warm half of the year, only on very high tides and then only when the sea is unusually heavy with plankton and

A high-water roost at Hilbre Island in the Cheshire Dee; Knots, with Oystercatchers and Herring Gulls in the background

50

its accompanying shoals of hungry little fish. Sharing in the plankton feast or preying on the multitudinous fishlets come the mullet and the bass, the shads, the smelts, the garfish. In pursuit of these come seals, porpoises, gulls, Cormorants, mergansers. Perhaps on only this one autumn tide can I watch such an unfolding of sea life so far inland.

Out in mid-estuary a confused glitter of flapping wings catches my eye. Evidently an upswelling of water has surfaced a supply of rich food which has attracted a great screaming, winnowing throng of Black-headed Gulls. Quickly the terns also gather and for a few minutes there is a snow-storm of plunging white bodies. Then the excitement gradually subsides. The terns go on up-river and the gulls settle quietly on the water.

Stillness all round: the breeze has dropped as it so often does towards night. The life has gone out of the water. It is quite still now, almost oily. Not a wavelet laps. No bird cries anywhere. It is the moment, I decide, of full tide. But when I look again at the gulls I see I am wrong. Already they are drifting very slowly seawards. It is a sign for all the rest to follow – the plankton, the fish, the porpoises and the seabirds. They have had their estuary holiday and must go. And so must I. As I walk back along the railway I hear the first Oystercatchers go yelping seawards, impatient for the mud to reappear. They will not have long to wait.

Eric Hosking

Martin-watching

I was staying for Whitsun one year at a little inn on the Upper Thames. Under the eaves a number of House Martins were building their mud nests. I was interested to find out something of their courtship, but there had been no courting in evidence during the Saturday afternoon and evening. So, knowing that such activities are often most pronounced in the early morning, I got up before dawn on the Sunday. To my surprise, there were no Martins to be seen – none in or by their nests, none flying round. I walked round the place, and up and down the towpath, along which spread a faint mist from the river, and still saw nothing of my birds. Then from the barn came a single Swallow, and flew steeply up into the sky. I followed its flight with my eyes, and suddenly saw why I had failed to find the Martins. They were all up there in the blue, circling round in company with some Barn Swallows and Chimney Swifts, from which I could just distinguish them at the height they were flying. The sun had not yet risen where I stood on the solid earth; but he already reached the birds high above my head. And as the earth spun and the sun's rays approached its surface, the birds sank with them, twittering all the time; until finally the light struck the inn and flooded the meadows, and the birds dispersed to the duties of the day.

Julian Huxley

Courtship and Family Life

Bird-song may be enjoyable for us to listen to, but the birds are not singing to please us! Of course language has various functions, and one kind of call (like the familiar churr of a Jay for instance) may give warning that a predator is about. It is disseminating information. Another call may serve to keep a group of birds in touch. Yet another kind may involve the language of love, person to person, bird to bird. But first and foremost we have to deal with full-throated song, proclaimed from the top of a tree, where the bird is positively drawing attention to itself.

This kind of behaviour, on the face of it, is so monumentally stupid, exposing the bird to the attentions of all its enemies, that there has to be a powerful justification. It must have survival value. Well, an Englishman's home may seem to be his castle, but it's actively defended by a whole host of other creatures each regarding it, in deadly seriousness, as uniquely *their* home. They defend it, and have an urgent need to perpetuate their species in it. And that is the nub of the matter: the principle function of bird-song is to proclaim a territory and to attract a mate.

In winter most birds are too busy to sing, and many of our breeding species are away in foreign parts. But as the sap begins to rise, so do the testosterone levels in the cock-bird's blood. His aggressive instincts refuelled, he turns his mind to land ownership and the acquisition of a mate. So, as light percolates the morning garden, it triggers a dawn chorus of naked aggression and lust.

Each species has its own distinctive 'brand image', an identifiable song. Warblers, finches, tits, thrushes – dozens of different species each with a clearly distinctive call, conveying the basic information – species and sex. And each individual within a species is clearly distinguishable by his fellows.

'That's the wise thrush; he sings each song twice over' wrote Browning. Good observation, that is. The Song thrush does tend to repeat each phrase twice, sometimes three times, and perhaps the best poetic version of the thrush call is: 'Summer is coming, summer is coming, I know it, I know it, I know it!' (Tennyson). The poets have rendered the song into plain English, but what does it mean? What is the thrush actually singing? When he gets up and opens his mouth the news comes pealing out. It is spring and the sap

The Robin

Even in the short dark days of winter, the garden Robin sings. While most birds are silent, or at best twittering feeding calls, and at worst thousands of miles away, our Robin entertains us with full song. Apart from the short moulting break he sings right throughout the year, for which much thanks! So it's not surprising that we develop such a fondness for the garden redbreast. He appears such a permanent resident that it seems churlish to point out that your garden friend may in fact, over a period of years, be a whole succession of individuals following each other as life's disasters take their toll. All Robins look alike to us, and you'll need to work very hard to learn to distinguish individuals. When a Robin dies he leaves vacant a comfortable 'freehold property', and there's precious little delay before a new occupant arrives.

has risen. I am a cock Song Thrush, I am in full breeding condition. I warn all male Song Thrushes that I own this patch and will defend it against all comers with my life. I hereby advertise for a female Song Thrush to present herself. Should we suit each other, I shall invite her to live with me and be my love, sharing this desirable property with suitable nest sites.

Now the effect of that broadcast depends on who is within reception range. A Chiffchaff will ignore it, a Robin will ignore it. A cock Song Thrush will prick up his ears and bristle, recognising the challenge and the opportunity. A female Song Thrush, if she's already suited, will ignore it. An unpaired thrush, clearly understanding the invitation, may approach closer. If no Song Thrush is within audible distance, nothing will happen and the incumbent male will continue to advertise. He will sing from somewhere effective, the top of a tree or the top of a telegraph pole. Either will do – indeed from his point of view they are both trees anyway, though one is a particularly poor specimen for

Eric Hoski

Robins defend their territories . . .

Dr M. S. Wood/Hosking

. . . with vigorous display

53

purposes other than a songpost. What he wants is a commanding view and the biggest potential audience.

Not all birds sing from the top of a tree or a rooftop. Sky Larks live in open country. But they solve the problem in the most elegant fashion, taking to the wing and singing from an invisible songpost in the sky. Many birds are reluctant to leave the dense cover of the shrubbery, but for them too what more effective way of conveying the message than by singing? Down on the lawn the grasshopper has this same problem of living in a dense medium, but he does the best he can, climbing to the top of a grass stem to increase his range and chirping out his message by rubbing his legs to and fro along the serrated edge of his wing. Some birds, too, do not produce their song vocally: woodpeckers, for instance, find themselves a tree with a good ringing acoustic, and then rap smartly with rapid blows of the bill, so drumming out the immortal message. Less poetically they'll even tap out the message on the junction box of a television aerial on someone's roof!

Swallows and Swifts are aerial species, but they often breed communally and share territorial air space. A mole's patch is underground, centering on the nest fortress and spreading out along the tunnels which may reach out as much as 150yd. He makes no territorial claims on the land or air above. Territories may overlap amongst different species, but that is not significant. They matter between individuals of the same species, and in essence, they represent a defended area. Territories are not necessarily defended at all times. Robins, for example, are very keen on land ownership, staking a claim after the summer moult and keeping it it right through winter to the breeding season. They are unsociable creatures – you only see them in groups on Christmas cards. Unless they are actually paired, Robins will not tolerate companionship. The song is loud and continuous – 'keep off'. At the other end of the scale, a Goldfinch may only establish his claim just before building a nest and even then the defended ground consists only of the area in which he nests and mates, just a few square yards. Different species, different attitudes.

What happens when the singer is challenged? Sometimes a bird which understands the significance of the song nevertheless decides to call the bluff in the hope of usurping the prize. The challenger approaches closer, deliberately invading the territory. And he sings. The two sing at each other in a slanging match. The invader comes closer, till there is an eyeball-to-eyeball confrontation. Once in visual contact they bring weapons other than song to bear. The splendid breeding plumage is displayed in all its glory, each bird presenting itself to the best advantage, fluffing itself up to look bigger. Both posture and strut in an overbearing manner – Mr World incarnate.

Aggressive postures are a part of everyday life for all of us, part of the struggle to corner the best food, the best roosting place, the best territory and the best partner. But

Into battle

A curious territorial battle occurs when a bird comes face to face with himself in a mirror; perhaps it is a car wing mirror or hub-cap or a reflecting window. Finding that his spirited posturing is returned in like measure, he is even more disconcerted when, on attacking the intruder, he finds that he is beating against glass. This kind of activity may take up a great deal of wasted time and exhausting effort for a bird. Pied Wagtails seem especially prone to it and it is a kindness to cover up the mirror to remove the 'threat'.

for birds they are most important in spring. Lengthening days make the task of finding food easier and allow more spare time but, most important, it is the onset of the breeding season. The bird-table is a likely place to see the action. Blackbirds which previously met there in peace will suddenly take to posturing and vocal threats, becoming uneasy when another bird is within a critical distance. A cock Chaffinch will not tolerate another cock Chaffinch close to him at this time, yet they spend the winter in an all-male club of great tolerance and camaraderie.

In a typical threatening situation a bird will thrust its head forward or upward and show its breast feathers boldly to its opponent. The feathers fluff out and it will spread its wings, perhaps showing off the colourful secondaries. The

Song Thrush at the nest with young

Eric & David Hosking

Pious Robin

In folklore, Robins are pious birds: a dull-brown bird is said to have plucked a thorn from Jesus' crown, wounding its own breast in the process, a stain which has remained ever since as a badge of honour.

And the 'pious bird with a scarlet breast' improved his reputation over the years by undertaking the task of covering the bodies of dead men in the woods. 'The Robin Redbreast, if he find a man or woman dead, will cover his face with moss; and some think if the body should remain unburied he will cover the whole body' (Johnson, *Cornucopia*).

When Victorian postmen sported waistcoats of ruddy hue, these welcome callers became known as 'robins'. The bird which was earlier associated with the crucifixion became a symbol of Christmas, as portrayed on Christmas cards delivered by 'robins'. And since Christmas is a time for warmth and fellowship amongst men, those desirable attributes were transferred by the greetings-card industry to the character of the already popular bird. On Christmas cards, ruddy-breasted Robins clustered on the snowy spruce and carolled goodwill.

Real-life Robins, of course, possess no such admirable bonhomie. With all their undoubted good points it's almost a relief to find that there is a darker side to their character. For they are thoroughly unsociable. Barely able to tolerate their own mates long enough to complete the breeding cycle, they won't tolerate another Robin anywhere near them in everyday life.

object of the exercise is to go through the motions of starting a fight but decidedly not to advance to the stage of combat. The hope is for a speedy stand-down by one of the contestants, long before the bell rings for the first round and mostly this is what happens. One of the sparring partners brings the affair to a speedy end by crouching down submissively with his head withdrawn and his feathers almost relaxed. The only damage is to his pride, and he promptly goes to elaborate lengths to display to the world at large that he was only joking really – nothing serious – and that had he wanted to he could have wiped the floor with his opponent. He engages busily in some unnecessary and irrelevant activity like preening, or pretending to feed.

This 'displacement activity' is rather like ear-scratching in humans – an effort to distract attention from a problem. In a confused situation in which fighting is possible, birds may peck the ground, pull out a beakful of grass, do almost anything to substitute for the activity they want to avoid. A popular feeding area may find half-a-dozen pairs of Blackbirds calling each other names and squaring up for interminable mock battles. Anything which produces an agreed winner and loser without bloodshed is acceptable. But threats have to be faced, and this leads to some comic situations, as when Blackbirds sing and posture at a car mirror or hubcap, or a garden window, believing their own image to be that of an intruder. This sort of behaviour is only evident during the breeding season.

Actual physical assault leading to grievous bodily harm only happens in territorial battles when all else has failed. Singing, posturing, screaming, making faces and chasing are all preliminaries to the fight, but even if they actually get to grips with each other there's usually more noise than damage. The consequences of actual damage are too serious, for an injured bird is in real and instant danger. At worst, the protagonists will lock themselves in combat, pecking and clawing, until one capitulates in flight and an ignominious exit. Fights are not always entirely mock, and indeed in rare cases they may end in tragedy. The result of one battle observed between rival Blue Tits ended in death, with the loser's skull dented like a collapsed table-tennis ball.

But our hero's problems are not over when he has fought his fight and established himself as king of the castle. Even when his choice is made and he turns his attentions to dalliance, the road is far from clear. Courtship, as we all know, is fraught with problems. Most animals, including ourselves, tend to shy away from actual touch most of the time, but perpetuation of the species requires physical contact. So to overcome that natural reserve there is the ritual of courtship. And the object of the ritual, no matter what the species, is to permit approach and copulation.

There is much anxiety, tension and fear to overcome and the very apparatus of aggression and combat are now employed to a totally different end. The screaming of land-grab becomes the language of love. The gorgeous colours of the plumage and facial expressions continue the process. Music and movement become the billing and cooing of love. But the mating situation is so fraught with conflicting emotions that one wonders that it ever results in success. For while the cock bird is pressing attentions on a hen, he may be distracted by a rival cock singing. He must break off one kind of engagement to enter another, using the same weapons for opposite purposes. No wonder the interval between the first meeting and the consummation is sometimes prolonged.

Pairing may take place well before Christmas in many species, but the first couple of months of the New Year are usual. The sexes instantly recognise each other, difficult though that may seem to us in cases where, male and female, their plumage is identical, as in the Robin or Woodpigeon.

When two male Woodpigeons meet, the tenant usually wins the mock battle, possession being nine-tenths of the law. The intruder may have to be jostled a bit, but he goes. But if the visitor is a female, she stands firm, albeit rather uneasily, while the male bows courteously, showing his white and green neck patches and his white wing bars to best advantage. He will sing his 'tak two coos, taffy' routine, or he will exhibit a short soaring display flight, with a spectacular stall and a clap of his wings. The female may stand her ground, or she may retreat a little before the wonder of it all. The male too may be confused, still uncertain whether he is called on to raise his head and stretch his wing-tips

Blackcocks joust for the favour of the Greyhen who watches from the sidelines

Georg Nystrand/FLPA

A BLUE TIT'S NEST

5 June. What remains of one of my legs having made an effective protest against the great heat, there was nothing I could do but, as in Ralph Hodgson's *Song of Honour*, 'stare into the sky'. A brisk note sounded and a Blue Tit alighted on the telegraph wire before disappearing into the nest within my guttering. I am pretty sure that this bird and its mate were the same pair that stripped the fruit-buds from two of my cordon pear trees in April and occasioned me hours of labour in black-cottoning the rest. In my compulsory inactivity, I watched the pair coming and going for some hours. Each bird was feeding the young roughly once every minute and a half or forty times an hour. Thus there were eighty visits to the nest per hour. But natural life escapes the yard-stick, and occasionally one bird would be away from a quarter or even half a minute longer than usual, while both of them used to pause for a few seconds on the wire in order to pant. I will therefore allow a quarter of an hour to each bird to account for these irregularities in the routine. Thus it is a conservative estimate to reduce these feedings from eighty per hour for the pair to forty. The birds continued to feed their young at this rate for the whole of the time I was watching them, about three hours. Counting the hours of daylight as eighteen at this time of the year, the paper calculation would be over two thousand feedings per day. Deducting a quarter of these for rests, distractions, personal meals, slowings up for weariness and occasionally longer excursions for prey, and I arrive at an all-round estimate of fifteen hundred meals for the young every day, or ten thousand or so a week.

While I was watching them, they certainly never crossed the boundaries of my land, and each bird pursued exactly the same course on

Nestling Blue Tits waiting for a feed

Eric & David Hosking

each journey to and fro. One went straight down south to the orchard, the other east by south to the cordon and espalier trees that run down towards the orchard. It is fairly safe to assume that the birds did not during the day swing their helms to any great degree port or starboard of these fixed points.

That brings me to the nature of the cargo. Since the birds were some 12ft directly above me and always alighted at the same place with their beaks facing me and the prey hanging from them against the blue sky, I could comfortably ascertain what it was on each visit to the nest. It consisted entirely and exclusively of one grub of the Apple Blossom Weevil and one maggot of the Apple Sawfly, never more than one, one hundred and twenty of them as I watched. Since the pair of Blue Tits was a cost-free labour force, ridding my trees of such pests at the rate of forty or fifty an hour, I could more than afford them their wages in advance when they stripped my two pear trees in March. Had I sprayed the trees with DDT for the weevils and arsenate of lead for the sawflies, I should have destroyed the insect predators as well as the grubs, poisoned the soil, killed many earthworms, spent a good deal of money and labour and presumably lost the services of the Blue Tits.

Admiring the selfless and indefatigable family I began to see them more for their own sakes than for mine. It was beautiful to see them swoop down from the telegraph wire and infallibly swing up into it again. Every motion of these jewelled atomies of life as a flash of certainty. Every feather in the fiery furnace of the sun had the metallic sheen of a Hummingbird. Everything they did was as purposive as an arrow. How felicitous for them this instantaneous response of fulfilment to need! There was nothing blurred nor fumbling nor meaningless in their lives. What acuity of the senses and brilliance of execution, however limited their range, what freedom of action within the bounds of family solicitude! Rummaging about in an old writing case today I found a quotation scribbled out from I know not what writer: 'The contemplative eye sees all things in their divine properties, but without that wakeful self all things remain extensive and literally nothing on earth can give us joy.'

The truth of that was made manifest in watching my Blue Tits.

H. J. Massingham

David Hosking

Woodpigeons in courtship display

in threat, or bow his head and raise his tail to convince the female that his intentions are honourable. For her part, she has to be convinced that the male is not going to attack her. And so the bowing continues, the neck is inflated to show the irridescent greens and the Persil-white patches, until they are both reassured and the next phase begins. It may be days before the birds are perching alongside each other on the same branch, billing and cooing their pleasure. Mutual preening will now serve to reinforce the rapidly growing bond. The cock bird will lean across and nibble at the little feathers on her forehead, which stimulates her pituitary gland so that soon she is ready to lay eggs. The sex act itself will be accompanied by much billing and feather-caressing, and the hen may solicit food from the cock in the manner of juveniles begging. This feeding further stimulates copulation and strengthens the pair bond.

Courtship feeding is typical of many species (including man!). You may see a hen Robin on the lawn, making the same call she made as a spotty juvenile. She crouches, with wings held down to the ground, quivering, then the cock bird passes a juicy grub to her, a token of his love.

It is not always the males which establish the breeding territory. Among Blackbirds, for instance, the females choose the home patch. Mostly the cock birds tend to gather in groups at roosting or bathing time, taking this opportunity to assert themselves and establish seniority. They pull rank on each other, with dancing displays, mock fights, chasing and bowing, chattering away. And as the days go by they direct their attentions more towards the hens. In the New Year pairs begin to emerge and, with bonds acknowledged, they confirm the territory and repel all boarders. Much of this is done before the cock bird begins to sing, a procedure which, untypically, comes late on the agenda, some time in February or March.

Basket of eggs

The female Robin's clutch of eggs is generally kept within reasonable bounds. The birds have evolved a maximum clutch that is the most that a single female can keep properly warm during incubation. For the Robin this seems to be seven although a very few eight-egg clutches are 100% successful. Egg collectors, by milking a nest – that is taking the freshly laid egg from an incomplete clutch each day – have often been able to induce hens to lay ten or eleven eggs. There is however, one amazing female that lost control. She nested in a strawberry basket in a garage in Kent during May 1944 and laid three batches of eggs, with a short gap between each 'clutch', ending with a total of twenty. Unfortunately, at this juncture, she was disturbed by a cat and had not started to incubate. The observer noted that the eggs were three deep in the nest and the Robin had some difficulty in balancing herself on the pile when she came to lay another!

Birds have evolved an astonishing number of ways in which to rear their young. Derek Goodwin discussed them in an article in the RSPB's magazine *Birds* . . .

Chaucer wrote 'the wedded turtel with her herte trewe' of the Turtle Dove, a symbol of lifelong fidelity. There can be no doubt that the parental care which nearly all birds give their young has most favourably impressed mankind, and in human societies where monogamy is looked on as the ideal, the lifelong pairing (whether fact or fiction) of certain species is also admired.

Birds have evolved many different mating and breeding patterns to enable them successfully to rear young. Of course, conditions may change, often very quickly in a world dominated by man with his modern techniques, and the behaviour some birds have developed may become less suitable. It may even become harmful, in which case, the species will decline.

One-to-one
The most widespread mating system is one in which the cock and hen form a pair and stay together only until their

LETTER FROM NORFOLK

Dear Sir,

On 31 October last year, we discovered that one of the Mallards resident on our pond had produced a brood of ten ducklings. Concern about their future lead us to 'duck-nap' them and rear them under a brooding lamp in the kitchen.

To our surprise, all ten survived to fledge in February and to be released. They hung around the house and pond and continued to be fed.

Imagine our dismay when we found one of the females in a ditch with a badly smashed leg. We assumed she had hit nearby power lines and had been found trying to make her way 'home' by 'walking' on her wings.

The leg was very badly broken, with bone shards protruding through the skin, but we have an excellent local vet who specialises in birds, and he set the leg in plaster. The rest was up to us. Sid (she was always hissing at us at first), took up residence in a box in the kitchen. We fed her, bathed her to keep her eyes and feathers in good condition, and in the evenings she would sit on an old towel on my husband's lap while he worked, read or watched the television.

Then I bought the BBC video *Wildfowl*. Sid was asleep on my husband's lap, but a few quacks from the TV engaged her immediate attention. She became excited during the swan section, and by the beginning of the geese, was balanced on her one good leg on my husband's knee, craning to see.

Into the geese section, her wings were out and her head thrust forward, eyes glued to the screen. When the Brents took off, we had to grab her, turn the video off and spend some time calming her down, out in the kitchen, away from the TV screen.

Needless to say, we were amazed that she had obviously recognised, either by sight or sound, or both, the ducks, swans and geese shown on the screen for what they really were.

I would welcome any comments that your experts might have to make on this occurence, and would be interested to know if any of your readers have had any similar experiences. (Though I suppose TV watching amongst ducks must be a rare occurence.) Tony Soper might be gratified to know his commentary was so appreciated.

By the way, Sid's leg healed beautifully, and, except for a slightly rolling gait, you'd never know how badly broken it was. She now lives on the pond with the other ducks, making frequent visits to the house for food, and bringing her 'mates' with her.

Yours faithfully,

Mrs. Pauline McGowan

young are well grown. This type of one-to-one pair bond is found among the majority of British species.

In some species, the pairs keep together even outside the breeding season, and such evidence as exists suggests that these species (among British birds, wild geese, Mute Swans, all the crow family and the Bullfinch) usually pair for life.

For other species, such as storks, herons, other finches, grebes, and the Turtle Dove, there is as yet no evidence that the members of a pair stay together outside the breeding period. There are, however, many records of the same two individuals pairing in consecutive breeding seasons. It is possible that, in some cases, they migrate and/or spend the winter together, but it is more likely that the fact that they returned to breed in the same place re-united them.

In many monogamous birds the males are usually ready, indeed eager, to copulate with any available female of the same species. From an evolutionary point of view, if a male can father a few 'extra' young, so much the better. Under natural conditions, males are rarely given such opportunities but, 'given half a chance', they are ready to take it. However, the cocks of monogamous species take care to 'guard' their mate during the period that she is sexually receptive, driving other males away from her, or driving her away from them.

In one-to-one pair bonds both cock and hen almost always assist in parental care, even though the precise activities of each parent may differ widely.

For example, in the true finches, most parrots, owls, thrushes, crows and some gamebirds, only the hen incubates the eggs and broods the young, but the cock helps to feed and protect the young and, in many species, also feeds the hen while she is incubating.

Take turns

However, the sexes in a number of other birds, including pigeons, gulls, Oystercatchers, the cockatoos among parrots and the nutcrackers among the Crow family, take turns in incubating and brooding and both feed the young.

In other species, such as plovers, both sexes (or the female only) incubate the brood and both sexes protect the young, but the young find all their own food.

Then there are mating systems in which the birds may be said to pair, but the pair bond does not usually last until the young hatch. In some species, the cock builds a nest or part nest, attracts a hen to it and to himself, courts and pairs with her. When she begins to incubate her eggs, he loses interest in her, builds another nest and courts a second hen. He may also assist in feeding *one* of the resultant broods of young. Many of the weaver-birds behave in this way. So, as the late E. A. Armstrong's studies showed, does our Wren, but only in those parts of its range where food is plentiful during the breeding season.

There is similar behaviour in the ducks of the temperate and cold parts of the northern hemisphere, but not in Shelducks or geese. The birds pair up, and stay together until

Brian Hawkes

Herring Gulls take turns in incubating the eggs

The long wait

Female Robins have a fairly standard length of time to sit on their nests: few have longer than a fortnight to wait before their eggs hatch. But, some unfortunate females who sit on infertile clutches do not seem to know when to call it a day. There are several records of these poor birds incubating, in vain, for more than twice the normal span. One lasted for five weeks and the record is forty-eight days! Eventually the frustrated bird will desert the nest but, if I come across such a tragedy, I always feel that it is kindest to destroy the clutch and allow the female some respite from her vigil.

Ducks

F. W. Harvey

From troubles of the world
I turn to ducks,
Beautiful comical things
Sleeping or curled
Their heads beneath white
    wings
By water cool,
Or finding curious things
To eat in various mucks
Beneath the pool,
Tails uppermost, or waddling
Sailor-like on the shores
Of ponds, or paddling
left! right! – with fanlike feet
which are for steady oars
When they (white galleys)
    float
Each bird a boat
Rippling at will the sweet
Wide waterway . . .
When night is fallen *you* creep
Upstairs, but drakes and
    dillies
Nest with pale water-stars,
Moonbeams and shadow
    bars,
And water lilies:
Fearful too much to sleep
Since they've no locks
To click against the teeth
Of weasel and fox.
And warm beneath
Are eggs of cloudy green.

the duck begins to incubate her eggs. The drake may stay nearby for some days or weeks and join his mate when she comes off to feed, but he usually deserts her before the eggs hatch.

In some species, of which the Mallard is one, if the drake has not begun his moult into eclipse plumage when the duck brings her ducklings to the water, he may join his family for a time. He shows no concern at all for his young, but if his mate is molested by other drakes he will attack them. The ducklings are led, brooded and protected by their mother only. Like young plovers, they have to find all their own food.

Unique system

The Red-legged Partridge has mating and parental systems which are unique, so far as is known, to its genus. A strong pair bond is formed in late winter or early spring. The pair stays together for many weeks during which the cock courts and feeds the hen and takes the lead in searching for nest sites. The hen lays eggs until a clutch has been deposited, then she seeks out another site and lays another clutch there. She then starts to sit on the second nest and the cock goes back to the first. If the eggs, which have been left uncovered and unvisited for a fortnight or more, have not been found and eaten by some predator, he then incubates them. Thus, if all goes well, both cock and hen hatch and rear a separate brood.

In some species only the cock incubates the eggs and cares for the young. Characteristics of these species are pair bonds which are very short in duration and in which cock and hen separate when or soon after the eggs are laid, or polyandry in which a hen copulates with two or more males within a short period. These hens, such as the Dotterel and Red-necked Phalarope, may be larger, brighter in colour, more aggressive and take a more active role in courtship than the cocks.

The Pheasant is often thought of as a polygynous (the male has more than one hen) gamebird. Certainly the cock Pheasant often associates with two, three or more hens to which he displays, calls to food that he has found, copulates with and which later hatch and rear their broods unaided by him. It is, however, uncertain whether such opportunities occur under truly natural conditions: where game is 'preserved' it is the usual policy to try to kill proportionately many more cock Pheasants than hens.

In at least two very different birds, the Tasmanian Native Hen (a kind of large, flightless Moorhen) and the Galapagos Hawk, the female has simultaneous pair bonds, if such they can be called, with each of a group of two or more cocks, all of which help to care for her brood.

Elaborate displays

Lastly, there are those birds in which the cock and hen are only together for copulation and the often protracted and

elaborate displays that precede it.

In some each breeding male is alone in his mating territory, though usually within sound and sometimes sight of his neighbours and rivals. Most remarkable of these are the Bower Birds of New Guinea and Australia in which the cocks build elaborate and beautiful ornamented 'bowers', 'gardens', 'huts' and other structures, in or around which they display to their female visitors. Although other birds which display alone in territories do not build any structures, like those of the Bower Birds, for display purposes, many of them clear an area of ground of dead leaves and other debris or remove live leaves from vegetation in order to have a clear space in which to display.

Striking

Most striking of all mating systems, at least to birdwatchers, are what are usually termed 'lek' displays. A lek is a relatively small area where the local would-be breeding males of a species gather. Each cock has his own very small territory, perhaps as little as a few square feet of ground or a single twig, where he displays and, if successful, copulates with a visiting hen. The males of lek species are usually conspicuously coloured or noisy, often both. Though they compete

Blackcocks display at traditional courting grounds known as 'leks'

Courtship

Chasing about the garden and shaping up for mock fights is typical Blackbird behaviour. Blackbirds are not particularly sociable, although they are tolerant enough most of the time, but in late winter you often see a gathering of cock birds throwing their weight about and establishing an order or precedence, hoping to impress the hens. They parade about with tails down and wings half open, measuring their strength one against the other, even though there may not be a female in sight. Part of the game is to chase each other round the herbaceous border. Most of these battles are entirely chivalrous affairs of honour. The object of the exercise is to produce a winner and a loser, with loss of face but no loss of blood. Even a few misplaced feathers can be serious for a bird, so both sides try hard to avoid damage, but occasionally mock battles develop into the real thing. The more pugnacious contender seizes his adversary with his beak and belabours him with his wings. Mute Swans are said to fight to the death but very rarely. Blackbirds, and other species for that matter, may sometimes be seen, ▶

with each other for the best (usually most central) display territories on the lek, their simultaneous displays or calls advertise the lek's location in a striking manner. A dozen big Black Grouse displaying in a clearing or a dozen tiny Hermit Hummingbirds all squeaking at once from their perches a foot above the forest floor make a greater impression on eye and ear than one possibly could.

Many grouse, some Bird of Paradise, and among waders the Ruff, have lek-mating systems. Some have helpless nestlings; others, like the Reeve (the female Ruff), have active chicks, but in all of them only the hen builds, incubates the eggs and cares for the young. Another feature of the lek system is that all the hens that visit the lek copulate with only a few of the most dominant or otherwise attractive of the many displaying cocks present.

Some lek species have evolved even more elaborate behaviour in that two or more males perform simultaneous, co-ordinated displays to the same hen. This is the case with the lovely blue, black and red Manakin which I was thrilled to see displaying when I was in Brazil. Something approaching this is seen in the Ruff, in which subordinate white or pale-ruffed males may be allowed to share a dominant, dark-ruffed male's territory and to display together with its owner.

To see such displays is an unforgettable experience, but the courtship of the Starling or Collared Dove, although less elaborate, has its own charm and certainly in terms of numbers they are more successful species in modern man's world.

Most birds mate for life, given the chance, but small birds do not live long, so it is the larger ones, like swans, which get the reputation for fidelity in marriage. The advantages of life partnership are real. If you already know your mate, then the annual courtship formalities may be shortened, leaving more time and energy for the practical side of breeding. But it is not easy to be dogmatic about the long-term effectiveness of the pair bond, since in spring the birds may be returning not so much to a known partner as to a known nest site, where last year's mate is conveniently to hand. Certainly, there is the bird equivalent of divorce as a result of incompatibility and, if one partner dies, the other will look for a replacement. Commonsense prevails. The survival advantages in a successful marriage ensure that the institution has an assured future.

There is a great deal of evidence in support of these assertions about marriage, especially from the waterfowl, which were easier to study as individuals in the days before numbered rings were invented. Marks on swan beaks revealed that the birds maintained stable relationships. In more recent studies at the Wildfowl Trust, it was found that the Bewick's Swans, birds which regularly fly in for the winter, once paired, stay together for a number of years, some of them for at least eight and the longest for more than thirteen years. Out of the 1,300 known birds, there was no record at all of a pair parting company and then re-appearing with a new mate, except in cases where one partner was missing, presumed dead. In other words, there were no divorces. Widowed females very soon found new partners, as females are always much in demand. This is not to suggest that birds lead sober, blameless lives with no hint of the darker sides of passion and philandery. Drake Mallards on any park pond will demonstrate their zest for the chase, forcing themselves on unaccompanied females. Seizing their necks, they will hold the females underwater while they struggle to couple, sometimes even drowning the unfortunate duck in the process. Even when paired, the behaviour of Mallard drakes leaves a lot to be desired. They hang about the nest site while the duck does all the work of incubation, then quietly slope off when the ducklings hatch and leave the mother to bring them up.

Courtship and pairing achieved, the next hurdle faced is the choice of a nest site . . .

The availability of nest sites is important, of course, but far and away the greatest attraction is a food supply that will make it possible to rear youngsters. This is why birds rarely have the temerity to nest in the winter; it can happen, but the odds against success are high and the evolutionary process soon stops it. Birds born during a food shortage do not survive to perpetuate the mistake. Natural selection determines the breeding season, as everything else. In spring and summer there is more plant material, more insect life,

▶ astonishingly, to mate or attempt to mate with foreign objects like tennis balls or dog's bones lying about on the lawn. This is only the sad evidence of frustration, and the bird is copulating with a substitute partner. Given the arrival in the garden of an unattached female, he will quickly find a more suitable object on which to lavish his all. Such aberrations are examples of 'redirection', a perfectly proper behaviour response directed at an improper subject as when a bird pecks at inedible things as substitutes for the food it really wants, and when a man bangs his desk when what he really wants to do is thump his boss.

A passing squabble between Avocet and Shelduck

Feathered fidelity

Do birds mate for life?
Probably most of them do,
given the chance. But small
birds do not live long so it is
the larger ones, like swans,
which get the benefit of a
reputation for fidelity in
marriage.

The advantages of life
partnership are real. If you
already know your mate, then
the annual courtship
formalities may be reduced,
leaving more time and energy
for the practical processes
and duties of breeding. But it
is not easy to be dogmatic
about the long-term
effectiveness of the pair bond,
since the birds may be
returning not so much to a
known partner as to a known
nest site, where last year's
mate is conveniently ready to
hand. Certainly there is the
bird equivalent of divorce as a
result of incompatibility, and
if one partner dies, the other
will look for a replacement.
Commonsense normally
prevails. There are survival
advantages in a successful
marriage, so it has an assured
future for wild creatures.

Long-tailed Tit collecting nest material

more warmth, more light and longer days, so that is when
the courtship comes to a climax. Small birds lay eggs in time
for the nestlings to benefit from the peak caterpillar population of May and June. Sparrowhawks lay a little later, so
that they benefit from the peak small-bird population! Second broods are less likely to succeed because they have
missed the insect peak. Pigeons breed almost through the
year, but that is because they feed their young on milk
which they can manufacture from whatever foods are available at the time.

Choosing the building site will be part of the courtship
activity, and may be decided long before construction work
begins. Resident birds may have spent the winter searching
for a plot, but summer visitors have less time to waste. They
may select a site and begin construction on the same day.
Either way the hole-nesters like tits have a more difficult
task, as suitable holes are not easy to find, even if they do
grow on trees! Even so, a cock Great Tit may find several
sites and take his hen on a tour of inspection. She makes
the final choice, displaying her pleasure with shivering wing
movements. A particular site may be attractive to more than
one pair of birds. Blue Tits may build a nest and lay eggs,
only to be evicted by Tree Sparrows which actually build
another nest on top of the existing one, eggs and all, and
proceed to lay their own clutch.

Building materials, as in all the most harmonious houses,
will be found nearby, and will depend on the local vegetation
and on the second-hand market. It is in the early stages of
nest-building that you have your best chance of identifying
the site, because you will see birds struggling to get airborne
with sticks and grass, before flying to the works. Much
material may be wasted as the main timbers fall to the
ground, to be left there while the bird goes off to find more.
But once the framework is stable the bird will shape the
cup by moving around, both ways, and working with its
breast and feet. Grasses and mosses will be packed tight,
and its bill will be used to work in odd strands. After the
main structure is finished, another layer may be added; for
instance, a Blackbird will have a mud layer. Swallows and
House Martins also need mud, so in a dry spell remember
to throw a pail of water on some bare earth for them –
mud-pie making is hard work without water.

Then comes the inner lining of soft stuff like feathers.
This is the stage at which birds will be grateful for any
offerings you may put out for them. Things like the dog's
hair combings, feathers and scraps of material (but not
lengths of cotton which might get into a leg tangle). Long-
tailed Tits will be especially grateful for feathers, as they
use prodigious quantities for nest lining. Hair of all kinds
is much prized; badger hairs have been picked from barbed
wire fences and pony hairs from the back of the animal.
Goldfinches use the silken thread from spider's webs as a
binding material when they are fastening the twig structure
and to bind the wood and grasses and dandelion fluff which

John Hawkins/Hosking

Speedy nest-building

Although Rome was not built in a day, the Robin, when it is nesting, can get a substantial structure built in a very short period. The fastest on record was a nest in Basingstoke. Between breakfast and lunchtime an almost complete nest had been built in a gardener's coat pocket. The coat had been hung in the toolshed and, although history does not record what happened to the nest, I would not have given it much chance of success. The old-fashioned gardener was not renowned for his sentimentality or love of birds – particularly in the spring when the Blackbirds seem to insist on making their nests from newly planted-out bedding subjects.

Another very fast nest proved successful. This bird, in Birmingham, started to build in an unmade bed whilst the legitimate occupant was having breakfast! In this instance the soft-hearted human left the birds alone and a brood was successfully reared. Robins seem to like beds in Birmingham as another built a nest in a cardboard box at the end of a bed. Young successfully fledged, the bed having been in normal use all the time. The bedroom windows were left open for the duration.

makes the inner lining. A Goldcrest even got itself trapped and tangled in the sticky web of a garden spider, but it flew away safely when a birdwatcher rescued it.

Tie-on plant labels are a favourite nest material, though Goldfinches actually untie the string, which involves quite intricate manipulative behaviour. One Jackdaw's nest held sixty-seven plant labels. Polystyrene chippings are popular, perhaps providing extra warmth and insulation — 1,500 were solemnly counted in the nest of one Long-tailed Tit. Pigeons go for sterner stuff, like stainless-steel wire. Short lengths of wire are not so very different from twigs, so there is really no behavioural significance in any of these odd uses of man-made materials. Birds just have nothing to learn from us in the field of low-impact technology; they use available resources to the best advantage.

Birds may build several nests. One Mistle Thrush actually started five, but finished two. The problem was that it was building on top of a pillar at a nuclear power station, and there wasn't just one pillar but dozens and dozens of them, regularly spaced 20ft apart in a rectangular block. The unfortunate bird became disorientated by the multiplicity of identical sites, and didn't always land on the same pillar.

Nest-building is part of a routine, and it has to start at the beginning, with the establishment of a territory and with courtship. Without this stimulus, an unmated hen is very unlikely to build a nest and lay eggs, although it does happen. (The domesticated chicken, is an example, but this is a bird which has been painstakingly selected for just this function). Cock Wrens build nests for a pastime, and in other countries the cock Weaver Birds build half a nest from which to display. But normally first things come first, and there's no nest without a partnership.

Birds are easily disturbed and may abandon the project in the early stages of nest-building. Many desert if they are fussed, so on the whole it is best to leave them alone al-

House Martins collecting material for their mud huts

Eric Hosking

Brian Hawkes

Goldfinch sitting tight amongst the raspberries

together. If you must go and look, do it in an ordinary, everyday sort of manner. Walk quietly up to the nest, talking as you go, and generally act like the blundering mammal that you are. At all costs avoid a slow approach with a direct gazing stare. The birds will resent this abnormal and inexplicable behaviour. Do not poke a finger into a hole-nest. Wrens, for instance, sit very tight, but will readily desert if you start touching them. Do not cut away leaves or twigs to see the nest more easily; this will simply be an invitation to the nearest predator. Photographers are the greatest menace in this respect. For my part I do not search for nests and I prefer to leave birds to get on with the job without my interference, and that goes as far as not getting in the way when Magpies are at their dirty work of egg-thieving, or woodpeckers are baby-snatching. If a bird deserts the nest, it has to start again elsewhere from the beginning. It takes an intelligent mammal, like a fox or you or me, to have the sense to pick up the juveniles and carry them off elsewhere to start a new life!

Most small birds lay one egg a day, usually in the early morning, and start incubating as soon as the clutch is complete. But some, Swifts and birds of prey like owls, for instance, lay on alternate days, or even at three-day intervals, but start incubating as soon as the first egg is laid. Thus their brood of nestlings always has a youngest – and therefore a weakest – individual. If times are hard and food is

RATHER A LOT TO SWALLOW?

Swallows are well known for their liking of man-made structures as nest sites and, hence, their tolerance of man's presence and even interference during their breeding cycle. However, as the following account will show, our resident pair had their tolerance well and truly tested in summer 1980 and emerged with flying colours, as well as flying young! I noted, on 28 April, that they were again building in the large shed at the back of our house. The nest was against the side of one of the roof support beams, the only support from below being a large nail sticking out from the beam. All must have gone well and by late May one bird was sitting tight. By the second week in June, the young had hatched and both parents were busy feeding them. Then on the night of Friday 13 June (definitely not their lucky day!) came tragedy. There had been heavy rain all night and it was still raining hard when, at around 10am, I went to get something from the shed. To my horror the nest, unfortunately positioned beneath a leak in the roof, had fallen down. There, amidst its remains in the coal scuttle, were four tiny, blind, naked young Swallows, and one addled egg. Of the parent birds there was no sign. I picked up the pathetic, stone-cold, soaking wet little 'corpses' and consigned them sadly to the dustbin.

On returning to the house, it occurred to me that my son might like to see the egg, miraculously unbroken, so I went back and opened the bin to retrieve it. Just as I was replacing the lid, I thought I saw the leg of one of the chicks move. I picked it out and held in in my warm hand, then the other three and, in a couple of minutes, three of the chicks were showing signs of life. I was still in two minds whether or not to attempt to save them, realising the difficulty of hand-rearing the young of insectivorous birds, and feeling sure they would die of pneumonia, if nothing else. Still, sentiment won the day and I took them indoors and handed them over to my son, who put them in a tissue-lined box in the airing cupboard. I then had to go out and did not get back till lunchtime. He said they were not only still alive, but looking stronger, so, as an emergency measure, we hard-boiled an egg and attempted to feed them some of the sieved yolk on the end of a matchstick. They took a little and began giving hunger cries whereupon to our surprise, the parent birds appeared, fluttering back and forth outside the bathroom window and calling in apparent distress.

Obviously the young birds would have a much better chance of survival if fed by their parents, so we decided to try making a substitute nest in the shed and putting the chicks in it. Again, I had to go out, so it was left to my husband to cope. He took a shallow plastic plant pot, cut a piece out of the side and nailed it to a beam in a dry part of the shed, so that it looked rather like a House Martin's nest. He lined it with torn-up paper tissues, then fetched the chicks and put them in it and offered food to get them to call. The parent birds came into the shed whilst he was doing this and, as soon as he left, recommenced feeding their offspring.

At around 11pm, we crept into the shed to see if all was well and, though both parents were there, to our consternation the young were not being brooded possibly we thought, because of the strangeness of the 'nest' and the rather small opening. I went off to bed, feeling that nature must now take its course, but my husband decided, once again, to give it a helping hand and fitted up the young birds with 'duvets' of tissue paper. When we looked next morning, these had been pulled out of the nest by the parents and they were busily feeding three apparently healthy youngsters. We did not again see the chicks brooded, though they possibly could have been, but they continued to thrive and left the nest on 28 June. Subsequently, a second brood was raised in 'our' nest, being brooded normally, and these fledged on or about 9 August.

Dorothy Underhill

Brian Hawkes

Well-appointed Linnet's nest – with strawberries for tea!

scarce, the youngest is the one to die, leaving more food and more hope for the older chicks.

Not all nests receive their complement of eggs. A cock Wren will build a whole series of trial nests in the early spring. Made of moss, grasses and leaves, they will be cunningly woven into a bundle of twigs, an old coat hanging in the shed, or a creeper-clad wall. One year we had an occupied Wren's nest in a coil of rope hanging in our boatstore. When the cock has successfully attracted a mate, she inspects the trial offerings and makes the final choice, finishing the job by lining the shell with feathers, then laying and incubating. But the cock still continues building nest shells and advertising for another hen, who in turn finishes a chosen nest. So the cock Wren, unusually among birds, is a bigamist, with perhaps as many as three wives at once. Not surprisingly, he hardly bothers to feed the young birds, but he may condescend to conduct parties of adolescents around the neighbourhood, teaching them the hunting trade.

Some birds lay an astonishing number of eggs. I have a record of tame Robins which, having laid two eggs on a garage shelf, deserted them to build another nest a couple of feet away and lay four eggs in it, which were successfully hatched and the nestlings fledged. Then the adults went back to the first nest, laying four more eggs and successfully rearing four more young. And after all that they returned yet again to nest number two and sat on four more eggs. But it is all part and parcel of the rather casual business of egg production. Among mammals, the burden of carrying the foetus for months on end and then having the responsibility of a helpless infant encourages a more sober approach to the whole process!

While on the nest, a hen Robin will be fed by the cock, thus continuing a process which started in courtship, when she begged food from him as part of the ritual. Now the behaviour pays dividends as it allows her to spend more time on the nest.

Martin B. Withers/FLPA
Robin in the traditional kettle

71

Eric Hoskng

Clutch sizes vary a great deal. First-time breeders lay fewer eggs than they will do in later, more experienced years. Farmland and woodland pairs lay more eggs than garden pairs because the feeding is better. In cold weather or a drought, there will be fewer eggs. Conditions may well improve between laying and hatching, but the birds have no way of foretelling this. Most of the tales which relate weather prospects to the actions of animals are so much nonsense. Unpopular though it may be to say it, meteorologists are the best weather forecasters in the animal kingdom!

Blackbird nestlings enjoy earthworms

Fledglings

Most garden-bird eggs take some twelve to fourteen days to hatch. The parent removes the broken eggshell, and starts the hard job of feeding those ever-open mouths. The most demanding and vigorous nestling will get the lion's share of the food, so that once again there tends to be a built-in survivor if the going gets rough.

Some young birds, like plovers and ducks, leave the nest a few days after hatching; if you have a Herring Gull nesting on your roof, its juveniles will soon be exploring the gutters and ridges. But most small birds stay in the nest, which now becomes their nursery. Straight away the problem of

Greenfinches eat seeds, but their young are fed with softer food like caterpillars

Brian Hawkes

Dartford Warbler as host to young Cuckoo – a poor exchange for British birdwatchers!

Home is where you make it

Robins have a fancy for an unusual range of nest sites, though mostly they go for a hedge-bank or a large hole in a wall, especially if it is well obscured with creeper or ivy. Discarded tin cans, buckets, kettles, are all pressed into service, while if they can gain access to a shed or house they will build on a shelf or in a coat pocket. A Robin even started one morning to build in someone's bedroom, choosing the attractive folds and comfort of an unmade bed. (In this event the bed and room were made over to the Robin till the resulting family was successfully fledged.) Once a Robin has learnt to find food inside a house, it will soon discover all the various methods of entrance; if one window is shut it will try another, mapping the internal geography of the house and threading its way about the labyrinth of passages and stairs and rooms.

sanitation arises, for as fast as food goes in one end, faeces appear at the other. But all is carefully ordered, as the droppings are elegantly encapsulated in a little gelatinous sac, and the parents carry the offering away in their beaks, dropping it at a discreet distance on to your lawn, where it should be a welcome source of nutrient.

When the young birds fledge they leave the nest for trial flights, doing their circuits and bumps and familiarising themselves with the landscape and its possibilities. On the lawn they will follow their foraging parents, begging for food with open beaks and fluttering wings. It is a hectic time for parents, and sometimes a House Sparrow, say, may find itself feeding a young Blackbird by mistake. The adult, carrying a juicy morsel, is stimulated by the sight of the juvenile's open gape. At this stage, in summer, the garden border will harbour many young birds which sit motionless, but flutter their wings and gape at you when you approach. Do not be misled into thinking that they have fallen out of a nest and are lost and hungry. It is a normal part of the process and they are not lost; the parent is busy looking for food and will find the baby very quickly with an interchange of calls. If you go away they will get on with it.

Sparrowhawks nest late so that their young get the benefit of the peak period of small-bird availability. Another bird which arrives late is the Cuckoo, usually in the third week of April, when small birds have already prepared nests and laid eggs and are all set to incubate on the hen Cuckoo's behalf. And of course if you discover a nest of eggs with a single maverick, then it belongs to a Cuckoo. Many other summer visitors, like the Chiffchaff, arrive earlier and are earlier announcers of spring than the Cuckoo, but in poetic terms he is the greatest. The male actually cuckoos, while the hen makes a bubbling noise. Cuckoos may superficially be mistaken for a Sparrowhawk, but they have none of the flashpast and bezazz of the hawk. The hen drops a single egg in each chosen foster-home, and in due course the young Cuckoo ejects the eggs or young of the rightful occupants, usually Dunnocks, or Robins, using its strong back specially constructed for the purpose.

Collared Dove in an industrial setting

Brian Hawkes

Cuckoo in the nest

The Cuckoo is unique, in Britain, where it is the only parasitic bird. Cuckoos opt out of family life altogether by fostering their eggs the moment they are laid. In other parts of the world, other birds use the same methods, while, for that matter, in other parts of the world, not all Cuckoo species are parasitic. In fact, most of them build nests in the conventional way but many are notoriously bad at nest-building and tend to lay eggs in an undisciplined way, at odd intervals and sometimes in someone else's nest. Cowbirds will steal another bird's nest but then incubate their own eggs in it. House Sparrows will take over a House Martin's nest by brute force, perhaps demonstrating one step along the road to parasitism.

Long ago, our Cuckoos found that they could perpetuate their species by producing eggs which mimicked those of some small bird. The Cuckoos then laid eggs in the nest of this bird, which became a 'host'. The system worked well from the point of view of the Cuckoo and not disastrously from the point of view of the host, since it is not in the interest of the parasitic Cuckoo for its host species to die out. The Cuckoo must not be *too* successful. Dunnocks have been prime targets for Cuckoos for many years yet it is estimated that there are over 3 million of them nesting in Britain alone.

Young Cuckoo ejecting Tree Pipit's egg to reduce the competition

Eric Hosking

Since it does not go to the trouble of building a nest, the Cuckoo has the luxury of a couple of extra weeks of winter warmth in Africa and is by no means the first of our summer visitors. Once on our shores, it returns to the kind of country where it was hatched and stakes out a territory, calling 'cuckoo' to attract a mate. The reason it returns to the habitat of its birth is because it is 'fixed' on a particular host species and will only parasitise a victim belonging to the species of its own foster-parents. We tend to speak of a 'Rock Pipit Cuckoo' or a 'Reed Warbler Cuckoo' or a 'Dunnock Cuckoo'. If the female was hatched in a Reed Warbler's nest, that is where she will lay her own eggs. She spies out the land and charts all the Reed Warbler activity. Timing is critical. The mated Cuckoo waits and watches. When the Reed Warbler lays its first egg, she must remove it and replace it with her own, without causing the rightful owners of the nest to desert. The moment the warbler has left its single egg in the nest and flown off, the hen Cuckoo flies in, picks up the warbler egg in her beak, turns to lay her own directly in its place and flies away, never to return. Her alien egg closely resembles the warbler's in both colour and size. Over the next few days, the host will complete her clutch in ignorance of the substitution. The Cuckoo's egg even has the same incubation period as the warbler but, laid first, it will be likely to hatch first, giving an important advantage to the nestling Cuckoo, who deals promptly with the opposition. He may be naked and blind but he has strong legs and wing stumps. Wriggling and manoeuvring, he heaves each of the warbler's eggs in turn onto his back, then pushes them out of the nest. If by chance he was not the first to hatch, he ejects the nestlings instead of the eggs. Once out of the nest, they will be totally ignored by the parents.

The gaping action of a hungry chick is a major stimulus to the returning foster-parent. They feed it. The Cuckoo needs all the food that his erstwhile nest-mates would have received, because he is going to grow faster and bigger than they would have, and he has assured himself of the full-time attention of his adoptive parents. In human terms, the affair is callous and horrific, but for the newborn Cuckoo, it is a simple question of survival. Either the Reed Warbler's rightful chicks go or he goes. His natural mother, meanwhile, has been busy finding anything up to a dozen nests, always of the same species. If she is successful, in due course she will have found homes for a dozen eggs which will produce monster chicks with monster gapes to tax the host's hunting prowess. The fat Cuckoos will be off to Africa at the end of summer, to return next spring to yet more Reed Warblers or Dunnocks or whatever it is that they are programmed to parasitise.

Although it never knew its mother's voice, the yearling Cuckoo will sing 'cuckoo' simply because this comes naturally to it. The rudiments of language are genetically implanted, then refined by exposure to other singers in the first season but, as the bird was deprived of experience, the

A. R. Hamblin/FLPA

Male Cuckoo singing for a mate

Is it true?

The Cuckoo is a dishonest bird, and is very slow, and does not stay in one place. In winter it is said to lose it's feathers; and it enters a hole in the earth or hollow trees; there in the summer it lays up that on which it lives in the winter. They have their own time of coming, and are borne upon the backs of kites, because of their short and small flight, lest they be tired in the long tracts of air and die. From their spittle grasshoppers are produced. In the winter it lies languishing and unfeathered, and looks like an owl.

Hortus Sanitatus (1485)

The cuckoo in winter-time

What becomes of the Cuckow in the winter-time, whether hiding herself in hollow-trees, or other holes and caverns, she lies torpid, and at the return of the spring revives again; or rather at the approach of winter, being impatient of cold, shifts place and departs into hot countrys, is not as yet to me certainly known. But seeing it is most certain that many sorts of birds do at certain seasons of the year shift places, and depart into other countrys, as for example Quails, Woodcocks, Fieldfares, Storks, etc, why may not Cuckows also do the same? For my part I never yet met with any credible person that dared affirm, that himself had found or seen a cuckow in winter-time taken out of a hollow-tree, or any other lurking-place.

John Ray writing in
Willoughby's Ornithology
(1678)

song, not surprisingly, is limited, and there is not much scope for polishing. The Cuckoo's song lacks the sophisticated variations which are so characteristic of more conventional songbirds. Though they may start with nothing more than a song-sheet, complete with what musicians call 'the dots', songsters like thrushes and Nightingales soon progress from a colourless sequence of notes to an imaginative and musical performance which improves with age.

Many birds nest in the comparative safety of a tree. Like the squirrel, Rooks and herons nest out in the open for all to see, protected by the safety of numbers and the difficulty of access. Other birds take advantage of the crevices and holes found in trees which are past their prime and where old branches have rotted and fallen away, leaving an open invitation to a decaying interior. Great Spotted Woodpeckers, favourite garden birds, mostly operate on dead or decaying branches, looking for both insects and for nest sites. They may damage a sound tree by barking it in order to enjoy the exuding sap (they are called sapsuckers in the United States) so they can be a nuisance to foresters, since the bark peeling opens the way to secondary infections by insects or fungi. Pines, oaks and limes are particular targets. But in the garden they can only be welcome. They have powerful chisel-tipped bills, and they use them to great effect in excavating tree-holes. They may even bore holes in telegraph posts, or in the cedar shingles of your house, all in the cause of foraging for insects! And if they find a brazil nut on the bird-table at Christmas they wiil take it to a tree and wedge it into a crack before splitting it with that multi-purpose tool of a beak. A Nuthatch will do the same, and indeed will take over a woodpecker's nest and convert it to his requirements, reducing the entrance to a more suitable Nuthatch size by plastering it with mud or clay. With its noisy liquid whistle, the Nuthatch is a welcome garden visitor in the south of England, preferring mature gardens with well-grown oaks, beeches, limes and chestnuts.

Woodpigeons have moved into the city . . .

Brian Hawkes

Eric Hosking

Young Cuckoo overflowing a Reed Warbler's nest

Woodpigeons are common garden tree-nesters these days. Originally a woodland species, over the last hundred years they have increased enormously in numbers and are now regarded much more as farm pests and city and suburban dwellers. Curiously shy in the country yet tame in the city, the Woodpigeon is even less scary than the street pigeon. A sociable bird but fiercely territorial in the breeding season, it defends it own nest tree against all comers. On the other hand Collared Doves like to nest sociably, with a preference for a stand of conifers in the corner of a park or mature well-treed garden. Collared Doves are now common garden birds, well established all over the country since their explosive arrival in 1955, after a rapid spread across Europe from India. Like Woodpigeons, they have been known to use wire netting to reinforce their nests. Not a menace to green vegetables, they have a great love of corn or grass seed, so watch out when you are seeding the lawn.

Tits are typically tree-nesters, and that accounts for their readiness to adopt nestboxes, which so far as they are concerned are an acceptable substitute for a conveniently decayed tree-trunk with an entrance hole.

KESTRELS IN THE CATHEDRAL

Every year Kestrels nest on the spire of Chichester cathedral. Perhaps they have done so since the building was completed in 1199, for the nest site is in one of several cavities within the thickness of the stone walls – about 4ft in length and height and 15in deep, with a single carved, quartrefoil opening, accessible only to birds. No structural reason exisits for these cavities, and a purely decorative feature would not require such careful construction. Perhaps they were designed for birds . . .

The site ownership appears to be vested in the male Kestrel and early in the year he does his best to attract a female. One year a couple of eligible brides arrived simultaneously and fought it out, with spectacular flying pursuits, and much shrieking of 'Keek, keek, keek!' Eventually, the stronger bird drove the rival from the scene, so reaching the top of the cathedral's avian hierarchy – other residents, such as Jackdaws, pigeons and Swifts, are obliged to nest at a discreet distance.

In autumn 1975, major repairs to the cathedral were started and two boarded gangways were erected near the nesting site. The following spring, I saw two Kestrels prospecting nearby, but that year and the next, they nested elsewhere. By spring 1978, the gangways had been moved up and, in March, I saw the male 'loitering with intent'. He must have decided it was safe to return because at the beginning of April he flew into the nestbox, quickly followed by his mate.

The aerial courtship acrobatics of Kestrels are especially thrilling when seen over such a large building. After a day's sunshine, the heated stonework creates thermals, which the birds exploit with dazzling virtuosity. Without flapping a wing, they soar round and round the spire, merely tilting their bodies to change direction, whilst their shrieks shoot like arrows through the humdrum bustle of the shopping streets below.

Their territory established, both birds bring their prey back to the cathedral – projecting bands of masonry on the spire are convenient for the smaller items, such as mice and sparrows, but larger meals take more room and may be devoured on the very top, directly beneath the gilded weathercock. After mating, the male often feeds the female, presumably proving he will be a good provider for the future family.

By mid-April, the eggs have been laid, and the male brings food for his incubating mate which he deposits in the dining end of the nestbox. The female flies up to a convenient part of the spire to eat, while the male takes her place on the eggs.

Towards the end of the incubating period the female becomes noticeably reluctant to leave the nest, even to feed and her posture shows when the young have hatched – she sits higher on the nest, instead of clamping her body down onto the eggs. For the first few days, she will not leave the nestlings because they require constant warmth. The furthest she will move is across to the dining area to tear the prey brought by the male into small morsels which she pushes into the tiny beaks of her nestlings, then she hurries back to brood them. In my ten years of observation all the broods have numbered three and, as their feeding demands grow, both parents have to forage for prey, the female concentrating on nearby areas, so that she is ready at the slightest hint of danger to defend her young. She continues to brood them at night and in cold weather.

When the nestlings are fully fledged, they start to shuffle awkwardly around the nest, indulging in wing-flapping exercises. They have been taught at quite an early age to manoeuvre their tails out of the lower part of the entrance, in order to drop their faeces clear of the nest, but this high level of hygiene is not maintained in the dining area. At this stage, the young are allowed to dissect their own food and the debris left behind attracts bluebottle flies – even at that altitude! I do not believe that this is accidental – the fledglings snap at the bluebottles gaining valuable experience in catching moving objects and sometimes a tasty snack!

During each of the three years since they resumed nesting on the cathedral the Kestrels have succeeded in rearing their brood, in spite of the scaffolding – indeed the thicket of steel 'twigs' has been put to good effect. Instead of facing a sheer drop on their first flight, the fledglings are now able to make a short hop across to the nearest pole; and regain the nest with ease. As a result, they can now leave the nest a week to ten days earlier than before. Previously, a youngster who made a clumsy first flight and landed on a roof far below had to be coaxed into attempting the much more-difficult feat of flying up to the safety of the nest, while the mother tried to guard not only the stranded youngster, but also its siblings in the nestbox, from the Carrion Crows nesting not very far away.

During the breeding season, neither Carrion Crows nor Herring Gulls are permitted to fly within a quarter of a mile of the cathedral. Both crows and gulls are expert on the wing, and larger than their assailants, but they are completely out-classed by the dive-bombing Kestrels.

The only birds not intimidated by the Kestrels' nest are the Swifts. They flit effortlessly by at close quarters, convinced that only Peregrines and Hobbies are fast enough to catch them – but their confidence is misplaced. One morning when the young Kestrels were still being brooded, the male was late bringing breakfast. The female craned her head out of the nest opening, trying in vain to catch a sight of him returning with food. Finally, she cocked her head sideways and stared at the sky, where a large party of Swifts were circling in a tight knot, presumably feeding on a swarm of insects. She slipped unobtrusively from her nest, flew round to the back of the building, then soared up until she was only just visible as a black spot against the blue of the sky. She turned, hovered for a second or two, then plunged in a Peregrine-like swoop, straight into the circling Swifts. At terrific speed, she caught one of their number as she hurtled past, and flew back at once to her hungry nestlings. This happened so quickly that even the Swifts hardly had time to notice that one of their party had gone for ever!

Such drama is not always appreciated. A Kestrel was once tactless enough to take a pigeon directly in front of some old ladies sitting near the cathedral and the Archdeacon received several letters of complaint about such 'unchristian' birds being allowed within the precincts of a sacred building. He replied that, since God had created birds of prey, it was not for us to question the wisdom of the Almighty. He might have added that, without them, the cathedral would become a colossal roost, every ledge thick with droppings . . .

Joy Crawshaw

Adult Kestrel returns to the front door . . .

David Grewcock/FLPA

Birds in Boxes

David Hosking

Fantails at an ornamental dovecote

Blue Tits and House Martins are both good examples of the sort of birds which take readily to artificially provided homes. But long before we bird gardeners started putting up nestboxes there were pigeon-houses with their serried ranks of pigeon-holes. Pigeon-house or dovecote, they both amount to the same thing . . .

'Pigeon' and 'dove' are interchangeable words to the ornithologist, and it is not easy to draw a line between them. All belong to the order Columbidae. But, in non-scientific terms, the smaller species are doves, the larger pigeons. And when poets are looking for an image of gentle innocence, purity and virtue, they usually turn to the dove, with the added bonus that it rhymes with love. Whatever you call it, the bird is greatly used as a symbol of fertility, not surprisingly since though it only lays two eggs to a clutch it may successfully breed nine or ten clutches in a year, an astonishing performance – and a characteristic that has been well and truly taken advantage of by man.

The intensive rearing of domesticated birds for fresh meat, especially in winter, really began with the Norman invasion, when the conquerers brought the science of the 'colombier' with them. No twelfth-century castle was complete without its rows of pigeon-holes, carefully built into a turret or high place, sheltered and southfacing. And soon the gentle pigeon became associated with less warlike places, the substantial stone-built dovecote being an important part of any manor house or monastery.

The pigeon-house was always carefully sited, to provide protection from prevailing winds. The Norman design involved a circular building, solidly planted on the ground with walls 3ft thick, no windows, gradually tapering, at the very top of the roof, to a 'lantern', which gave entrance for the birds. A single door at ground level allowed entrance for the pigeon-keeper. Inside, the walls were covered with row after row of pigeon-holes, 'three handfulles in length, and ledged from hole to hole for them to walke upon'. An ingenious device called a 'potence' allowed the keeper to reach any nest by means of a ladder which rotated on a central pillar passing within a couple of inches of the wall as it was pushed around. The interior was dim, to the liking of the pigeons, and each pair of birds had a double nest

David Hosking

Tits take readily to artificial nestboxes

site, because before one set of squabs is ready to leave the nest the hen might well have laid her next clutch of eggs.

Up on the roof, the pigeons would have a promenading area, sheltered from cold winds and facing south to catch the best of the sun. Under the whole structure there might well be room for a stable or cow house, giving the additional benefit of extra warmth in winter, to encourage breeding. Everything was done to aid these 'wondrous fruitefull' birds. Each year the best of the early squabs were carefully selected for future breeding. The less satisfactory – 'unfruitful and naughtie coloured, and otherwise faulty' – quickly found themselves fattened and on their way to the kitchen. But the right to husband pigeons was a privilege enjoyed only by the chosen few.

One way and another, both the Lord of the Manor and the Church regarded their exclusive rights as of great value, and it was many years before the social abuses of the system were righted. The problem was simply stated. Pigeons might well be housed by and belong to one man, but they flew free and ranged widely, taking their corn wherever they

Street-wise pigeons

Feral street pigeons choose nest sites which owe a lot to their ancestral sea caves: ledges under railway bridges, ventilation holes, roof overhangs, crevices behind statues, ornamental window railings, etc – with the tidal roar of traffic flowing below. Foraging over the open spaces of the streets and parks, they prefer grain when they can get it, grass and weed seeds as second-best. But mostly they rely on handouts of bread and scraps. Fortunate for them that many people in towns are lonely, and feeding birds is one of the ways in which they can establish a relationship with a fellow creature. The population of pigeons in towns and cities would reduce itself very sharply if people stopped feeding them, but in spite of official encouragement that event is highly unlikely.

could find it. In the early seventeenth century the jurist John Selden could write:

> Some men may make it a case of conscience, whether a man may have a pigeon-house, because his pigeons eat other folks' corn. But there is no such thing as conscience in the business: the matter is, whether he be a man of such quality that the state allows him to have a dove house: if so, there is an end of the business: his pigeons have a right to eat where they please themselves.

But it is only too easy to imagine the thoughts of the tenant farmer or the yeoman whose corn was being eaten. And in spite of what Selden thought, pigeon law rested on shaky foundations which were not easy to sustain in the courts. So as the years went by, small farmers and freeholders built their own pigeon-houses, with rows of nest holes along the walls of their barns and farmhouses. This was not without a good deal of trouble on the way; the depredations of the lordly pigeons were one of the contributory causes, for instance, of the French Revolution. New agricultural practices, making it possible to feed cattle and sheep through the winter, using root crops, have made fresh butcher's meat available throughout the year, and most pigeon-houses now lie derelict.

The descendants of those wild Rock Pigeons have lasted well, for though they may not flourish in dovecotes they are plentiful in our streets today. But how have their wild cousins fared? Sadly, they are rare, and increasingly rarer. However, a number of small populations of the pure-bred birds exist, confined to the north and west coasts and Scottish and Irish islands: bluish-grey birds, with two striking black bars across the folded wing, neck and breast an iridescent purple and green. The species is in decline partly because of the use of toxic seed-dressings, and perhaps because it was in direct competition with the Stock Dove; the catastrophic use of toxic agrichemicals in the late fifties knocked that species badly, too, but unlike the Rock Pigeon it has recovered. Apart from those far-flung Celtic outposts of pure-bred birds, Rock Pigeons are now represented only by the cliffside colonies of racing pigeons which have given up the sport, and by the ubiquitous street pigeon, which itself represents a hopeless mix of long-ago-escaped dovecote stock and more recent racing pigeon drop-outs. Mixed or not, all domestic pigeons, racers, dovecot, messenger and fancy breeds owe common ancestry to the Rock Pigeon.

Apart from pigeons, wildfowl have provided the earliest examples of artificial nesting devices. Various duck have been encouraged to nest in places convenient for their harvesting. Goldeneyes, for instance, nest naturally in tree-holes or tree-stumps, and by the late Middle Ages the Lapps were improving natural sites to attract them as a food source, mainly for the eggs.

Not long after the Viking colonisation of Iceland, coastal farmers realised the special qualities of the breast feathers

Feral pigeons on the garden shed

of Eiders. Lining the nest with its breast feathers, this sea duck arranges an eider-down quilt to cover and retain the warmth of the eggs if she leaves the nest for any reason. By the cunning provision of carefully placed sticks and stones (the birds like to nest *against* something), the farmers create conditions which suit the ducks and so encourage the formation of a colony in places which are convenient for the down collector. The practice is still followed today, and the farmers go to great lengths to please their worker birds, which are fortunately very tame. They provide music in the form of wind-activated instruments and hang coloured ribbons in strings, both of which are supposed to act as added attractions. Some of the Eider colonies are large, with anything up to 10,000 pairs nesting. The down is taken twice in each season, once just before the eggs hatch, when the lining is removed, and then later the remainder is taken after the young have left the nest. The down, which is carefully cleansed of any dirt and grass or large feathers, represents a substantial income to the farmers. They have a vested interest, of course, in making sure the wild duck breeds successfully and continues to patronise the facilities so carefully provided.

Eiders are one of the most numerous duck species in the world, their winter population in Europe totalling more than two million. Since the mid-nineteenth century their range has been expanding and we now have sizeable breeding numbers in Scotland – perhaps one day we shall see the

Arthur Christiansen/FLPA

Kestrel at nestbox

birth of a new British industry. In passing, we should note that the same basic technique pioneered for attracting Eiders to nest, that is the provision of suitably shaped sticks or stones in a featureless landscape, has been used by egg collectors wanting to plunder the eggs of Greenshanks, whose moorland nests are notoriously difficult to find. (Nowadays it is illegal to take any eggs.)

Doubtless Mallard Ducks, and others, have been provided with convenient nest sites (convenient for the plunderer, that is) in Britain for centuries, but it is not easy to find evidence of them. Decoys, which date back to somewhere around the thirteenth century, were set to live-trap migrant wildfowl in winter, and this practice certainly led to a small-scale provision of nesting facilities in the breeding season. Perhaps the first record of duck boxes in Britain comes from the diarist John Evelyn, a friend of Samuel Pepys and a mine of information on the times of Charles I. In his diary entry for 9 February 1665, he writes:

'I went to St James's Park . . . at this time stored with numerous flocks of . . . wildfowl, breeding about the Decoy, which for being so near so great a city, and among such a concourse of soldiers and people, is a singular and diverting thing . . . There were withy-potts or nests for wildfowl to lay their eggs in, a little above the surface of the water.'

The designer of the decoy, incidentally, was a Dutchman, Sydrach Hileus, who had been brought over especially to do the job.

In North America, the Indians used nestboxes made from bottle gourds to attract birds to nest and offer themselves as a food source. The disadvantage of this method is that the gourd had to be smashed to get at the contents. But they also, more effectively, farmed their wildfowl. Canada Geese, relatively tame and easy going in their choice of nest sites, were obvious targets. Over the years they have been greatly exploited by men who found that they took freely to haystacks and sheltered positions in the lee of a fence or hut. Introduced to Britain as a status symbol to decorate the fashionable landscaped lake in the eighteenth century, they bred freely on the islands so conveniently provided for them. Indeed, they flourished to become a common feral goose breeding all over England, a fair part of Wales and with outposts in Scotland. They enjoy popular protection in city parks and places like gravel pits and semi-natural reservoirs.

Black-headed Gulls have been farmed for their eggs in times past. Breeding colonially, they patronise lake islands, sand and shingle banks at the coast and inland. From the eighteenth century onwards traditional gulleries were further encouraged by the preparation of man-made islands called hafts. In midwinter great quantities of reeds and rushes were cut and level places laid out to greet the return of the breeding birds in spring. These gulls lay in April, and their pairs were so numerous that at Scoulton Mere, East Dereham, in Norfolk, for instance, some 30,000 eggs were taken annually with 44,000 marking one particularly successful year. At Pallinsburn Hall, in Northumberland, a 7 acre lake was said to be 'covered so thick, when they are disturbed and on the wing, as if a shower of snow were falling on it'! (F. O. Morris, *History of British Birds*, 1857.) The young birds were also considered good eating, some gullery proprietors making £50–80 a year by their sale. At the beginning of June, when the young were near fledging, they were driven onto the bank and netted, 'an occasion for jollity and Gentry'. In Staffordshire, three days of netting, over a period of a fortnight, gathered fifty dozen fat gull chicks at each drive.

FUN AND GAMES

One of the great charms of House Martins is their playfulness. They have fun even in the cradle. I have watched a young one stretching half its body out of the nest to play with a smaller martin in a neighbouring nest. Twittering excitedly, with head craned forward, it just managed to touch the tip of the other baby's beak. The smaller one entered into the fun and bobbed up from its nest to take the kiss, both withdrawing directly afterwards. Then the bigger one, behaving excitedly began poking its brother – or sister – as if trying to egg it on to join in the fun, but getting no response, the merry martin again turned to the neighbouring baby and, with a terrific effort, heaved almost all its body outside the nest, with eager twitterings touching the small one's beak. This touch or kiss was received with obvious amusement by the little one, who repeatedly retired into its nest then bobbed up again to thrust its head forward for another touch of beaks. The game continued for some time, the enjoyment of the martins so infectious it was impossible to watch without laughter. The elder one, in its eager excitement, made stretching efforts that could easily end in falling from the nest and the parents evidently disapproved. When preparing for their second brood they wisely sealed up the old entrance hole, making another on the opposite side of their nest where there were no neighbours, so the young of their next brood were not tempted to play risky games, with neighbouring young before they were fledged.

Len Howard

A Faulkner Taylor/FLPA

Nestboxes for pleasure

So far, all these examples of artificial nestboxes or man-assisted nesting have had a culinary or commercial significance. Perhaps the first known record of birds attracted to an artificial nest site purely for aesthetic reasons, was that of Gilbert White's brother Thomas, who, as Gilbert recorded in his journal for 5 June 1782:

> . . . nailed up several large scallop shells under the eaves of his house at South Lambeth, to see if the House Martins would build in them. These conveniences had not been fixed half an hour before several pairs settled upon them; and expressing great complacency began to build immediately. The shells were nailed on horizontally with the hollow side upward; and should, I think, have a hole drilled in their bottoms to let off moisture from driving rains.

Charles Waterton, developed the use of nestboxes in the early nineteenth century, as also did the other pioneer field ornithologist, J. F. Dovaston. Unfortunately, although we know Dovaston used boxes in connection with his experiments, which may have been the first to consider the principles of territory in bird behaviour, he left precious little published information on them – a terrible lesson for all amateur scientists who fail to record their findings! Waterton wrote fully, so we know for example that he made (possibly in 1816) an artificial sand quarry with fifty deep holes in a sheltered and sunny part of the grounds of Walton Park. And we can imagine his pleasure and delight when, the very next summer, Sand Martins arrived in his reserve for the first time to found a thriving colony. (A similar experiment, equally successful, may be seen today at the RSPB's Minsmere reserve in Suffolk.)

Waterton improved hollow trees to make them more attractive for Tawny Owls, and developed a Barn Owl house:

> . . . on the ruin of the old gateway, against which, tradition says, the waves of the lake have dashed for the best part of a thousand years. I made a place with stone and mortar, about four feet square, and fixed a thick oaken stick firmly into it. In about a month or so after it was finished, a pair of Barn Owls came and took up their abode in it. I threatened to strangle the keeper if ever, after this, he molested either the old birds or their young ones.

Waterton was so delighted with his succcess that he subsequently built four other owl establishments, all of which were occupied. He also built a tower for Jackdaws and Starlings, rather in the style of a garden dovecote. Its stone pillar, smooth and vertical, was surmounted by a flat circular stone with sharply sloping edges, measures all designed to discourage rats. On top of this he placed a circular stone house, with conical roof, each course of stones having some loose ones, channelled to allow inspection access to the nest

Odd nest sites

A pair of wagtails built their nest between the radiator and the grille of the RSPB's Bedford van at Sandy. Staff decided that it would be better to leave the nest *in situ* rather than remove it, and continued to use the van for daily trips to the town. The wagtails eventually fledged four young from this centrally heated mobile home and an RSPB staff spokesman commented that the family 'even seemed to enjoy the ride'.

But wagtails by no means have the monopoly on odd nest sites. Black Guillemots have nested on the Yell ferry in the Shetland Islands, despite daily journeys, while House Martins nesting on boats will tolerate regular trips into the English Channel.

chamber behind. Although Waterton was regarded as little more than an eccentric in his own time, many of his ideas sowed the seeds of a whole new attitude to wildlife which were to bear a great deal of fruit later.

By 1897, twenty species were known to have bred in boxes or platforms of some kind in Britain. But the pioneer of large scale bird manipulation by the use of nestboxes was the Baron von Berlepsch. His primary interest was the control of insect pests in his woodland, but there is no doubt he had aesthetic considerations firmly in mind. His main interest was in methods of increasing woodland bird populations in areas where foresters were intolerant of trees past their maturity, and nestboxes played an important part in his operations. Before his time, these devices had been relatively ineffective. He brought a cold and logical eye to the requirements and pursued them with relentless efficiency, pouring scorn on bird 'inventions' which had suffered failures in the past, not being based on what he saw as an understanding of bird nature.

HOUSE-PROUD

When I started putting up nesting-boxes for the birds I did not clean the used ones, thinking they would prefer them undisturbed. Experience taught me this was wrong. I found the tits who used uncleaned boxes were very restless at night and continually woke up to preen, while those from clean boxes were free of parasite troubles and never needed night preening. I used to watch tits go to their uncleaned nesting-boxes, peep inside then hurriedly make one or two preening movements and fly away without entering. On examining the boxes I saw lice round the interior of the entrance hole. Directly I cleaned the boxes (a kettle of quite boiling water poured over all sides the surest and quickest method), the tits occupied the boxes, and preening movements were not again made on looking inside. All the boxes I clean are used for roosting in winter and nesting in spring, those left uncleaned are not entered again, unless driven by necessity, through scarcity of safe nesting-holes. Some people think 'leaving it to nature' is best. But in supplying birds with artificial water-tight boxes we encourage them to use something not quite natural. The hole in a tree probably gets enough moisture through it for cleansing purposes. Also, I notice ants enter tree-holes where tits have nested, not to nest there themselves, but for some definite reason. This, I think, may be for eating the lice. I have a good reason for thinking this as the other day, when cleaning out the tit's roost-boxes, some ants appeared and I watched them walk off with the bird lice I was scraping out of one of the boxes. Many species of birds, when suffering from this pest, pick up ants and place them between their feathers.

Len Howard

Eric Hosking

The photograph is credited vertically at the right edge: *David Hosking*

A semi-detached development – Blue Tits on the left, Wren's nest on the right being visited by the neighbour

Pied Flycatchers are enthusiastic nestbox customers

Much of his experimentation, in the 500 acre bird park set aside for the purpose, lay in attempts to design the perfect woodpecker nestbox, having observed that woodpecker nest holes, deserted or uninhabited, were preferred nest sites by many other species. He proposed that his all-purpose box, whether destined for Tits, Nuthatches, Starlings or indeed woodpeckers, was to resemble the natural woodpecker design in every exact respect. He proposed no mere invention, but exact copies of nature. He cut down several hundred trees in his search to reveal the woodpecker's secrets, discovering, to his surprise, that the nest cavities were all constructed to exactly the same general principles whether the carpenter was a Black, Green or Spotted Woodpecker. He then set about reproducing, in quantity, the perfect nestbox.

In fact, Berlepsch went too far, since as we know only too well, birds will occupy boxes of almost any shape, size or colour provided they offer certain fundamental design advantages – most particularly that the entrance hole is of the correct size. But, after measuring hundreds of natural woodpecker excavations, he specified that his boxes should

reproduce those measurements precisely. He wouldn't allow tin guards around the entrance holes (to discourage Great Spotted Woodpeckers from taking over from tits) on the grounds that they destroyed the natural appearance of the boxes ('their chief merit'), and said that such 'guarded' boxes were never occupied, a claim which seems nonsensical today.

In one wood he set up 2,000 of his boxes, and claimed 90 per cent occupancy; and in his bird park, he had 300 boxes occupied by birds of fourteen species. But although he went to some lengths to provide additional food for his birds in order to sustain an abundant population, it is not clear that he fully understood the overriding importance that food availability has in controlling bird numbers. He believed that the provision of nest sites was of paramount importance. Nevertheless, he was the first to make nestboxing popular; his boxes were successful, they were manufactured

From the correspondence columns of The Times
18 April 1988

To make a cat laugh
Sir, Like so many things learnt in childhood, a sacrosanct habit has been to put all loose hair and combings from a hairbrush out of the bedroom window for the birds to line their nests with.

Now that golden tresses are thin and grey, with no insulation properties, the copious combings from a large cat are hooked to a thorny branch of a pyracantha tree.

Imagine our joyous mirth this morning to see our (?) Robin flying past weighed down by a tabby moustache twice his size!
Yours faithfully,
Cecilia Preuss,
Thames Ditton, Surrey.

(But be careful that if you offer hair clippings or lengths of cotton or wool they are cut to short lengths, so that the birds do not tangle their legs.)

5 May 1988

Sir, Apropos the recent correspondence, my neighbour bought her daughter a vivid turquoise blue angora jumper, which unaccountably went into small holes after it was washed and dried on the clothes-line.

When I cleared my Blue Tits' box in the autumn their nest lining solved the mystery!
Yours faithfully,
Joyce Robson,
Whitton,
Twickenham, Middlesex.

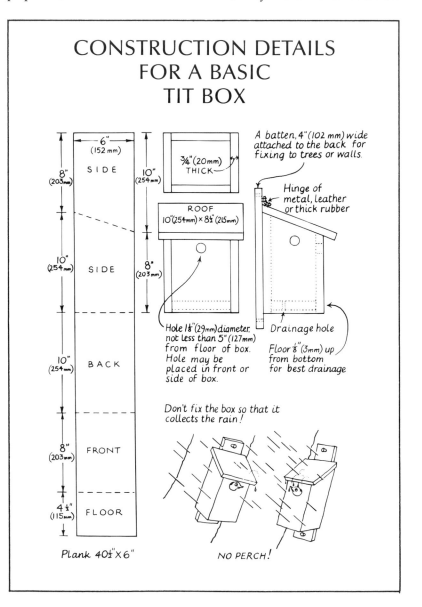

CONSTRUCTION DETAILS FOR A BASIC TIT BOX

6" (152 mm)
8" (203mm)   SIDE
10" (254mm)
3/4" (20mm) THICK
10" (254mm)   SIDE
ROOF 10" (254mm) × 8½" (215mm)
8" (203mm)

A batten, 4" (102 mm) wide attached to the back for fixing to trees or walls.

Hinge of metal, leather or thick rubber

Hole 1⅛" (29mm) diameter, not less than 5" (127mm) from floor of box. Hole may be placed in front or side of box.

10" (254mm)   BACK

Drainage hole

Floor ⅛" (3mm) up from bottom for best drainage

8" (203mm)   FRONT

Don't fix the box so that it collects the rain!

4½" (115mm)   FLOOR

Plank 40½" × 6"

NO PERCH!

GOLDENEYE

One of the most interesting British ornithological phenomena of the past ten to twenty years has been the successful breeding of several species of Scandinavian birds in Scotland. Climatic change is the usual reason given for this population expansion, though the exact extent and nature of the change are still uncertain.

Nevertheless, the birds are there, and they include passerines such as Redwing, *Turdus iliacus* and Lapland Bunting *Calcarius lapponicus*; a primitive woodpecker, the Wryneck *Jynx torquilla*; waders such as the Sanderling *Calidris alba*; a predator, the Snowy Owl *Nyctea scandiaca*; and a sea duck, the Goldeneye *Bucephala clangula*.

The first Scottish nesting Goldeneyes were spotted about fifteen years ago in the Spey valley; and by 1981 more than fifty pairs were breeding in various places, and almost 300 chicks had hatched. Goldeneyes nest in holes in trees – with the result that there is intense competition for sites, particularly with other arboreal ducks such as mergansers – and have taken readily to nestboxes custom-built by welcoming birdwatchers.

This colonisation has been aided by special protection from the Nature Conservancy Council, which has banned interference with the duck to the extent that even the people who built the nestboxes need licences to inspect them.

But there is nothing rare about the Goldeneye in Europe as a whole, and the big flocks along the coasts number in the tens of thousands, widely dispersed over extensive shellfish beds. In Britain coastal wintering flocks are generally on a smaller scale. Inland flocks also range across the Continent and lowland Britain, where they have wintered ever since man began building large reservoirs for canals and drinking water and digging huge gravel pits.

Many people wonder how young tree ducklings, hatched in a nest with an entrance three, four or even five metres above the ground, make the daunting descent. The answer is simplicity itself: they trust mother and jump – as tiny balls of down on the morning after the day they hatch. The female calls them off the nest and the whole brood, quite often more than ten ducklings, pop out and plop down to the ground in the space of a minute or so. The mother then leads them to water and rears them there.

Chris Mead

in large quantities both in Germany and – under licence – abroad. In the early years of this century the newly formed RSPB offered them in various sizes, for sale at prices varying from 1s 6d (7½p) to 5s 6d (27½p). Berlepsch left his mark, if nowhere else, on the commercial world of nestbox production, and it was years before cheaper, less natural, but equally effective, versions were on the market. In one major respect Berlepsch strayed off the path of righteousness: he believed firmly in controlling predators, creatures he called the enemies of his birds. These included cats, squirrels, weasels, martens, polecats, House and Tree Sparrows, shrikes, Sparrowhawks, Goshawks, Jays, Magpies and Carrion Crows – his blacklist for whose demise he offered rewards.

From Berlepsch's time, boxes were used systematically by scientists engaged in population studies. In the case of the Pied Flycatcher, which takes to nestboxes as ducks take to water, whole woodland populations have preferred the artificial sites to anything a tree has to offer, and tens of thousands of birds have been ringed in research directed towards analysing their life-style. A great deal of work has also been done on the nesting behaviour of Blue and Great Tits, and of Tawny Owls.

Bird Gardening

J. Watkins/FLPA

There are three essentials in any good bird garden – food, water and cover. Most of the trees and shrubs planted will provide all the cover necessary but a certain amount of pruning at an early age will ensure that they do not become too tall so that the birds pass over, not through the garden. Water is important, but a square of black plastic camouflaged around the edges and sunk 3–4in into the ground is all that is required. The provision of a tank – a 5gal drum perhaps – to drip steadily into the pond below is a worthwhile addition.

Trees are a problem. Most are far too big for the average garden and newly planted specimens usually take too long to produce seed or fruit. Rowan is good, except that hordes of Blackbirds, thrushes and Starlings usually strip it long before the winter, and one of the ornamental crab apples is very useful. The variety Golden Hornet produces a vast crop of tiny yellow fruit annually and the apples remain on the tree long after the leaves have fallen. All the thrushes, including Redwings and Fieldfares will eat the fruit, and Marsh Tits will spend happy hours hacking away at the exterior to get at the pips.

But berry-bearing shrubs should be our main concern; their great advantage is that they can be used in so many ways. Some, with a little training in their early stages will make small standard trees far superior for the average small garden than the sterile double-flowered cherries one so often sees. Some may be trained as wall shrubs or clipped to form a child or animal-proof hedge attractive at all seasons and there are others which are ideal for ground cover on rough banks or even beneath trees.

Berberis come in many forms, both species and hybrids. It is not at all unusual to find a nursery listing fifty or more varieties. In a case like this it is obviously best to see the growing plants and choose them on the spot. For a hedge there is no reason why several varieties should not be used since this will mean that the berries ripen at different times, thereby prolonging the useful season. All *Berberis* have attractive foliage; many colour well in the autumn; some have red fruit, some, for which the birds seem to have a slight preference, have black.

Cotoneasters vary even more than *Berberis. C. dammeri* and

Why spades?

One of the traditional pictures of the tame Robin shows it perching on a gardener's spade. Why does it do it so often? The answer is simple. The Robin's preferred feeding technique is to use a low perch to survey an area and then to fly down to take any prey it sees. The spade is an ideal perch. Add to this the presence of the gardener, turning the soil and exposing such useful food as earthworms, leather-jackets and other grubs. Heaven for any garden Robin!

C. microphylla are two completely prostrate, ground hugging varieties; in the 4–6ft range are *C. conspicua* and *C. franchetti sterniana* (often listed as *C. wardii*) with grey foliage and orange berries and larger still is *C. bullata* (which attracted our first Ring Ouzel into the garden in 1971). Finally both *C. aldenhamensis* and *C. watereri* will make small trees in time. As a fan-shaped cover for a low wall (up to about 6ft) *C. horizontalis* is already an almost automatic choice.

Larger walls (eg the areas between windows) call for one of the *Pyracanthas* which will have the additional merit of producing fruit on even the most depressing north wall. To scramble over a trellis or a fence at least one honeysuckle should be included – our native *Lonicera periclymenum* is as good as any. Few birds eat the berries but wintering Blackcaps will take them and Marsh Tits seem to find them irresistible. Marsh Tits do have the oddest tastes! Rose species, some of which produce large quantities of very attractive hips, are not particularly sought after by birds although Greenfinches will shred them to get all the seeds within.

There are a number of less well-known species which will be taken. In fact of all the berry-bearing shrubs we have tried there are only two which birds never touch – the Guelder Rose (*Viburnum opulus*) which grows wild all over the South Downs, and *Skimmia japonica*. The American Chokeberry (*Aronia*) comes in two forms; *A. prunifolia* (or *A. floribunda*) has dark crimson fruit but a much superior form is *A. melanocarpa* with brilliant autumn foliage and huge black berries which are invariably taken as soon as they are ripe. *Stransvaesia davidiana* is a tallish evergreen

A pond or bird-bath is an essential part of any bird garden, patronised here by a pair of Collared Doves

Peggy Heard/FLPA

'Top ten'

The 'Top Ten' customers at garden bird feeding stations, from a BTO survey 1982/3:

Blue Tit (Chart topper)
Blackbird
Robin
House Sparrow
Chaffinch
Dunnock
Starling
Great Tit
Greenfinch
Song Thrush

Collared Dove and Coal Tit didn't quite make it.

with bunches of scarlet berries which are taken somewhat reluctantly towards the end of winter. Two less common shrubs are *Callicarpa*, with violet berries in October, and *Coriaria xanthocarpa*, a suckering sub-shrub which will eventually cover several square yards and is worth every inch of it. This has foot long racemes of translucent yellow fruit at the end of every shoot. The Royal Horticultural Society's *Dictionary of Gardening* assures me that the birds do not eat these, but my birds – Robins, Blackbirds, Blackcaps and Whitethroats – do not read the dictionary so they strip the bushes every year with no apparent ill effects.

This is by no means the end of the list, there are many others – *Daphne* species, *Pernettya*, *Gaultheria* and *Vaccinium* (American Blueberries) – but on the whole the quantity of fruit produced is hardly sufficient to justify their inclusion unless space is unlimited: and one could, of course, always add a row or two of raspberries or strawberries except that the cook would inevitably claim them.

An open and well-kept lawn is almost essential to a good bird garden. Lawn-watching is the easiest way of discovering some of the different adaptations and techniques used by birds for feeding. One of the constant wonders of the natural world is its diversity, the extraordinary range of plants and animals in any given habitat, and the way they all manage to make a living by occupying slightly different niches. Superficially the 'nature red in tooth and claw' approach may seem justified, but it would be more just to see communities of different creatures living in tolerable harmony. Birds come in all shapes and sizes. Some hunt by day, some by night. Some are vegetarian, some are meat-eaters, some eat anything they can get hold of, including other birds. Some walk after their food, some hop for it, some fly for it, some dive and swim for it. And each is specially equipped for the chosen job. One way or another anything which grows or moves gets eaten by something. Fruit, nuts, seeds, leaves, bark, living matter and decaying matter, all is grist to the mill.

Very roughly we can divide birds into four categories according to the shape of their beaks: the hard-billed birds like sparrows or finches which have nutcracker bills; the soft-billed birds like Robins which deal with insects; the dual-purpose bills which take on all comers; and the hook-billed predators like Sparrow-Hawks.

On the lawn, the most obvious visitors are the birds searching for worms and soft grubs. The old saying about the early bird getting the worm is an exact observation of fact. Worms are creatures of moisture and mildness; early morning dew suits them, sunrise and sun warmth does not and they retire underground. So thrushes and Blackbirds comb the lawn at first light and this is when you may see the bigger Blackbird steal worms from the Song Thrush, getting his breakfast the easy way.

Birds have a well-developed sense of hearing, but they hunt almost entirely by the use of sight, and to some extent

A fine meal for Tony Soper's garden visitors

Sow four grains in a row,
One to rot, one to grow,
One for the pigeon,
One for the crow.
Traditional rhyme

touch; at least that is true of those most active by day. When the thrush catches a worm, he does it because he has seen it first. The longstanding mis-observation that birds listen for worms is based on a characteristically human weakness: people make the classic mistake of regarding birds, or any other animal for that matter, as if they too were people. The worm-hunting thrush hops a few paces, then stands very still and cocks its head to one side. A pause, and then the stab. So we deduce that the bird had its head cocked to listen for the sound of the worm. But the observation failed to take note of the fact that the bird's *eye* happens to be in the position where the human *ear* is found. When a man cocks his head in that attitude, he is listening intently; when a thrush does it, he is watching intently.

People are strangely slow to believe that bird sight is an improvement on their own. I am often asked by what strange sixth sense birds know that a particular delicacy has been thrown onto the lawn for them. Why are distant seagulls so quick to respond to scraps of meat and fat but take their time for stale bread, they ask. But the answer is simple: gulls can see what is on offer as well as you can, but from a greater distance. And what's more, when one gull is excited about a find, his very behaviour in flying down to it attracts distant gulls. Seabirds like gulls and, more spectacularly, Gannets, can keep in touch with the news over large expanses of sea by watching each other. This, incidentally, accounts for their white plumage. Other species may have drab camouflage, but seabirds have fewer predators and don't mind being seen.

Woodland species like Buzzards can see a beetle from hundreds of feet in the air. Certainly it isn't the sense of smell that's used; birds *can* smell, but seem not to use this ability. Sight – and sometimes sound – is what is important.

Green Woodpeckers search the lawn for ant nests

Eric & David Hosking

Eric Hosking

As it is the early bird which catches the worm, Starlings tend to miss out on the morning feast. Roosting in city centres outside the breeding season, they tend to arrive late on the lawn scene, and will be probing for leather-jackets and insect grubs, as well as picking up the kitchen scraps. They are much maligned: if they were rare we should be delighted to see them. In breeding plumage they fully justify their name – little star. Their sociable habits and skill as mimics just do not seem to be able to make up for their supposed bullying character in the bird garden. One of the problems of success!

The bird which is a universal favourite when he swoops onto the lawn is the Green Woodpecker, with his striking green plumage and red head. His curious flight – a few flaps followed by a glide with wings clasped tight to body – and yaffling call bring him switchbacking into the garden. So remarkable is his appearance that many people can't believe he is a British bird at all, working on the dismal

Great Spotted Woodpeckers enjoy peanuts

assumption that home-grown species are bound to be dull and dowdy! But British he is, and a delight to see, working over the lawn and exploring for ants and ant nests. The other woodpeckers, equally striking in their red and white livery, are less attracted to ground level, but the Green Woodpecker, with his long, mobile tongue tipped with sticky mucus, searches out larvae from their hidey-holes in crevices. He may spear out larger bugs and grubs, but ants are his speciality. In hard weather when ants are scarce he may become a nuisance to bee-keepers by breaking and entering hives to eat the bees; and he may vandalise nestboxes by enlarging the tit-sized holes in order to gain entry to search for bugs inside.

Some of the lawn visitors are looking for grass and weed seeds, and of these perhaps the most attractive is the Goldfinch. The sight of a charm of Goldfinches attacking the golden dandelions ought to be enough to convert any gardener into a dandelion fan. They approach them with zest, leapfrogging into the stems, landing about half way up towards the head so that they weigh it down to the ground. Then they get to work. All finches are seed-eaters, with powerful jaw muscles and bills modified for husking. They have two grooves inside the bill which locate the nut or seed, then the tongue rotates it as the mandibles crush. The husk peels off, leaving the kernel to be swallowed. Different finches go for different seeds, a Hawfinch, for example, is tough enough to cope with cherry and plum

MAN, PREDATORS AND VERMIN

Birds and beasts of prey do not hunt for sport except in very rare cases: a fox killing a Pheasant is going about his lawful business; an eagle taking a grouse is doing so to enable him to exist. The larger cats and all hawks kill in a more humane fashion than does man. There is very little wounding, and death is usually instantaneous.

Man's desire to kill predatory animals probably survives from the days when he had to compete with cave bears and sabre-toothed tigers and when gangs of hairy Neanderthalers would mob the lion with the same noise and fuss which accompany the mobbing of an owl by tits and thrushes today, except that Neanderthal man probably threw stones and logs of wood. Today it is seldom that a gamekeeper can resist shooting any hawk or owl he sees – the larger and more unusual the bird, the more readily he will shoot. That type of man probably constitutes the greatest danger and does the greatest harm to many forms of wildlife; and the sportsman with the gamekeeper's mentality is little better – possibly worse – for he should know better. The excuse is that objectionable word 'vermin'. Every conceivable form of wildlife which might possibly disturb game is classed as vermin, whereas the most dangerous disturber of wildlife and the greatest vermin of all is man himself. The sportsman, the egg-collector, the bird-lover, bird-photographer and bird-watcher are all greater disturbers and destroyers of wildlife than any wild predator, who after all is going about his lawful business – survival. I am not preaching anti-bloodsport propaganda and I recognise man's right to kill for food, for science, or to protect his own property; but he has no right to kill for the love of killing or endeavour to exterminate animals whose lawful pursuit is killing for food. 'No animal species should be outlawed – in doing so we greatly overestimate our present level of knowledge' (Rudebeck, *Oikos*, 1950).

R. Meinertzhagen

stones. Goldfinches, at the weaker end of the finch scale, use their relatively long narrow bills rather like a pair of tweezers, probing deep into the seed-head.

Even a Magpie will weigh down a plant stem to attack the seed-head, and is representative of those birds which will eat almost anything, including other birds and eggs if it gets the chance. It has even been alleged to lift dustbin lids to get at the contents.

Swallows will occasionally settle on a lawn to pick up flies, but most of the time they are concerned with airborne flies. Their beaks are wide and flattened, designed to scoop quantities of insects out of the air. With their forked tail streamers they are easy to distinguish from the white-rumped House Martins, although they may mix together as they feed in the air space above your garden. But the Swift is the most completely aerial bird, in this country anyway. He not only catches his food on the wing but he mates, and probably even sleeps, in flight. Indeed he would probably never touch down at all if it weren't impossible to incubate an egg while airborne. Perhaps in the course of evolution he will manage that, as may many seabirds which would never come ashore if only they could make a nest on the surface of the sea. The Swift flies from near ground level up to 1,000ft, grazing the insect pastures of the air, and filling it with those screams which nostalgically recall continental holidays. Like the Swallow, he has a big head and a wide mouth with bristles round it, designed to act like an aerial shrimp net.

Sometimes exotic visitors arrive in gardens: escaped cage birds may turn up to puzzle and confuse the local birdwatchers; Budgies or Canaries will visit a bird-table for weeks or even months in the summer. The harsh weather of winter usually finishes them, even if they survive the Sparrowhawks and crows, but there are some astonishing success stories, like the Rose-ringed Parakeets which have established themselves around London and are keen visitors to bird-tables for peanuts. Mild winters certainly help.

Perhaps the most spectacular lawn visitor, but one that you're only likely to see if you live on the south coast, is the Hoopoe. With its pinkish-brown plumage, barred black on the wings and back, it swoops in to the grass with a lazy flight. On landing it shows a remarkable crest in the shape of a fan, pink with black tips. Then it struts about, probing into the soil with its long curved bill. Typically it prefers parkland, orchard and open wooded country, but it is fond of the vicinity of houses, where it feeds on lawns and paths for insect larvae. A very few stay with us to nest, in holes in trees or buildings, and some years there is a considerable influx of them, so keep an eye open. One of the Hoopoe's most endearing traits is its tameness and tolerance of man; even the French are fond of it and refrain from shooting it. It gets its name from its voice – a low, but penetrating sexy 'hoop-oop-oop'. The scientific name is *Upupa epops* – both onomatopoeic and charming!

Birdwise

The Hobby, a summer migrant, is undoubtedly the most acrobatic of our raptors, quartering the rich undulating lowlands of southern England in search not only of small birds, but also of aerial insects, such as moths and dragonflies, which provide a valuable supplement to its diet. But when weather conditions are bad, reducing insect availability, how does the Hobby respond?

Reporting on his study of Hobbies, during the pre-incubation stage, at a site in the New Forest, Tim Milsom suggests that there is a temperature threshold of 13°C below which hunting for insects is not attempted. He bases this on observations of aerial hunting activities which, he noted, were confined to the warmest part of each day, and were not observed below 13°C. There are good reasons for this. Firstly, as air temperatures fall, thermal updraughts, on which the birds rely for soaring flight, become weaker and in order to continue hunting the bird must switch to flapping flight. This uses much more energy. Secondly, the rate at which Hobbies encounter insect prey also declines with falling temperatures so that the birds must fly for longer to catch the same amount of food. These factors combine to make it simply not worthwhile hunting below the threshold temperature.

The message for birdwatchers is clear: if you want to see Hobbies in action choose a nice warm day!

When you have a well-stocked and varied bird garden, the next step in encouraging a superabundance of birds is to set up a bird-table. Put it somewhere within easy flying distance of cover, for the sake of the bird's comfort, and within viewing distance of a convenient window for your enjoyment . . .

Bird-tables
Many species come to a table, especially Robins, finches and sparrows, and hanging bags of nuts attract tits and Greenfinches. A bird-table has the added advantage of being high enough to see from the comfort of an easy chair!

Scatter
Not all birds will feed from a raised table – Dunnocks, thrushes and Blackbirds like food on the ground. If you put food in several places, or scatter it widely, more birds will feed than will eat happily together in one place. In bad weather it is important to give as many birds as possible the best chance of a good feed, without continually bickering.

Dying for a drink
Water is every bit as important as food. Not only must birds drink, but they must bathe to keep their insulating feathers in perfect condition. Although it looks less attractive than a pond, a simple dish or tray, or upturned dustbin lid is just as effective.

Keep water clean and free from ice and remember to top

Great, Blue and Long-tailed Tits at the bird-table

Eric & David Hosking

Hoopoes sometimes overshoot the Channel and visit lawns on the South Coast

it up. Ingenious devices from night lights to aeration pumps can be used to prevent the water freezing. A useful tip is to use an old frying pan as a bird-bath. When the water freezes, melt it on the cooker, allow to cool and return to the garden.

Menu

Here are just a few suggestions for a varied diet for your wild birds.

Bones (for the marrow)	Dried fruit
Fat (including suet)	Baked potatoes
Cheese	Cooked rice
Oats/coarse oatmeal	Moistened cake
Sunflower seeds	and bread
Peanuts (not salted)	Fresh coconut
Bacon rind, chopped	Windfall apples

Fruitful exercise

If you have bruised apples or windfalls from the autumn, put them out in spells of cold weather. Blackbirds and other thrushes love them and you might get Redwings and Fieldfares if you are lucky.

Robins

Robins cannot eat seeds or nuts but will be attracted by suet or grated cheese. If you really wanted to indulge your Robins, you can buy them mealworms from pet or angling shops – but make sure they are alive, or they can cause salmonella poisoning.

Cracks and crevices

Bags and baskets are not the only way to provide food and attract interesting birds. If you have an old tree or stump in the garden, especially a gnarled apple or oak, use the bark. Wedge nuts and seed in the crevices and smear cheese, fat or suet in the cracks. Even shy visitors such as Treecreepers, Wrens and Goldcrests can be helped in this way.

Roger Wilmshurst/FLPA

A very fruitful exercise for ten birds from four species – Fieldfare, Mistle Thrush, Redwing and Blackbird

Nuts

Natural, unsalted peanuts are ideal food for many types of bird. Blue, Great and Coal Tits, House Sparrows, Greenfinches and Siskins all love them and are able to feed on a suspended bag or basket. Place them all over the garden to attract as many birds as possible. Even Nuthatches and Great Spotted Woodpeckers may come to a nut bag in a garden close to woodland. Some feeders exclude sparrows and finches and allow in only the Tits, but beware of making it too difficult for birds to feed. The whole point is to help them to survive, not to test their ingenuity!

Bags and baskets

A plastic mesh bag is as good a holder as any for shelled peanuts, but if you find it is torn by birds or squirrels, a wire basket may be a better buy. Plastic-coated wire is safer for the birds and lasts for years. Spiral feeders should not be used unless they are rigid and unlikely to trap a bird by its foot.

Feeders may be hung from bird-tables, but try other sites too – a bracket on a fence or wall, a branch of a tree, even a hook on a window frame will make likely spots for some entertaining birdwatching.

Seed and grain

Greenfinches and Chaffinches like grain and large seeds from sunflowers and melons. Put them on the bird-table and scatter some on the ground beneath. You can buy wild birdseed and sun-flower seeds, or save your own each autumn. They make a change from peanuts and invite a greater variety of birds to feed near your window. You may even attract Bramblings, winter-visiting finches from Scandinavia.

Passing through

The same half-dozen Blue Tits and handful of Greenfinches come to feed each day – or do they? Appearances are deceptive. In many gardens there will be at least ten times the number of birds coming to feed during the day as can be counted at any one time. The Blue Tits may be part of a roaming flock of several dozens, all of which come to the bird-table at different times.

Winter feeders

Birds derive advantage from the autumn plenty by putting on fat and by laying up a winter store. It is at this time of year, when berries and seeds are plentiful, that you are least likely to have a well-attended bird-table – the natural food available is a greater attraction. But it may be that your bird-table is not particularly successful in a winter which follows a bumper seeding season. In other words, there is no substitute for natural food, and birds will prefer it given a choice. As well as seeds, there will still be a measure of life-support in the hibernating flies, spiders, woodlice, cen-

---

Earthworm culture

Earthworms, *Lumbricus terrestris*, are bisexual, each individual exhibiting both male and female characteristics. But it still needs two to start a family. Use a suitable box in a shady position. Fill with a mixture of sand, well-ground manure (which may include a generous helping of household peelings and greens), rich loamy soil and peat moss in equal parts. Water and mix well. Turn and sprinkle with yet more water every few days. Introduce your breeding stock after two weeks, when the mix has cooled to betwen 66°F and 75°F (19° and 24°C). In three months you will have a powerhouse of worm production, to be culled for your ground-feeders' tray.

tipedes and so on, which find just enough warmth to over-winter in the fallen leaves of undergrowth. One of the characteristic sounds of winter is the crunching noise made by Blackbirds as they thunder about in the shrubbery, foraging.

It is in hard weather, when the extreme cold requires more energy output by birds to maintain their body temp-ratures, that the bird-table is a life-saver. The most obvious effect of the arrival of a cold snap is that more species will

Offer a variety of food at the bird-table

Derek Washington/Jamie Wood Ltd

come for the food. There will be Mistle Thrushes, Green-finches, Long-tailed Tits, and more Blackbirds. Fieldfares and Redwings will visit the garden lawn and the bird-table, and there will be Bramblings feeding under the nut bags for fallen morsels. In extreme conditions, even the fiercely territorial Robins will feed side by side. Other species will find their way in from exposed country to enjoy the relative shelter, including Reed Buntings and Yellowhammers, Grey Wagtails, Sky Larks and Meadow Pipits, Pheasants and Moorhens. Wrens may take crumbs from bird-tables in a way that is entirely untypical.

It is perhaps true that the existence of bird-table food has made it possible for some normally migrant birds to stay with us and stick out our British winter. Blackcaps, which are overwintering in increasing numbers, mostly in the mild

RECIPES FROM THE BIRD-TABLE SCHOOL OF COOKERY

Basic Pud
Take seeds, peanuts, cheese, oatmeal, dry cake and scraps. Put them in a container, pour hot fat over the mixture until it is covered, and leave to set. Turn out onto a table, unless you have prepared it in a tit-bell or coconut holder. Rough quantities: 1lb (400g) of mixture to ½lb (200g) of melted fat.

Tit-bell Recipe
Fill the upturned bell with seeds, peanuts, cheese, oatmeal, sultanas, cake crumbs and other scraps. Pour in hot fat to the brim. Insert a short piece of twig into the mixture to act as a learner's perch, if necessary. Leave to harden. Turn the bell over and hang in a suitable place where small birds like Blue Tits are already accustomed to come for food.

Edwin Cohen's Pudding
Mix 8oz (200g) melted beef suet, 12oz (300g) coarse oatmeal and 2–3oz (50–75g) flour with 5oz (125g) water to stiff paste. Bake in shallow pie dish to form flat cake at 175°C (350°F, Gas Mark 4) for approximately 1 hour.

Miss Turner's Maize Cake
Mix 3oz (75g) maize meal in a bowl with equal quantities of chopped nuts, hemp, canary and millet seed. Stir with boiling water till coagulated, and add two beaten eggs. Tie tightly in a cloth and bake at 175° (350°F, Gas Mark 4) for fifty minutes to one hour.

Tim's Bird Cake
Mix 2lb (1kg) self-raising flour, 8oz (200g) margarine and a little sugar with water and bake like a rock bun.

Max Knight Mix
Mix stale cake and fat with a few dried currants and sultanas. Imprisoned in a 5–8in (12.5–20cm) wire-mesh bag, it keeps birds busy and prevents too much scatter.

Anti-sparrow Pudding
Boil together one cup of sugar and one cup of water for five minutes. Mix with one cup of melted fat (suet, bacon or ordinary shortening) and leave it to cool. Then mix with breadcrumbs, flour, birdseed, a little boiled rice and scraps, until the mixture is very stiff. Pack into any kind of tin can or glass jar. Lay the can on its side in a tree, on the windowsill, or any place where birds can perch and pick out the food. The can must be placed securely so that the birds cannot dislodge it, nor rain get inside. May not fool sparrows for long though, so don't take it too seriously.

Eric & David Hosking

Birds need water for drinking as well as bathing

south and south-west, are particularly vulnerable to severe winters. They rely heavily on berries, such as those of *Cotoneaster* and honeysuckle, will eat the holly berries which are not exactly popular generally, and turn to ivy berries during the early spring as their preferred food. Rotting windfall apples are also important to them, and they have even been seen to take mistletoe berries, a fruit which seems of little interest to most birds apart from thrushes. It is in hard weather that Blackcaps are most likely to be seen at bird-tables, looking for cake crumbs, fat, nuts and seeds, and this is the time when a tray of rejected fruit from the shop will be most welcome. Overwintering Chiffchaffs will come to the bird-table too, for crumbs and suet.

It is possible that bird-table offerings have fuelled the range expansion of an exotic invader, the Ring-necked Parakeet. This attractive-looking parrot, originating from Africa and India, escaped from captivity, or was perhaps deliberately released in some numbers (as a human response to its unrewarding behaviour in captivity), at the end of the 1960s. Since then, starting from a nucleus in the London suburbs and Kent, it has slowly but surely colonised the south-east and established itself as a feral species and something of a pest. Omnivorous by nature, it prefers fruit and has a devastating effect on apple orchards with its tendency to take just a couple of pecks at each fruit. It comes freely to bird-tables and, breeding in tree-holes, will presumably take to nestboxes. Even the most severe winters have failed to halt its spread, in spite of knowledgeable predictions that it could not survive the cold. Broadly speaking, it is true that birds are perfectly able to withstand the lowest temperatures, provided they are well fed and protected by healthy plumage.

In extreme winter conditions, when water is frozen and mud-flats glazed by ice, water birds and waders suffer greatly. Herons and Kingfishers must go down to the sea to find open water. Pied Wagtails cannot find their ditchside insects; thrushes and Robins cannot penetrate the frozen

Some hazards of garden bird feeding

We begin to wonder if a time will arrive when we shall have to offer danger money to at least some of our contributors to the Garden Bird Feeding Survey. Can we quote from three recent reports to illustrate our thinking:

From a small town in Northern Ireland. '150lb bomb outside the shop that keeps peanuts. I was going to get some when it blew up, so the tits will have to wait until I can get to Belfast. I'll hang out suet and cheese instead.'

From a Devon observer. 'My squirrel-proof nut feeders have been a complete success, saving many pounds in lost nuts. Unfortunately the squirrels have developed a *passion* for seed! Instead of one squirrel after the nuts I now have at least four at any one time on each table after the seed! Someone has tried to shoot them with a 4.10 but as the squirrels are so quick, all they have got is the table, which is becoming somewhat holey! If you have any ideas for a squirrel-proof seed-feeder I will be very glad to hear as we are becoming desperate.

From a North Devon village. 'I have not yet been able to tempt a Buzzard into the garden, although last summer one sat on a tree staring for at least an hour and a half watching my daughter sunbathing. I am not sure whether he was just disapproving or sizing up the chances of carrying her off!'
BTO News

earth. And small birds like Long-tailed Tits, Wrens and Goldcrests may die because there aren't enough feeding hours in the day for them to meet their high energy requirements. So, once you start operating a winter bird-table, it is of the utmost importance that you keep it well supplied through the dark months until April.

And, once you start enjoying your bird-table, why not record the comings and goings-on? The BTO runs a Garden Bird Feeding Survey and welcomes new information . . .

The great thing about the Garden Bird Feeding Survey is that it focusses attention on cycles: the slow build-up of numbers to a midwinter plateau, followed by a decline as they leave in the spring. Of course not all species follow such a simple pattern, and one of the frustrations referred to is that so many interesting cycles occur at least partly outside the period covered by the survey. This is obviously true of the arrival and departure of our House Martins (which don't take artificial food) and of the Linnets and

ON SAFARI

It is not so much a garden – more a wildlife park. There are nettles for the *Vanessa* butterflies and thistles for the Goldfinches; Jackdaws in the chimney and bats in the – well, wherever bats do live! The rabbits which live off the vegetable garden and the fox that trots across the lawn at 'dimpsy-time' to live off the rabbits. And a charming weasel that sometimes sallies forth to do its fantastic dance in front of a bewitched Blackbird (the Blackbird collected its wits just in time, but I have seen the weasel take a young rabbit with this ploy). To say nothing of the Sparrowhawk which slithers between the hedge and the shrubbery at such speed that one could have imagined it, were it not for the chilling hush its visits impose on the garden.

But that is all by the way, for the real delight of my 'safari park' is, as for the past twenty-five years, the pond which lies just beyond the sitting-room window – so near that binoculars are not needed to identify the odd rare visitor such as Hawfinch or Black Redstart.

For two springs now, 1984 and 1985, a Kingfisher has made occasional forays after the goldfish. I like to think its presence says something positive about the state of the nearby stream since Woodbury got its new sewage treatment plant. And I happily sacrifice the fish for that flash of brilliant colour as it dives from the overhanging crab-apple tree. It never misses, taking the victim back to the perch and thwacking it several times before manoeuvring it round till it is head-first and ready for swallowing. Sometimes the fish tail can be seen sticking out for a minute or two until the final gulp. Then the bird tucks its head down into its neck and switches off for about twenty minutes. Suddenly, up pops its head and it takes a quizzical, sideways look at the pond and the whole process is repeated. The heron is quite another matter. There never seems to come a time when a heron says: 'Ugh! Not fish again today!' What is more, one bird can virtually clear the pond in a few nightly visits and seldom desists until it has cleared it of all but a few small fry; and they will take three years to restock the pond. This summer it has been an immature heron (from Powderham, I suppose) a smoky, purplish-grey bird without the distinctive markings of the adults, and as bold as brass. He would arrive every evening as the light faded, a ghostly figure drifting with great wings over the lawn and alighting close to the pond. I was torn between the instinct to frighten him off in an effort to save the fish and a deep sense of curiosity to see how he went about it. Curiosity mostly won, as it was pointless to try to save the fish. The heron would return and fish throughout the night. He was usually there first thing in the morning when I got up and it was amazing to see with what ease so large a bird lifted himself out of the water and over

Goldfinches, which at least come for water. So far as the garden is concerned, both finch species are total migrants, arriving in April and leaving in September. On the other hand, the Blue Tit is pre-eminently a GBFS species, and yet it seems to us that its cycle starts two months before the survey. Young Blue Tits start to come to the feeders in late July or early August, the numbers building up as newly moulted adults join them, but every year numbers drop sharply in late September and remain at a low level until late October, when the main winter influx begins. This October absence has occurred consistently over eight seasons, and is confirmed by ringing, but we do not know what causes it. One hypothesis is that in late September the tits change diet for a while, feeding on the blackberry harvest.

A Reed Bunting first visited us one frosty February morning and fed on crushed oats scattered on the lawn. It was gradually joined by others so that on one occasion we could count eighteen at once. Each winter since then they have arrived progressively earlier, so that we may nowadays ex-

---

the trees. But if I kept very still he would cautiously and slowly go about his business, always with one glassy yellow eye on the figure in the window, and he reacted if I so much as blinked.

As the pond is too big to net, I was at a loss to know what to do. Then a friend said, 'Oh you just buy one of those plastic herons and stick it by the pool and he won't come when he sees it.'

I said, 'Why won't he look down and say, "Oh, look, there's Charlie; let's go and see what he's doing. Hi-ya Charlie! Alright then?"'

'Because herons are *territorial*,' said my friend, knowingly. So I phoned a local garden centre, explained my problem and asked if they had a plastic heron.

'Well, we've had them,' they said, 'but the Americans buy them all up as fast as we can get them in.'

'What do the Americans want them for?'

'Same as you, I expect,' came the answer. I had a fleeting vision of Concorde packed with rows of plastic herons all sitting in first-class seats and being served with dainty trays of plastic goldfish. I tracked plastic herons down to another garden centre.

'Do they really work?' I asked.

'I guess they do, or why would the fish farms use them? Herons are territorial, you see.'

'Yes, I know,' I said without much conviction and returned home with a plastic heron

tucked hopefully under my arm. Charlie, as he was called, was a totally convincing imitation, standing there in the bog garden, so lifelike that he gave me the fright of my life every time I caught sight of him, glassy yellow eye and all.

I awaited dusk with some impatience, but at about the usual time the real heron flew low over the area and veered off. Perhaps it really does work! The next night there was no sign of him. But on the third evening the heron arrived on time and alighted about 5ft away from the plastic bird. 'Hi-ya Charlie, alright then?' he said, and held his wings up high and flapped them in Charlie's direction. Charlie never said a dickie-bird and our bluff was well and truly called.

A few days later I revisited the garden centre. 'One plastic heron coming home in disgrace,' I said. I must say, they were awfully nice about it and I shall certainly go there again – if only to buy more goldfish!

All in all, and despite the drawbacks, I'd recommend a safari park to all who have difficulties in keeping top-side of the garden. You'll never had a dull moment. In the meantime, if any readers have a good idea about herons and fish-ponds . . .

Ursula Brighouse

pect at least a temporary visit on the first frosty morning in November. In spring they linger surprisingly late, sometimes paying at least an evening visit each day until late April. We know as a result of ringing and colour ringing that some of them breed at the local reservoirs, the nearest of which is less than a mile away.

In a recently established garden on, say, a housing estate, it is probable that for several years the bulk of the winter food available to birds will be that put out by householders, and under these conditions the GBFS will produce reliable figures. However, ours is a mature garden with plenty of trees (some of them rather rotten), fallen apples for several months in good fruit years, and a long herbaceous border full of the seed-heads of helenium, Michaelmas daisy, etc. In short, there is a fair amount of natural food, but the rules of the survey do not allow us to count the birds seen taking it. Are they attracted first by the artificial food, and then to

PURE ORANGE BLUE TIT?

Milk-bottle top opening by birds is a well-known habit, on record since 1921. When James Fisher and R. A. Hinde wrote on the subject in 1949 (*British Birds 42*) they were able to report instances in Britain and Ireland of (in order of frequency): House Sparrow, Blackbird, Starling, Robin, Chaffinch, Song Thrush, Marsh Tit and Hedge Sparrow opening milk-bottle tops as well as the more usual Blue, Great and Coal Tits. Foreign records reported in a subsequent paper by the same authors added Magpie (Sweden), Great Spotted Woodpecker and Jackdaw (Denmark) and Steller's Jay (USA) to the list.

Doorstep diets proved diverse too. Tits were seen drinking from 'coffee cream bottles' in Sweden and tasting butter and wrapped meat in East Germany (Hinde and Fisher, *British Birds 44*). Subsequently, Magpies have been spotted stealing boxed eggs in Surrey and South Yorks (Chris Mead, *British Birds 70*). Further variants have occurred in our Cheshire village in recent weeks: the milkman has reported a raid by an unidentified titmouse on a half-pint carton of cream, and an early morning delivery of packeted bread unwittingly left uncovered on the steps of the village shop suffered a savage attack by avians unknown. Further afield I dare say some readers will have also spotted the Christmas advert showing a Robin bringing colour to its breast thanks to a sip from a can of beer that reaches parts that other beers can't reach.

With these events in mind, and remembering that paper tearing is a well-known tit pastime, I was not surprised the other day to find a Blue Tit making a prolonged attack on a carton of pure orange juice delivered along with our daily pintas. The cardboard carton proved too strong however and eventually the Blue Tit gave up. But I wondered, would the Blue Tit have enjoyed the orange juice if it had found a way through the carton? A little experiment with a milk bottle filled with orange juice and capped with foil soon gave the answer. I cannot claim to detect distaste on the face of a Blue Tit, but it did only try one sip!

Tom Wall

the natural, or vice versa? Could one argue that by not cutting off the heads of the Michaelmas daisies (and the gardening books tell us we should) we are really providing food?

Some species seem rarely to take any of the conventional food items we put out, the best example perhaps being the Bullfinch. Yet they are fairly frequent visitors to the garden and gradually we are beginning to detect an annual cycle based on different food crops. In January and February they are often to be seen feeding on the seeds on weigela, systematically cracking open the long pods. March, April and May visits are unmistakably associated with fruit buds, but they usually leave us a surplus of fruit. In July and August raspberries and redcurrants are the attraction, and I can usually mist-net up to a dozen during this period. Then come the delphinium pods and in late autumn we have watched them feed on the seeds of antirrhinum and *Campanula carpatica*.

Data collected from a large number of observers have to be simple and capable of being expressed in figures, but the great opportunity for the really hooked garden birdwatcher lies in bird behaviour. We have been fascinated to watch a young Song Thrush make its first encounter with water, when it came across our small pool. On three or four occasions we have watched Blackbirds go through all the motions of bathing, not in the pool but in prostrate rock plants just a few feet from the water. On several occasions we have been puzzled and horrified to inspect a nestbox known to have been occupied by Blue Tits, only to find a Tree Sparrow, with eggs, in a nest built on top of a brood of dead Blue Tits. This year we saw for the first time how this is done. When the Tree Sparrows wish to acquire the nest-box, they simply prevent the Blue Tits from feeding their young, time after time driving them away until, presumably, the brood die of hunger or cold.

In a conservation-orientated society, it is inevitable that people should be concerned about population levels – which is really what the GBFS is about, and why the trust is so grateful to those who support it. But don't leave it at that: a garden and a chair by the window offer splendid opportunities to get to know birds well, and even to understand them a little.

Feeding Squabbles

Study the behaviour of your breakfast guests over a period of time, and you should be able to work out a pecking order. Birds are easily inclined to quarrel over their food, and these feeding squabbles are well observed at the bird-table, where they inevitably come into close contact. One threatens another by posturing ie gaping aggressively, spreading wings and tail. It is largely a game of bluff, since neither individual wants to come to blows, wasting energy and risking the loss of precious feathers, to say nothing of the danger from predators if they aren't keeping a proper watch.

Feeding station

'We finally got the severe weather we have been waiting for since the start of the survey – too extreme though, with 10ft drifts and 18 degrees of frost. We were snowed in with power cuts lasting 30 hours and saw no one for a week! I kept the snow drifts cleared from under the bird-tables, and this attracted the largest number of Blackbirds we have ever had, also Redwings feeding on seed for the first time. A pair of Sparrowhawks became very bold and the male would wait on the roof of the bird-table. We also had Snipe and Lapwing feeding on the lawn, the first time they have come so close to the house. Near another table, not included in the survey, a Kestrel has taken to roosting on a sill, leaving mounds of pellets within sight of the table. During this time my two hand-tame Blue Tits multiplied until I had fifteen or more, also two Coal Tits, one Great Tit and two Chaffinches. About sixty other birds would come for nuts when thrown including Nuthatches, Marsh Tit and Greenfinches. It was quite a sight being followed, with no exaggeration, by such a large flock of birds. (Letter from a BTO Garden Bird Feeding Survey contributor.)

Robin's favourites

Everyone knows that Robins are fond of crumbs, but mealworms are their favourite titbit, followed closely by cheese. They are enthusiastic bird-table customers, prepared to sample anything that's going. Their bird-table technique is much the same as their typical twig-to-ground forays for wild food: appraisal from a safe distance, then the firm approach and grab, and removal of the food to a safe place for enjoyment. They will soon learn to come and tap on the window for a daily ration of currants or sultanas. Some individuals have even learnt to take their turn on the peanut bag, along with the tits and Greenfinches.

But the game has a serious object, because the winner gets the choicest titbit (and at other times, the best perch, the best breeding territory and the most desirable mate). So the establishment of a pecking order is a meaningful affair, and it plays a real part in everyday bird life, as in our own.

The peck order, or more scientifically, dominance hierarchy, is so called because the experimental work which demonstrated its validity was carried out with domestic hens. They establish dominance by pecking about the head and shoulders of rivals. It applies to species which live social or colonial lives, involving a great deal of shoulder-rubbing with other birds, not necessarily of their own species. The process involves fights, bickering and bluff which continues until an order emerges. From the boss bird downwards, everyone knows his place, though bickering is constant, with individuals jostling and 'trying it on' with the object of improving their rating. The dominant cock has it all his own way, eating the best food and fathering the most chicks on the most attractive hens. He therefore leads an aggressive life, defending and consolidating his position till he is inevitably toppled as age creeps up on him. In a mixed flock there will still be a peck order, which explains why the greedy Starlings take precedence at the bird-table, followed in the hierarchy by House Sparrows, Great, Blue, Marsh or Willow and Coal Tits in that order. In fact Blue Tits will rob Great Tits almost as often as they are robbed by them, but without a doubt these two species dominate the other tits, with Coal Tits decidedly the weakest in the hierarchy.

Safety in numbers

Why do you never see more than one Robin feeding on your bird-table except perhaps in the severest winter weather? If a second Robin does arrive, there is a brief argument and one or other beats a hasty retreat. But then a Starling arrives and seconds later there is a flurry of wings and half a dozen more pitch in. They gobble anything they can lay their beaks on, with hardly any bickering, until the food has been consumed and, as one bird, they fly off together.

Can we explain why living in a flock is a good thing for Starlings – and sparrows, Woodpigeons, Lapwings and geese – but not for Robins – and Dunnocks, Kingfishers, flycatchers and Kestrels? Research has shown how birds benefit from living in a flock, but if flocking is sauce for the geese why isn't it sauce for the ganders? There must be good reasons why some birds do not live in flocks.

There are two broad advantages for a bird living in a flock – the chances of being caught by a predator are reduced, and finding food is easier.

Predation can be reduced in several ways. A bird in a flock is less likely to be singled out by a predator if it is in a crowd. It is possible that the predator finds it difficult to concentrate on singling out a victim from a compact, fast-moving mass of birds. It also runs the risk of a damaging collision as it dives among them. Flocks of geese and waders bunch together when harassed by a bird of prey. Moreover, many pairs of eyes on the look-out make it harder for a predator to make a surprise attack.

This group vigilance has a useful spin-off because it allows the birds to spend more time feeding. With its companions helping to keep watch, each bird needs to spend less time scanning its surroundings for danger. As well as detecting danger, the birds benefit from watching each other. When food is dispersed over the countryside in 'clumps', for example, a hedgerow rich in berries, it pays a bird to find where other birds are feeding and join them. If the feeding is good, more birds gather and the flock grows. Then, as food begins to run out, birds start to leave in search of more food and the flock dwindles and reassembles elsewhere.

In a less obvious way, tits in a flock working their way through a wood are helping each other to find food. Tits feed on insects which are often camouflaged or hidden. When one tit finds a caterpillar under a leaf, not only does it start to look under other leaves in the expectation of finding more caterpillars, but its companions follow its example and switch to hunting caterpillars. The result is an efficient exploitation of a locally abundant supply of food.

Hand bills!

If you take a close look at garden birds you will often find that some of them display abnormalities of the beak, and Starlings seem particularly prone. It is not uncommon to see a bird with a down-curved bill as much as a couple of inches long, curlew-like. Such birds seem to manage well enough, although sometimes this must be because they are paid special attention at bird-tables, for they find it very difficult to pick up natural food. A bird's bill, of course, acts as its hand. The horny sheath is a projection of the jaws, and like a finger-nail it is growing all the time. Normally wear and tear compensate for the rate of growth and the bill remains at a useful operating length; a tool used in nest-building, preening and feeding. If damaged, the bill will regenerate, but the process takes time, and the bird must be at a disadvantage meanwhile. Oddly shaped bills are not always caused by an accident; they can result from a genetic abnormality. On the whole it is surprising how little annoyance they seem to cause – though we just don't see the worst-afflicted birds because they don't survive.

As a general rule, birds that live in flocks feed on 'clumped' food, such as crops of seeds and fruit or animals that live in swarms, whereas solitary birds feed on animals that live at low densities and are distributed evenly, or which disappear when disturbed. The relative benefits of social and solitary feeding are best shown by the few birds that alter their behaviour as the distribution of their prey changes.

When Pied Wagtails feed on dungflies gathered on cowpats, they defend temporary territories and drive other wagtails away to reduce the disturbance which would scatter the flies into the grass making them hard to find. However, dungflies occupy cowpats during the middle of the day only, so in the morning and evening the wagtails gather in flocks to feed on swarming midges. Midges are not so easily disturbed so the wagtails can feed in a flock without interfering with each other.

Whether to flock or not is illustrated by the behaviour of Redshanks. Compared with some other waders that feed on mud-flats, Redshanks usually feed separately, but under certain circumstances they gather into compact flocks. Their favourite food is amphipod shrimps which live in burrows with their tails sticking out, and the Redshanks hunt them by sight. But the shrimps are very sensitive to vibrations and duck below the surface as the Redshank walks past. So it is better to defend a territory as an exclusive feeding ground. If there are too many Redshanks in one area, they interfere with each other's feeding by driving all the shrimps down. When this happens the Redshanks switch to hunting by touch – probing with their beaks for hidden animals –

THE KINGFISHER

W. H. Davies

It was the Rainbow gave thee birth,
　And left thee all her lovely hues:
And, as her mother's name was Tears,
　So runs it in my blood to choose
For haunts the lonely pools, and keep
In company with trees that weep.

Go you and, with such glorious hues,
　Live with proud Peacocks in green parks;
On lawns as smooth as shining glass,
　Let every feather show its marks;
Get thee on boughs and clap thy wings
Before the windows of proud kings.

Nay, lovely Bird, thou art not vain;
　Thou hast no proud, ambitious mind;
I also love a quiet place
　That's green, away from all mankind;
A lonely pool and let a tree
Sigh with her bosom over me.

Eric & David Hosking

but the animals they catch are less favoured food. This pattern can be seen among other waders too. Ringed Plovers that hunt by sight are well spaced while dense flocks of Knots probe the mud to find food by touch.

Why do Redshanks sometimes form flocks if it interferes with their feeding? Compact flocks are formed at night when they cannot feed by sight anyway. They could remain well spaced but the advantage now is that of safety in numbers. Although feeding efficiently is crucial to survival there is a greater risk of predation – it is no use being well fed if you are caught and eaten. Redshanks also gather together in sheltered places during gales when the strong wind buffets them and prevents them aiming their pecks accurately.

So, with the help of these examples we can try to explain why your bird-table attracts both a single Robin and a flock of Starlings. While it is quite easy to see the benefit of a flock of Starlings, it is less obvious why Robins preserve their independence.

Starlings have a liberal diet of animal and plant food, but it mostly consists of worms and insects, such as leatherjackets, beetle larvae and caterpillars, which live at or near the surface of the soil. The Robin's diet also mostly consists of insects and other small animals, particularly caterpillars in summer and beetles in winter, as well as small fruits in season. The essential difference between the two species lies in their habitats and methods of feeding. The Starling typically strides across open grassland, probing and peering for prey, while the Robin is a woodland bird whose technique, familiar to many gardeners, is to wait on a low perch and drop on any animal which is careless enough to show itself.

Starlings take advantage of group tactics to find food which may appear in 'clumps'. Flocking also gives them safety in numbers in open country so they are less likely to be caught while their beaks are thrust into the ground. Experiments show that a lone Starling takes one second longer to react to danger than a small flock and that it spends half its time looking around compared with only one-tenth while in a flock.

A solitary Robin flitting about under the woodland foliage is probably better concealed and less likely to attract a predator than a flock. Its food is thinly and evenly spread – each item has to be individually sought out. Like the Pied Wagtails feeding on dungflies, its best tactic is to defend its resource against other Robins.

Messmates

Sparrows are sociable, gregarious birds. They have thrown in their lot with man in a very close and long-standing relationship. Long years ago, when men first broke and tilled the soil to produce cereal crops, the sparrows moved in to help eat the seeds. And they have stayed with us ever since. They are parasitic on us, sharing in the fruits of our labours in cultivation and urbanisation. They eat at the same

Brian Hawkes

Blue Tit poised for a little mild thievery

Nesting Habits

You wonder, with good reason, that the Hedge Sparrows, etc can be induced at all to sit on the egg of the Cuckoo without being scandalised at the vast disproportioned size of the suppositious egg; but the brute creation, I suppose have very little idea of size, colour or number. For the common hen, I know, when the fury of incubation is on her, will sit on a single shapeless stone, instead of a nest full of eggs that have been withdrawn: and, moreover, a hen turkey, in the same circumstances, would sit on in the empty nest till she perished with hunger.
Gilbert White
The Natural History of Selborne

table, in effect, and are our messmates – commensal species, whose success story runs parallel with our own. When men desert an unprofitable farm or a remote island, the sparrow very shortly leaves as well. But where there is cultivation or free food, there is a sparrow. One of the most widely distributed land birds, you'll find it as comfortably at home in Moscow as in Paris, and as an introduced species it flourishes all the way from New York to Buenos Aires and Sydney.

Enjoying the farmer's corn, it soon made sense for the sparrow to share his house as well, so it moved in and nested conveniently close to the dining-table. When the poultry were fed, the sparrows joined in. The warmth and safety of buildings suited very well, so sparrows flourished as man flourished. And as villages grew into towns and cities, sparrows quickly became accustomed to the new scene and the new possibilities. Since the main means of transport was the horse, vast quantities of straw and grain were available, and sparrows took their share.

With easy pickings all year round, there was never any need to indulge in dangerous activities like migration. Sparrows became sedentary birds enjoying an easy life. Yet nobody loves them the way they love Robins. Sparrows live with us, but we have never really become friends. Farmers don't like them because of their appetites and householders don't like them because they hog the bird-table. Even in folklore they have a bad image. When the cross was being prepared for Christ, Swallows carried away the nails in an effort to delay the crucifixion; but the sparrows promptly bought them back, to curry favour. And in Russia they say

the sparrow is an unwelcome guest, whose entry into a cottage foretells trouble. As a punishment for its sins its legs were fastened together by invisible bonds, since when it has been unable to run, and must always hop. Horrid thought.

It is hardly surprising that sparrows have been persecuted. When the farmer's wife put down corn for the pigeons and poultry she begrudged the share taken by the sparrow, from whom she got nothing in return except a lot of noisy chirrups. The eighteenth-century French naturalist Count de Buffon summed up the general attitude to the sparrow: 'It is extremely destructive, its plumage is entirely useless, its flesh indifferent food, its notes are grating to the ear, and its familiarity and petulance disgusting.' Only John Clare had a good word to say for it, and indeed he often paid cash he could ill spare to 'tyrant boys', buying liberty for captives.

> And chirping sparrows dropping from the eaves
> For offal kernels that the poultry leaves
> Oft signal calls of danger chittering high
> At skulking cats and dogs encroaching nigh.
> (John Clare, *Rural Morning*)

William Cowper writes in a style more likely to be welcomed by the farmer:

> The sparrow, meanest of the feathered race,
> His fit companion finds in every place,
> With whom he filches the grain that suits him best,
> Flits here and there, and late returns to rest.
> And whom if chance the falcon makes his prey,
> Or hedger with his well-aimed arrow slay,
> In no such loss the gay survivor grieves,
> New love he seeks, and new delight receives.

The last line is actionable, since in reality the sparrow is a faithful bird, the pair bond being particularly strong. Be that as it may, all men's hands were turned against the thieving brown bird. But the sparrow is a tough cookie. In its time it has suffered onslaught from stones, lead shot, poison and every known trapping device, but it has proved impossible to exterminate. In World War II the Ministry of Agriculture appealed to patriotic Britons to destroy sparrows nests, in order to lessen their effects on the harvest, but although plenty of small boys wrecked every nest they could lay hands on, whether or not it belonged to a sparrow, the bird war was lost before it began. However hard you try you can't defeat sparrows. Hit as hard as you like, they just bob up for more. As long as there's food and a warm safe building nearby, they will be there to enjoy them. Best to learn to live with them.

In fact they sustained a temporary setback with the invention of the internal combustion engine. With the decrease in town-stabled horses, they inevitably suffered from the loss of feed-corn. They are still less common in city centres

Two sparrows

Humbert Wolfe

Two sparrows, feeding
heard a thrush
sing to the dawn.
The first said 'Tush!'

'In all my life
I never heard
a more affected
singing-bird.'

The second said
'It's you and me,
who slave to keep
the likes of he.'

'And if we cared.'
both sparrows said.
'we'd do that singing
on our head.'

The thrush pecked sideways,
and was dumb.
'And now,' they screamed.
'he's pinched our crumb.'

than they were at the turn of the century. But as one door closed another opened, and with the rise of suburbia and gardens the town sparrows flourished again. As skilled free-loaders they will enjoy lunchtime sandwich ends in the city and bird-table food in the suburb. In winter, the time of greatest difficulty for most birds, our sparrows may even be better off because this is the time when people are most generous with their handouts.

They are tough customers at the bird-table, scattering food about in a tiresome manner, and ousting all non-sparrow competition. Tending to operate in pugnacious gangs, they terrorise other small birds and take what they want by virtue of aggressiveness and sheer numbers. Thrusting and showing their muscle, they sweep the Dunnocks and Chaffinches and tits out of the way. What can be done about it? Not much, but we may take advantage of one of their characteristics, at least for a short respite. They are cocky birds, and impudent: yet they are at the same time cautious by nature, suspicious of anything new. So food placed in a different position may be left free for other species for a while. Putting offerings in several different places may help, too. A novel food basket or bag will be safe from their attentions for a few days, though they will always win through in the end. Less than ten years ago they were foiled by hanging wire-mesh nut baskets of the sort designed for the acrobatic tits and much used by Greenfinches. The sparrows showed interest in them and fluttered alongside ineffectively, but failed to get a grip on the mesh – then hung about to pick up any pieces of nut which fell to the ground. As the years went by they learnt to grasp the side of the basket and pick out the nuts in Greenfinch fashion. Now this habit is wide-spread, another example of the learning ability so strikingly demonstrated by the Blue Tits with their milk bottles.

A device which has beaten most sparrows so far is a suspended wooden box giving access to its nuts only through a grill across the bottom face. This is no problem for the tits, but sparrows, which have learnt to grip and work at nuts from a vertical position, are less keen on hanging upside-down. However, it's only a matter of time before they solve this puzzle, and indeed there have already been records of isolated individuals extracting nuts from a hovering position under the box, and others who have begun to land and grip while upside-down. Such versatile performers, who take seeds from seed-heads in the manner of a Goldfinch, work over a tree like a woodpecker, and like a flycatcher hawk for flying insects, are pretty well invincible.

Sparrows have even learnt to take stale bread to water in order to soften it and make it more palatable, a behaviour pioneered by a few individuals, but likely to spread and be learnt by many more. Birds are well able to learn from experience and others soon get the message. Peanuts are not exactly a natural food in our gardens, any more than bread is, yet they have become a staple bird-table offering. The saga of the milk-bottle cream is a classic example of birds

Garden badges

Robins are not particularly long-lived. The record is currently held by an Irish bird which lasted eleven years, and other ringed birds have approached that span, but these are exceptions. The average lifespan is said to be little more than a year. So there's small doubt that 'our' garden Robin is a string of individuals over any period of years. One thing we can be sure of: there won't be an extended period of vacancy when one dies. The garden won't stay long without its badge of flashing red.

learning from experience, a case where wildlife-watching from windows revealed a remarkable story. Anyone who provisions a bird-table will know that tits have a great craving for fat, often suet or bacon rinds, and their most spectacular technique for satisfying that craving is to prise off milk-bottle tops and drink the cream from your daily pinta.

It's not surprising that tits were first to exploit the free milk. They're lively, acrobatic birds, with that sense of curiosity which leads them to explore and investigate. Tits are good at intelligence tests. You've probably seen those amusing films showing them hauling up peanuts on string, hand over hand (or should I say beak over claw) and heaving 00 gauge railway trucks loaded with peanuts up an inclined plane. So it's not too much to imagine one particular Blue Tit with an exceptionally high IQ, perching on top of a shiny white bottle and hacking his way through the cardboard top. This was first recorded in 1921 near Southampton. But other tits imitated and the habit spread through the suburbs like wildfire. Rather like gulls following the plough, parties of tits followed the milk cart, and attacked the bottles within minutes of them hitting the doorstep.

Years ago milk bottles were sealed with a waxy cardboard disc and if it wasn't too well sealed, they'd rip it out and chuck it away. Or they'd just take out the central disc, or they'd peel off layer after layer of paper till the cap was thin enough to smash. And then the ecstasy of the cream – what a way to start the day. They'd drink as much as the top 2in learning further and further into the bottle; indeed, many tits have leaned too far, and drowned in a sea of milk.

Some people say that the tits go for Channel Islands milk especially and – unkindly – have tried switching foil tops, between Channel Islands and ordinary milk; but the bird sticks with the gold top, not the gold taste. Probably each bird tends to keep to the colour it first learnt to open. If you think that the birds are getting the best part of the milk by drinking the cream, remember that the really nutritious part is the milk underneath, so the Blue Tit is doing you a good turn by drinking off the fatty top.

Eric & David Hosking

The southern spread of the Siskin has been encouraged by garden peanuts

Brian Hawkes

Feeding birds is a pleasure

When aluminium-foil tops were introduced, the dairymen thought they'd foiled the birds as well as the milk bottle. But the beak of a titmouse, scaled down, is as powerful as the building contractor's pneumatic drill: a few thumps, a crack, a hole, and off we go again. People have tried all sorts of ways to keep their milk intact. Everything, that is, except getting out of bed when the milkman calls. They've persuaded the milkman to cover the bottles with flat stones – one tit removed the stone three times in quick succession; or with a paint-tin lid – the bird just sat on the edge and tipped it off. They've persuaded the milkman to cover bottles with a tea cloth, an interesting one because it meant that the bird was denied the stimulus of *seeing* the milk. But they even beat that. I think the prize story is the one about the school in Surrey. One November morning the milkman delivered 300 bottles of milk. By the time the caretaker had arrived, the birds had opened fifty-seven of them.

Only one kind of milk-bottle top foils them: the crown cork – that heavy tinny one with a sharp crinkly edge used on sterilised milk bottles – and also beer bottles. It's a comforting thought that birds are defeated by beer bottles – anybody's Saturday night would be ruined by a band of drunken Blue Tits.

Of course, in behaviour terms, opening a milk bottle re-

Plenty of peanuts for Great Tit and Blue Tit

Mr & Mrs R. P. Lawrence/FLPA

quires no new technique for a tit. As part of his normal daily activity he searches trees for insects and will peel away the bark as part of the search; the milk bottle pioneers were really looking for bugs. But that is not to suggest that birds do everything on an automatic, programmed basis. If you define intelligence as the capacity to learn and to adapt behaviour as a result of experience, birds definitely have it. They have some programmed responses; the essential movements of flight are innate, so that the young bird knows instinctively what he has to do. But trial and error improves the performance. Birds quickly learn to ignore noises or movements which prove to be harmless, the young learn from their parents, adults learn from each other. And the classic case is that of the tits and the milk.

It is just as well that Blue Tits are pretty, and have an amusing and acrobatic way of behaving, because they sometimes indulge in other bad habits, such as putty-eating and paper-tearing. They can do a lot of damage when they enter a room and start to strip the wallpaper, perching by the edge of the paper and tearing it away with sideways movements of the head. Yet, this is probably just another version of the bark-tearing behaviour. Even when there is plenty of food on a nearby bird-table and the bird is not hungry, an urgent drive is in operation, just as with a fox which enters a chicken run and kills every single fowl; it is not because he needs to eat them or because he finds it fun, but because it is in his nature and his purpose in life to pounce on and kill anything suitable *which moves*. He is unable to stop himself once the killing starts. So the Blue Tit continues searching for food by tearing away the wallpaper, or the putty on the window, even though he is not hungry. Having said that, though, it is also true that outbreaks of paper-tearing may be most prevalent in years when natural food is scarce and when continental tits may invade us in large numbers. Fortunately they do some good work round the house by taking the odd house-fly or spider.

There is good feeding for small birds around the windows of a house, especially if it's a rather old house with peeling paint and slightly neglected stone or brickwork. There will be many bugs and spiders for the questing Wren and tit. But sometimes birds actually fly into the windows, at best giving themselves a bruise, and at worst killing themselves. The trouble often occurs when there are windows on opposite walls of a room and the bird can see right through from the front to the back garden, or whatever. Then it flies through full of confidence, only to be brought up with a smart jerk when it hits the glass. Venetian blinds may be the answer or, dare I say it, dirty windows – anything to show the bird that the glass is there. On sunny days the problem may be caused by a reflection of the garden, and in this case blinds or curtains are of no use. Outside netting will serve, but it is not very attractive. Cut-out shapes of Sparrowhawks often work. one man who worked in a modern office block with a plethora of glass and concrete found

Mr & Mrs R. P. Lawrence/FLPA

Waiting room only for the Great Tit while a pair of Blue Tits gets down to the job

121

that an average of six birds were being killed every week and stuck up a Buzzard silhouette with some success. But probably any sort of pattern which breaks up the apparently empty window will do. In Denmark they sell oval glass shapes for hanging in windows, and in Switzerland they etch hawk shapes on the glass. When the Young Ornithologists Club carried out a survey on this subject, they found that the problem mainly occurred in spring and summer, when birds are busy and fledglings learning to fly. It is not confined to diurnal birds; often enough owls will fly into windows at night. If you find birds stunned under your window, the best treatment is to put them somewhere dark and very warm for an hour or so. That will often do the trick.

The actual fabric of a house provides many a happy hunting ground and homesite for animals. Try to see your home through their eyes and consider its potential for both wild plants and animals. Imagine yourself a bat or an owl and the roof cavity immediately becomes just another kind of cave. Holes in the tiles or in the wall are just another version

FESTIVE FARE

It had been snowing for three days when my mother telephoned. 'Thermal underwear and warm, filling stews' predicted my husband as he battled grimly to unfreeze the pipes in the downstairs loo. But no . . . 'Darling, you know the bird-table your father and I gave you both for Christmas . . . well, have you put it up yet?' I replied that we had, omitting to mention that the bird-table had disappeared under a frozen billow of snow, and that the corkscrew hazel I had selected as a perching post was now a misshapen snowman in an arctic landscape. 'Hundreds of small birds will die unless *you* do something to help them.' 'What do you have in mind?' I asked cautiously. 'The RSPB has written all that you need to know in *The Times*,' she said firmly.

Mum is inclined to panic, so I did not venture the information that, just as we had been unable to get out for three days, the milkman, postman and paper boy had been unable to get to us.

'Just provide whatever you can from the list . . . and none of that junk food you eat up your way,' she added darkly. Mum watches too much television and is convinced that north of Newark we subsist on black pudding, chip butties and Chinese take-aways.

'What have you been putting out?' I asked. There followed a list which sounded like a shopping spree in a health food store. 'High calorie food for maximum energy – keeps out

the cold,' she explained. I went back to the kitchen deep in thought. High in the beech tree outside the window sat a Robin, puffed out like the bright, woolly pompom on a child's bobble hat. I removed the last two rashers of bacon from the fridge and it began to whistle in an encouraging sort of way.

'Hey! What are you doing with my bacon?' demanded a voice emerging from the loo.

'Chopping it up for the birds,' I said resolutely. 'They need the calories more than you.' The Robin whistled its approval. 'Now for the cheese,' I muttered. I had grated the last of the Edam to liven up the lentil and ham, well, ham bone really, soup which I intended to concoct for our supper. 'Half each,' I promised, and added it to the tray. Apples were easy. Those stored in the garage had been frozen solid, so I chipped away at a couple of Cox's congratulating myself on my resourcefulness. When I explained to Paul that this was not a Food-Aid-for-the-Frozen recipe, but life or death to countless small birds, he overlooked his yearly battle with the Bullfinches which wantonly disbud his apple trees, and hunted around for the last of the Christmas nuts. These were mostly fiddly little hazelnuts and uncrackable almonds, but he persisted until his thumb, still frozen from the plumbing job, got nipped in the nutcrackers, and spurred on by pain and annoyance went off to telephone the local council offices about the mythical of a hole in a tree for a tit or a Starling. The eaves represent a rocky cliff-overhang for a House Martin. The walls are cliffsides for ferns, especially if there are cracks and crevices which may hold a little soil. Limestone is perhaps the most sympathetic of wall materials, but plants will get a foothold almost anywhere, given half a chance. Lichens are well suited to living on walls and roofs. They are compound plants, part fungus and part algae, with the algae growing inside the fungus and providing sun-ripened food for it to feed on. So they are a nice example of symbiosis – two different species living together to their mutual benefit.

Creeper of any kind growing on your walls will improve the wildlife possibilities enormously. That much-maligned plant ivy is the best of all, providing cover right through the year for birds and insects, nest sites and, best of all, berries which fruit very late into the winter and provide a valuable food source at a difficult time. Ivy is a beautiful plant and is very attractive to insects in the autumn when it flowers – so in turn it has yet more attractions for birds!

snow-plough we had been promised.

The Robin's song sounded weaker now. 'Hang on,' I counselled it as I hunted in vain for calorie-laden goodies. We had finished the Christmas Cake yesterday and the biscuit tin was empty. Inspiration! I crumbled a few remaining liqueur chocs onto the tray, struggled into my overcoat and wellies, and headed for the great outdoors. The biting north-east wind shipped the entire contents of the tray back into my face in a cheese-flavoured blizzard. As I scrabbled to retrieve what crumbs I could, the snowdrift drifted down my wellies and the tray slid away from me like a sledge on the Cresta run. I could no longer see the Robin through the blowing snow and feared I was too late. 'I've got a plan!' I shrieked into the wind, rushed inside, grabbed the supper soup ham bone and a piece of string and then the phone rang. News of the snow plough I hoped.

'It's your mother again.' Hurriedly I kicked off the wellies, put down the ham bone and rushed to the telephone.

'Waxwings' was all she said.

'Wax wings?' I queried. The cold had obviously numbed my brain. Was this I wondered another suggestion from the RSPB – Icarus insulation for frozen flight feathers?

'Don't be silly, Diane, Waxwings. In the garden, feeding on the holly berries. They must have flown from Scandinavia to escape the cold. It's so exc . . .

Hastily I cut her short, 'Sorry Mum, I've got to dash, I can hear polar bears rummaging in the dustbin.' I reached the garage just in time to see Harry, the dirty dog from next door, disappearing with the ham bone . . . Most of my abuse was drowned by the wind – but what was that noise? Yes. The steady chug of a snow plough battling up the lane. We should be able to get to the shops tomorrow.

'Hold on, chaps,' I cried to the waiting birds. 'Meals on Wellies will be resumed as soon as possible.' I dashed inside, making a mental shopping list – cheese, raisins, bacon . . . but what I needed right now was a receptacle so large and heavy that the wind could not blow it away. Got it! I grabbed the packet of muesli, jammed my woolly hat upon my head and sprinted for the door.

When the snow-plough driver was interviewed by the local press, he stated that he was kept going by the warm welcome he received, especially from the lady at the top of the hill, who rushed out to greet him with a tea cosy on her head and in her hand a muesli-filled rose-sprigged Victorian chamberpot.

Diane Williams

A Bird in the Hand

By the time your bird-table is well supplied and your garden is a riot of berry-bearing shrubs and your pond is full of gossiping birds, you will certainly be regarding 'your' garden birds as personal friends. And nothing gives more pleasure than being able to take the relationship one stage further so that you come even closer. Food is the key to unlocking this door, of course. Everybody knows that Robins will sell their grandmothers (even though not many Robins have grandmothers to sell) for mealworms. But plenty of other species may be persuaded to perch on your finger, or at least take food from them. Ducks at the duck pond, pigeons in the city square, sparrows at the open air café, they'll all take crumbs from you, though they will certainly prefer corn or, in the case of pigeons, a little piece of cheese. But there's something about a Robin which makes him a strong candidate for individual hand-taming. One of the first to write on this subject was the distinguished statesman Viscount Grey of Fallodon.

In *The Charm of Birds*, which he published in 1927, he writes of his experiences in hand-taming his garden birds . . .

My own experience has been mainly with Robins. Several of these were tamed at different times, not with any intention of scientific observation, but solely for the pleasure of being on terms of intimacy with birds in a free and natural state. None of these Robins were quite close to the house: none of them became house-birds, nor were they induced to lead an artificial life. They were visited once every day, each in its own territory, and offered mealworms; but except for this supplement to their natural food, there was nothing to disturb or distort their natural habits.

The first Robin had a small white feather on the right wing by which it was easy to identify him. This freak feather was constant, either it was never moulted or it reappeared after each moult. His territory included both sides of one end of a pond. The water was about 10yd wide, and on either side were trees and bushes. The bird had a good strip of territory on each side of the pond, but more on the west than on the east side. In the winter of 1921–2 he would sit on my fingers and eat mealworms out of a little box held open on the hand. In the nesting season he was feeding

To feed or not to feed

Millions of people annually derive an enormous amount of pleasure and benefit from feeding wild birds, while others raise their eyebrows at the wisdom of the exercise and query the actual benefit to the birds. Artificial feeding is certainly much on the increase today, both in gardens and other habitats, and the subject really merits more thought and more facts.

One fact which cannot be disputed is the enjoyment to be gained from securing the confidence of a wild bird and from watching it at close quarters. Two personal incidents come to mind. The first involved migrant Sanderlings on a remote beach in Iceland, the second a juvenile Robin in a Hampshire garden: the Sanderlings were successfully enticed to take maggots from the hand, while the Robin boldly hopped onto my wheelchair to devour its first piece of cheese. Both were memorable moments.
David Glue

With patience, a Blue Tit can be encouraged to feed from the hand

young birds: about the middle of July he disappeared and was not seen again till well on in August, when he presented himself once more and came on the hand as usual, and reoccupied precisely the same territory. Here he remained tame, but alone, till the spring of 1923, when a female was admitted to the territory. She would make a small note and he would feed her with mealworms, just as if she were a young bird. If I appeared and held out the box when he was not near, the female would sit in a bush uttering the little notes till he came and fed her. She never offered to help herself. About the middle of July he disappeared, but again showed himself in the latter part of August. The following months were a repetition of those of other years, including the admission and feeding of a female in the spring of 1924. In 1924 there was the same disappearance for the moult in July after the breeding season. In August he reappeared, with the white feather either still intact or renewed after moulting. It had become convenient to distinguish this bird by the name of 'White Feather', and so he was always called. After he reappeared this time there was trouble about territory, and eventually the east side of the pond was annexed by another Robin, and White Feather was restricted entirely to the west side. Here he was visited

Can't catch me

'Little Robin Redbreast
    sat upon a tree,
Up went pussy cat,
    and down went he.'

and fed. He had now become very tame, and after satisfying his appetite would sometimes sit on the hand so long that it was necessary to give him a gentle hint to go. On the last day of the year 1924, he came to me at the usual spot; after that I never saw him again, and his place was taken by another Robin. I searched in the hope that White Feather might only have been driven farther west; but there was no sign, and I fear that there had been combat to the death.

The observation of another Robin showed similar habits with certain variations.

There is a white seat by another pond, where it is the habit for someone to sit about midday to feed such waterfowl as care to come out of the water for bread. On the right of this seat and close to it is a clump of dogwood. Here in February 1924 a Robin and his mate were tamed. The male bird would sit on the hand and eat several mealworms; the female would only perch for a moment, snatch a single mealworm at a time and fly off with it. As spring advanced the female ceased to feed herself, but sat in the dogwood, uttering the plaintive note, and was fed attentively by the male. In time the female ceased coming to the seat, and the male would pack his beak with mealworms, fly with them over the water to some bushes a hundred yards away, and return time after time to get more. The nest was evidently in the distant bushes, but I made no search for it, lest by finding I should betray it to some enemy. In July the male also disappeared, and it was not till September that I found him expecting to be fed, not at the seat, but in the bushes near the site of the nest. He was as tame as before, and for several days endeavoured to come to me at the seat. But the dogwood was in possession of another robin, that attacked him furiously. Finally he gave up the attempt to come to me at the seat, and it was a recognised thing that he was fed in the bushes at a safe distance from the virago in the dogwood. So matters continued through the autumn and winter. The bird in the dogwood never came on my hand, and whether it was the female of the previous spring, or indeed whether it was a female at all, I cannot be certain. In the spring of 1925, however, the tame robin was admitted to the seat and to the dogwood, where it fed a mate. It seems probable that this mate was the same bird that drove him from the seat in the autumn and had been in the dogwood territory throughout the winter; but as it was not hand-tame and had no distinct mark, I cannot be sure of this. In the nesting season the female went out of sight as before. The last time I saw the male, in July that year, he was pursued by two speckled and importunate young birds: he gave them a meal-worm or two from my box, but seemed more anxious to escape from than to feed them. After the moult he reappeared in the bushes as in 1924, and there was an exact repetition of the proceedings of the previous year: exclusion from the seat and dogwood territory till the early part of 1926, then admission to it, and feeding of a female in the dogwood. In April there was trouble: the tame

John Hawkins/Hosking

Robins are easily persuaded to come and feed

robin appeared with his breast feathers dreadfully disordered: he held his ground so for some days in April, and I fed him daily: then one day no robin came to the seat and the proffered box of meal-worms. High up in a young tree close by a robin was singing very loud and bold: I stood underneath with the box of meal-worms open on outstretched hand. All my overtures were ignored; the robin was a stranger, and sang there daily thereafter with an indifference that seemed ostentatious. My white-seat robin was never seen again. The new bird never was tame, and remained an example of

"The simple rule, the good old plan,
That those should take who have the power,
And those should keep who can."

Table Service

A Robin's method of feeding is to pick up a mealworm crosswise in its beak and hold it thus for a second or two, then suddenly – there is no mealworm, the act of swallowing is so quick that it is hardly perceptible. The first mealworms are taken one after the other with little delay, but after these the bird has long pauses and stands pensively on the hand. In cold weather it is disagreeable to keep the bare hand extended so long, but one does not like to disturb the bird. The last mealworm is generally taken to a bush or to the ground to be eaten, and this is a sign that the bird is satisfied.

Whether the conqueror possessed himself of the mate as well as the territory of the tame bird I could not tell.

Besides the white-seat Robin I had three others that were hand-tame in the winter of 1925–6. Their territories adjoined and apparently met in a large spiraea bush. Two, and sometimes all three, birds came to this bush together, and whenever this was so, feeding was impossible; each bird as it perched on my hand was knocked off by another before it could eat. The incessant combats were wearisome, almost disgusting, and I had to manoeuvre to get each bird fed peacefully in its own territory. One of these birds I judged to be a female, for it would snatch mealworms from the box and not sit on my hand and eat quietly as the other birds did. By March one of the males was settled in a territory that adjoined the east of a greenhouse. He was a particularly delightful bird and very tame. His singing place was high up in a sycamore tree. I would hold out the box; the singing would stop; there would be a short pause of silence, and then he would fly straight down to my hand and sit there, till satisfied; when he would again fly up to his sycamore perch and sing. If he saw me in the greenhouse he would come to me through the open ventilator at the top. Once after eating a few mealworms he sang while on my hand: a full and proper song, loud and sustained, very ear-piercing at such close quarters. White Feather often sang a few notes before he left the hand, but this bird is the only one that has ever treated my hand as a real singing perch. I could not discover that he had a mate, and in April he disappeared, though I saw no sign of his territory being disputed and no other Robin sang in his place.

Of the other two Robins, the one that 'snatched' was, as I had supposed, a female; they paired; their two territories, which were next to each other, were amalgamated: as in old days a king would marry the queen or heiress to the throne of a neighbouring country and combine the two kingdoms in one realm.

Any male Robin can be tamed; such at least is my experience. The bird is first attracted by crumbs of bread thrown on the ground; then a mealworm is thrown to it; then a box – such as one of the small metal boxes in which chemists sell lozenges – is placed open on the ground with mealworms in it. When the bird has become used to this, the next step is to kneel down and place the back of one hand flat upon the ground with the box open on the upturned palm, and the fingers projecting beyond the box. This is the most difficult stage, but Robins will risk their lives for mealworms, and the bird will soon face the fingers and stand on them. The final stage, that of getting the bird to come on to the hand when raised above the ground, is easy. The whole process may be a matter of only two or three days in hard weather, when birds are hungry; and when once it has been accomplished the Robin does not lose its tameness: confidence has been established and does not diminish when weather becomes mild and food plentiful.

Maxwell Knight was a bird gardener who wrote about his experiences a generation after Grey of Fallodon. He had a great facility for making friends with wild animals but at one time or another he kept fair numbers of them in his Camberley house either as guests or as patients. Well aware of the pitfalls of 'rescuing' young birds which had not been lost or 'abandoned' by their parents he nevertheless had to deal with a lot of needy juveniles . . .

Nearly every bird gardener at some time or other will encounter the problem of the young bird. This means a bird that is not yet able to feed itself and which has been deserted by its parents, or which has fallen from the nest, or has been injured; or more frequently, one which has been found in a hedgerow, field, or garden.

All these categories of young birds may require different treatment. If the bird is a nestling that has been deserted, or if a whole brood of young has been left without parents owing to a cat or other predator, the wise bird gardener should consider the situation carefully.

The stage which the young have reached is important. If the birds are very young indeed – only a few days old in fact – the chances of rearing them are few, for the feeding

THE SPARROW ORPHAN

One day in early spring, as by this time the young musician could usually be relied upon to honour his engagements, I arranged a little informal concert so that he could make his debut as an operatic tenor. Six or seven people accepted the invitation and, after tea, the stage was set for the First Appearance of the Infant Prodigy. The audience was seated, breathless and expectant, at some distance from the piano, and the doors, both of the music-room and of an apartment opposite which served as the Artist's Room, were opened wide. I took my seat at the keyboard, and all eyes were focussed on the floor at the threshold.

For several minutes after I began to play nothing happened. There was neither sight nor sound of the artist, and my heart sank. Then someone said in a stage-whisper, 'Hugh! He's coming!' and a moment later a minute figure appeared in the doorway. I cannot truthfully say that his entrance was a success. It was not impressive and it lacked style. Perhaps he felt some tenseness in the atmosphere that he did not understand. However, after stopping on the hearthrug to arrange his coat-tails or, to be more exact, to draw the feathers of his tail one by one through his beak, he half ran and half flew across the room – as if the cat were after him – and scrambled up my leg and on to my shoulder. The silence could be felt. Once again there was an anti-climax and it looked as if the money for the tickets would have to be returned, for he sat there for several minutes, quietly preening his feathers.

At long last, after more rapid trilling and rippling from me in the upper register of the piano, he began to tune up and suddenly burst into full song to the accompaniment of the *Black Study*. This, alas! was his swan-song as a concert artiste, for the applause so terrified him that he disappeared down my neck and never sang in public again.

Nevertheless, our own private and intimate recitals continued to be a joy to me for several years. He loved music that trilled, and scales played rapidly in the treble; and, though I do not for a moment suggest that he knew one piece from another, some undoubtedly had a special appeal and inspired him to more spontaneous outbursts. I always think that he learned to trill from Chopin's *Berceuse*, but that of course is impossible to prove. He never sang so well as in the early morning and, as I played faster and faster, and higher and higher in the treble, he would pour out his soul in an ecstasy as great, if not as melodious, as any Sky Lark.

Clare Kipps

of a brood of five young Robins, for instance, would be beyond the average person's powers and diligence. Such a brood should be painlessly destroyed by a capable person who will wring their necks. No attempt should be made to place the nestful of young in the vicinity of another pair of birds engaged in feeding a family; for even if these birds do respond to the movements, and, later on, the squeakings of the orphans, one of the two broods (or both) will suffer and will very probably perish from under-nourishment or starvation. Another objection to this type of rescue work is that though would-be foster-parents might be obtained, these could not keep two broods in two different nests equally warm at one and the same time – hence, one or the other of the broods will be bound to die.

A single nestling, if only a few days old, is also a well-nigh hopeless proposition, as keeping it warm and fed is a full-time task; and it is often the case that the bird has already been chilled before it is found – there is little future for such a bird.

If you find a young bird all but fully feathered and looking bright-eyed and active, though not able to fly properly, do not imagine, as so many people do, that it is injured. Many birds die before their time each year through the misguided kindness of children and others who come upon them when they have just left the nest. Because these birds cannot yet fly, or because they are 'cheeping' to let their parents know where they are, their finders think that such fledglings are ill or damaged. They then proceed to pick them up and carry them away from their parents and food, thus probably signing their death-warrants.

Such young birds should be left where they are. If they are found in your garden, then of course you should be doubly vigilant about cats and squirrels; but if they are encountered when on a walk in the country – leave them alone.

Young birds after they have left the nest are fed by their parents for periods which vary according to the species and if left to take their chance in the care of their parents, they have a much greater expectation of life than if they are taken away to be either liberated far from some sure source of food, or maybe left in the charge of an uninformed person who will endeavour to hand-rear them – probably in the wrong way.

I myself have brought up and liberated sparrows, Robins, thrushes, Blackbirds, Magpies, Jackdaws and owls but my most interesting adoptions have been a House Martin and a young Cuckoo.

The basic requirements of young birds are warmth, food and cleanliness. In nature the first is obtained in the early stages of growth through brooding by the parent; and later on, when feathers start to grow and feeding is in full force, the young tend to keep each other warm when they are alone in the nest. In captivity they must have a nice even temperature; and if they are on the young side – with few

Pigeon time

Once literally thousands of country railway stations had baskets full of racing pigeons consigned to them. When the train that brought them had been sent on its way, the stationmaster or porter would open the lid, watch the birds gain height and circle overhead while they got their bearings, and then fill in the certificate of release to be returned by the next train. Inevitably things occasionally went amiss, such as the pigeons being sent to the wrong station – or forgotten overnight. Certificates could be incorrectly completed, giving the impression of unduly slow or rapid flights home. It was not even unknown for the certificate (fastened to the outside of the basket) to be received at the sending station before the pigeons had been released. The porter at one lonely country junction always delayed releasing the birds beyond the stated time because he enjoyed their company while sitting on a bench outside the parcels office having his sandwiches.
David St John Thomas

feathers – a piece of soft flannel laid gently over the birds in the box in which they are placed will help to provide the necessary warmth. Even when they are better clad they should still be protected from draughts and sudden changes of temperature.

Nest sanitation is very important. In the wild, very few species of birds allow their nests to become dirty, and their naturally clean instincts are helped by an internal process which delivers the waste matter from the bowels of the young birds in the form of a little bag, the outer covering of which is composed of a remarkably strong, jelly-like substance. This prevents the contents from fouling the nest.

These little faecal sacs are voided by the young birds at very frequent intervals; and in the early stages of nestling development these sacs are picked up in the beak of the parent birds and taken right away from the nest site. When the young have advanced a little and are less helpless, they themselves develop an instinct which prompts them to turn their hind parts outwards and over the edge of the nest so that their sacs are shot clear. It will be seen from this that great care must be taken by all human foster-parents to see that this aspect of rearing young birds is dealt with. It will be found that these sacs will be ejected after each meal, and they should be studied carefully, as they are reliable indicators of the bird's state of health.

If the sac is chiefly white and chalky-looking, and is shaped like a lozenge tapered at one end and if it is unruptured – then all is well. If the excreta are not in this bag, but are loose, and they appear more brownish than white, then something is wrong which must be speedily adjusted. It should be quite possible to pick up these sacs with a pair of tweezers without breaking them, and this again is a test of normality. The tweezers, gently but firmly used, will not penetrate the outer covering of the sac. Each one should be taken away from the nest as soon as possible; and an inspection of the nest or box in which the bird or birds are kept, should be made from time to time. This is in case one sac has accidentally got under the young bird and has been burst in the process. Should this happen, the contents get dried out on the underside of the bird, a stoppage may occur, and death follows very quickly in such cases.

Of course, when your charge gets to the stage when the faeces are ejected well away from the bird, it is still necessary to remove them completely – the cleaner the bird's surroundings are the better chance it has of survival.

How to house your nestling is worth some thought. An old nest will do, if it is clean and soft inside; but it should be placed in a cardboard box for warmth, convenience and tidiness. An artificial nest may be made with soft hay and, if the bird is very young, a piece of flannel used to cover it up between feedings. For some time you will not have to worry about other accommodation, and you will have to be guided about future housing by considering what you eventually intend to do with your bird. The bird's own behaviour

Eric & David Hosking

Feeding an injured Great Spotted Woodpecker

Harry Lacey/FLPA

Young Cuckoo being hand-reared

will show you when it wants more room: for instance, there will come a stage when it wants to sit on the edge of its nest and stretch its wings and begin to flap them. You must encourage it to do this. You should also take the bird on your finger and get it to raise itself up on its legs for short periods. This can be done by keeping the food you offer it a little out of reach.

With regard to feeding and food, the difficulties are not necessarily so great as is so often imagined. What horrifies people about the prospect of bringing up young birds by hand is the thought that it will be necessary to feed the nestling every few minutes. It is true that in nature parent birds often do give feeds at intervals as short as three or five minutes. But it must be remembered that these feeds are usually made up of a few small flies and insect larvae; and the lack of 'body' and the meagre nature of some of the flies is compensated for by the constant stream of feeding visits paid to the nest. In captivity this can be adjusted by giving more substantial types of food and feeding less frequently. I have reared dozens of young birds in my time, but I have never fed at much more frequent intervals than once every one and a half hours. Even my House Martin and Cuckoo were not fed more regularly than that, except when showing them off to admiring visitors.

It is important to realise that nearly all birds which are likely to be adopted will want live food, or rather animal food. Mealworms are excellent and full of nourishment; and

THE YOUNG CUCKOO

It was early in June 1952 that a radio listener wrote to ask what I could advise in the case of a young Cuckoo about a week old which was in a Hedge Sparrow's nest in his garden, and which was daily being stalked by a cat. For years it had been my ambition to try my hand at rearing a young Cuckoo, and it occured to me that here was an opportunity to do so without having a guilty conscience.

On 6 June I visited my correspondent's home and was escorted by his wife to the nest. The young Cuckoo, which was already occupying three-quarters of the space available had been hatched on either the 28 or 29 May. Now, when one approaches a nest with young birds in it, it is usual to receive a greeting of craning heads and open beaks, but there was none of this sort of thing about the young Cuckoo. It fluffed itself out, gave vent to a sort of juvenile scream and pecked savagely at my finger. I was interested to see that two of the Hedge Sparrow's eggs, which this vigorous youngster had ejected, were caught up in some

moss on the edge of the nest. I packed the fledgling–nest, eggs and all – into a cardboard box and returned home.

My feeding system was operated satisfactorily, and on a diet of soft food, earthworms and mealworms, varied with an occasional slug or green caterpillar, this young Cuckoo thrived and grew. It was never fed at more frequent intervals than ninety minutes, and on occasions when it had to be left for a greater length of time, a ration of about six or seven mealworms would keep it in good trim for two hours or more. A crisis did develop once, when its digestion seemed to have been a little upset, but several doses of whisky and water worked wonders, and the next day it was normal again.

It is difficult to make up my mind which of the many interesting things I observed about this bird are most worthy of comment. I think perhaps that its rapid development in every way; its amazing tameness; and what I can only dare to describe as its intelligence, were the things that impressed me most.

as the usual supply of mealworms which one buys from a store or breeds for oneself is bound to consist of larvae of varying ages (and therefore sizes) it is easy to fit the size of worm to the size of the young bird. With very small birds it is perhaps an advantage, at least in the early stages, to break up the mealworm before feeding, though my House Martin took entire mealworms without any digestive troubles.

Earthworms are equally good, more easily obtained, and a great stand-by. I do not think, however, that they should form the sole diet of a young bird, as they seem to have a somewhat aperient effect if not varied with other forms of food. Very small earthworms may be fed entire, but it may be necessary to chop up large worms for the consumption of really small 'infants'. If you are not prepared to do this – then don't try to rear nestlings. Gentles (maggots) are *not* good for young birds. It would appear that their extremely tough skin cannot be attacked by the digestive juices of young birds, and they are therefore passed through the bird's system complete – generally with dire results. If they are to be used at all they must mashed up – a messy process that a really keen bird gardener will not shrink from, but which will deter many people. Once the digestive juices of the bird can reach the inside of the gentle all will go well. On the whole it is better not to feed maggots, unless no other live food can be obtained.

What about 'soft foods'? This is the name given to pastes

Its physical growth was certainly not adversely affected by having large nutritious meals at much longer intervals than it would have had in nature. Most authorities state that a Cuckoo leaves the foster-parents' nest on or about the twenty-third day after hatching. This particular one was encouraged to try and feed *itself* when it was three weeks old, and after two or three days it was able to do this without any difficulty! Like most other young birds it found drinking more of a problem, and for quite a long time it had to take drops of water off the tip of a finger.

One expects hand-reared birds to be tame; but this one was fantastically so – particularly when one remembers that at first it resented approach so much that it went through all the movements of attack. Its tameness persisted, even after it was given practically complete freedom; and later, when the bird had no restriction at all placed upon its movements, it showed its confidence and some sort of rudimentary affection for its friends. It would come when called or whistled, and – provided of course that it could see me – it would actually come in response to my beckoning finger. It flew about my garden and neighbouring gardens; it flew in and out of the house; it came and sat in my dressing-room first thing in the morning; and it visited the table quite regularly at meal times. It had some peculiar tastes in food, for in addition to what it got for itself, and the mealworms which were provided in order to keep it around the place, it had a passion for butter and magarine.

Although I had hoped to keep it with me for longer, the migratory urge was too strong, and my Cuckoo left me during the last week in July – a sad, but much wiser man. I would not have missed this experience for anything; and I think that my young Cuckoo was the most attractive bird I have ever had anything to do with.

Maxwell Knight

of various kinds which can be made up for feeding to the young birds, and also for feeding those adult birds which are termed by aviculturists 'soft-billed birds'. There are several brands of commercial products of this kind. These are in the form of powders which can be made up into crumbly pastes with water or milk. These differ a little in their composition, but most of them are fundamentally the same. Avoid cheap brands.

Though the proprietary foods save a little time in preparation and are supposed to be balanced in the constituents, I myself prefer to make up my own paste. At the same time it is important to point out that such food is not to be regarded as a substitute for live food; it is only a *supplementary* food which is useful when your charge has to be taken with you on a journey, or when you are going to be away from home for some hours. This is a contingency to which you will have to resign yourself.

Mr C. A. Bartlett used to make up a most effective and luxurious paste in the days before the war when foodstuffs of all kinds were unrationed and plentiful. His formula was elaborate, but it contained nearly every dietary requirement that a bird needs. There were vegetable fats, animal fats, egg, ground flies, ground ants' eggs, honey and crushed biscuit! It shows to what trouble a first-class aviculturist will go in an endeavour to rear young birds.

A very good substitute can be made up by scrambling an egg with the minimum amount of fat, and adding enough crushed biscuit to make a nice smooth paste. The best liquid to use when mixing is water. Milk is sometimes too strong for the young birds, and in any case it will go sour in hot weather and will obviously not last for twenty-four hours. It is better to make up the paste every day if possible. In addition to its value as food, paste, so long as it is not too moist, is a good corrective to the aperient action of an excess of earthworm diet. If the droppings show signs of being loose, cut down on the earthworms and give an extra meal or two of paste. By the way, if you can get some fresh ants' eggs (free from ants) and mix them into your paste it will much increase its nutritional value.

How much to give, and at what intervals is the next problem. It is clear from what I have already said that the more frequent the meals the less they should be in quantity; and while it is good to keep the bird's system working regularly, it is a mistake to feed every quarter of an hour just because you have nothing else to do, and then, from pressure of circumstances, leave the bird for two hours before it gets another meal. It is better, particularly in the early stages of growth, to fix an interval, say every one and a half hours, and stick to it. I have found that it helps to make the task less strenuous, and does not apparently do any harm if, when you find you have to leave the bird unfed for a little longer than usual you cover up the box or cage so that it is completely dark. This seems to quieten the bird down and make it less eager. Perhaps it actually slows down the diges-

Robins in cold weather

Undoubtedly the most desperate time for Robin survival happens, in Britain, every few years when we have a severe winter. During mild winters most Robins are easily able to find enough food to survive – provided that they hold a good territory in a suitable area. When really cold weather strikes all sorts of problems arise and many birds may die. For instance, in Mid December 1981 the exceptionally cold weather led to almost four times as many ringing recoveries as usual.

The problems are all to do with food and shelter. The cold weather comes at a time of year when there is the least daylight and so the birds have only a short time each day when they can see to feed. Snow may cover many suitable feeding areas and bury food supplies that would otherwise have been available. Severe cold weather cools the birds, who must find sheltered places to roost in and, in any case, will almost certainly have to eat more food to provide metabolic heat for survival. The cold weather will also drive many of the small arthropods on which the Robins feed to hide in nooks and crannies where the birds are unable to reach them.

Chris Mead

B. S. Turner/FLPA

A bird in the hand . . .

live processes, and so stills the pangs of hunger.

I have not found it necessary to feed young birds before 7am, if they are covered up last thing at night. Birds in the wild are fed from dawn until dusk, but you can compensate quite satisfactorily for the hours between dawn and 7am, if you give two or three late feeds between dusk and your own bedtime.

Of course, birds will often give a hunger response to your approach, even when they do not really require a meal, and this arouses alarm in the novice; but on the whole it is better to give too little than too much. If you stuff a young bird till you get no further reaction from it, when you next come to feed and you still get no reaction, you will be unable to tell if it is merely satisfied, or if it is upset from an overloaded stomach!

Many people get worried over the question of drinking. Do young birds drink? Well, many of them certainly require water and with some species of bird, water is brought to the nest by the parents. Of course there is a high water content in caterpillars, but it would seem that this is not always enough. I doubt if anyone knows exactly which birds bring water to their young and which do not. Perhaps they all do so at times. I can only say that I have successfully reared young owls without any water at all, yet I have had some which liked to have a drink at a very early age. As far as my experience goes, water in small quantities does not do any harm; and I would favour a few drinks during the day – particularly if the weather is hot. Water is best given drop by drop on the tip of a finger – about three drops being enough. The water should not be warm and stale, nor should it be very cold. I usually give fresh water with the chill just off it.

The question of water naturally makes one think of bathing, and here caution is necessary. No young bird should be bathed or sprinkled with water until it is really well feathered; certainly not until it has left the nest and is perching properly. The feathers of a young bird are very delicate and if they lose their 'bloom' it is very often a sign that something is up with the youngster. By the same token, you should watch carefully to see that when the nestling begins to show signs of leaving its nest and hops about its box or cage, the tail feathers, which will by then be growing, do not get broken or damaged or fouled. Encourage the bird to sit on a perch, or a small log, so that it can keep its tail well clear of the floor. If the tail does get dirty don't wash it. Let the sand, etc, dry out, then gently remove it with your fingers and stroke the feathers between your thumb and finger to set the plumage right again.

Your next feeding problem will be to start the process of teaching your foster-child to fend for itself. The difficulty of this varies with different species, and also with individual birds of the same species. My little Cuckoo, learnt amazingly quickly. This is a curious feature, since Cuckoos are usually fed by their foster-parents – and other birds as well – for a long time after they leave the nest. My Cuckoo could feed itself at three weeks old. I encouraged it to do this by keeping it waiting a little longer than usual for its meal, and then placing some mealworms, or pieces of earthworm in a shallow white dish so that they could be easily seen. The young Cuckoo was curious, as are all birds, and it dabbed at the worms with its beak. Occasionally, more by luck than good judgement, it got hold of a morsel, and it was most interesting to see how the instinctive swallowing motion followed. It was very funny at times, because this swallowing reaction was so very instinctive and mechanical that even if the worm was dropped from the beak, or missed altogether, the gulping movement still occurred.

After a time – a few days only – the self-feeding attempts became more and more successful, and as they improved a longer interval was allowed between 'hand-feeds', a few items of food being left in the dish in the intervals. If this sort of procedure is followed most young birds will learn to feed themselves. Learning to drink, however seems much more difficult, but it comes in time.

When the young bird can really fly strongly and can perch where it wishes without difficulty, you must harden your heart, let it go free, and refuse to feed it. Otherwise it will tie itself to you and tend to become a fixture, which is really unkind to the bird. In most cases, if left unfed by hand for some days, it will generally go farther and farther afield until it leaves you altogether. Sometimes though, birds will

go away for a whole season and yet return to your garden later. This is very gratifying. Of course, if you wish, you can take the bird right out of your neighbourhood and give it its liberty elsewhere; but see that it does not behave like a Jackdaw which belonged to a friend of mine.

It was taken some miles to a nice sheltered piece of woodland – far away from cats – and was set free. My friend got into his car and drove home. Arriving there he went to put his car away when he felt something alight on his shoulder. It was the Jackdaw which had, unseen by him, perched on some part of the car and managed to stay there during the whole of the return journey.

All this business of rearing young birds may seem a lot of trouble, but think of how much you will learn in the process, quite apart from the satisfaction of having saved life and given the chance of survival when little may have existed in the first place.

Maxwell Knight actually enjoyed rearing birds and the problems of releasing them back to the wild. Most of us try to avoid the time-consuming and often heart-breaking process. The bird artist Eric Ennion decidedly disapproved of keeping animals in any kind of captivity. But, in running his celebrated Bird Observatory at Monks' House on the Northumberland coast, he couldn't avoid it . . .

Frankly, much as I love birds, I have no use for them as pets. If you like to saddle yourself with Canaries or Budgies, or for that matter with a dog or a cat or a goldfish, go ahead: it is up to you. There will be one more job to be looked to before you can shut up your house. Birds born and bred in captivity have long since forgotten the wild. Tend them well and I would agree with Coleridge:

A melancholy bird? Oh! idle thought!
In Nature there is nothing melancholy.

Nevertheless, no bird born and bred in a briar-bush has any business in a cage.

But all these pious resolutions do not prevent me keeping birds. I have to. Every so often a little procession arrives at the door: father carrying a cardboard box with holes punched in it or an oiled Guillemot bundled in a bit of rag, children dolefully bringing up the rear. They may come in a car, in a van, in a bicycle-basket, in a pram, in a hand, in a paper bag, these casualties of beach and road and telegraph wire. One procession we have got to know quite well: anything up to half a dozen small boys and girls pulling a little cart made of a fishbox mounted on an old set of pram wheels, all the way from Seahouses; and in the box either a storm-battered Shag or a big gull with a badly damaged wing.

Sometimes the birds bring themselves. A young Goldeneye one stormy evening walked into the kitchen of Fair Isle Bird Observatory, a Little Auk went into a suburban surgery, to be met by the astonished doctor walking out. One morning after a dirty night I myself went into an open

---

Land locked

As a veterinary surgeon in a country practice, I frequently have brought to me wild birds that require attention. Unusual ones in the past year have included a Sparrowhawk, a Grey Heron and a Tawny Owl.

These birds are all native to the area, but recently I was surprised, to say the least, when a client arrived with a Guillemot which had been found in a hedgerow near her garden on the southerly slopes of Clee Hill, near Ludlow.

Clee Hill is approximately 30 miles west of Birmingham with the River Teme about 8 miles to the south. The bird had a small flesh wound to its left wing, but even without this, it is almost inconceivable that it had flown inland, even with the help of the River Teme.

It was an attractive bird, in winter plumage and probably a youngster. We kept it for a week during which it fed voraciously on all the fish we could feed it, and took great pleasure from a daily swim in our bath.

Seven days later I took it to the Worms Head on the Gower Peninsula and released it near the Guillemot colony there. It really appreciated its reunion with the sea and spent two hours preening itself in the salty pools, apparently trying to get sea-water into every feather.

Gareth B. Thomas

(This is the first known record of a Guillemot in Shropshire this century, although there were a few in the nineteenth century. They are generally very rare inland.)

coke-shed to find a young Shag standing in the corner; and a local publican once rang me up to say he had found a queer bird on his doorstep as he was locking-up at closing time. He put it in his car and brought it along. It was a Black-throated Diver, a beauty and so far as I could see completely unharmed. It had been raining and I think the diver had mistaken the wet road with its reflected lights for water. We kept it overnight and launched it from the beach next morning, none the worse: in fact, all the better for a hearty meal of fish.

Oiled Guillemots need careful treatment . . .

Eric Hosking

138

Monks' House beach has seen many another launching. Some like the diver's, with no misgivings; or the dabchick rescued by a quarryman from a pocket in the snow; or the young Red-necked Grebe found at high water mark bogged down in loose sand, carried there presumably on the wash of a seventh wave. Grebes and divers will not of their own accord alight on land. Their streamlining for underwater travelling is such that they would have the greatest difficulty in taking off again: pocketing in snow or sand might easily prevent it. Fulmars too find difficulty. These when discovered landbound and brought in, we launch from a height, from Stag Rocks or from the harbour breakwater, for they prefer to glide rather than swim out to sea. One we rescued from the bottom of an old kiln shaft in the fields, fetching a long ladder from the nearest farm to go down to recover it; and, at Bamburgh Castle where the Fulmars breed, the caretaker keeps a long-handled scoop to deal with any that get lodged behind the parapets.

David Hosking

. . . the plumage must be cleaned meticulously

Some launchings, on the other hand, we don't feel quite so happy about: these stormridden Shags and Cormorants and young Gannets – we once had a call to rescue a Cormorant that had come down in a chicken run and bitten the village policeman! – Guillemots, Razorbills and Little Auks. Many of them, if they are not oiled as well, improve greatly after a night's rest and a feed of fish – our 'bed-and-breakfast' convalescents. They will not feed themselves, at first: a fish to them is a silver streak to be chased underwater, not a messy white slip held in human fingers. Force-feeding for a few times is inevitable, but once they get the hang of things there is no further difficulty. I have been almost chased upstairs by a hungry and raucous Razorbill: as 'de jay-bird say ter de squinch-owl, "I'm sickly but sassy".'

Then there was Charlie, the first of a long queue of Gannets. Young Gannets in their grey-speckled juvenile plumage take to the sea from their nursery cliffs – the Bass Rock in our case – and swim away, being too fat to fly until fasting and exercise has thinned them down a bit. It is a critical period in their lives. In stormy weather they may drift inshore and get themselves beached. Exhausted and perhaps injured by being thrown against rocks they soon seem to lose the will to survive and quickly deteriorate. Some die. Others, like Charlie, after a few days in hospital, begin to look up and recover; but, probably because they have used up in the struggles the reserves of fat that should have carried them over their drifting period, it is no good releasing them until they can fly – for Gannets catch the submerged fish on which they live by diving in after it from the air. In the midst of plenty they would starve unless they can rise above the surface of the waves. So Charlie, and others after him, had to be kept and fed – and young Gannets put away a pound or two of fish a day. There were times when heavy seas kept the fishing boats in harbour. There was no fresh fish to be had for love or money. Would Charlie mind a 'wee bit haddie, very lightly smoked?'

Charlie was on the lawn. He fixed me with his pale china-blue eyes and their appalling convergent squint, slowly opening his bill and then his wide grey gullet. He took first a few bits of 'fresh' fish saved from previous days (by now distinctly *passé*), then a couple of wee split haddies, and I topped him up with a bit more 'fresh', as one used to use jam to mask grey powders. He gulped a few times, preened a little and settled down to the pleasures of digestion. All's well thought I . . .

Irks care the crop-full bird?
Frets doubt that maw-crammed beast?

DRAWING BIRDS

Draw from tame or familiar wild birds to begin with. The better you know a bird, the more confidently you will be able to respond to it. Those seen fleetingly through binoculars are best ignored until you have more experience, and can retain a lot of what you see in your memory. Birds at a winter feeding-table, which can be watched from a window, ducks coming for food on a park lake, or gulls to a fishing harbour – any occasion where a situation is repeated, will give more chance for your drawing fragments to turn into completed birds. Wild birds attracted to a local farm or a zoo by easy pickings are less timid than usual, and one can watch finches, Starlings, crows, wagtails, gulls, Moorhens and pigeons, without taking extreme measures to hide. A car is often ignored by birds, and it makes a comfortable, if not very manoeuvrable viewing hide, with the advantage of support from partly wound-down windows for binoculars or telescopes. (You can buy telescope brackets which attach to a car door frame.)

Hides provided by organisations like the RSPB on nature reserves are a godsend to the artist, but to me, there is nothing better than sharing the birds' environment (and weather conditions). Without the enclosed feeling of a hide one can be alert to sounds and to movement seen out of the corner of an eye, and open to the unexpected. A bird artist has all the excitement and frustrations of a hunter, and the need for similar subtlety of field-craft. It is a hopeless task to pursue birds with pencil at the ready! However careful you are as a stalker, you can be certain that the birds have seen you coming and know just how close they will let you come. It is far better to sit and wait for birds to come to you or approach them casually, avoiding stealth. Birds wake early in their search for food, and you will usually see more activity between dawn and breakfast than at any other time of day.

As field knowledge accumulates, the odds against seeing wild birds close enough to draw can be shortened. Many patterns of behaviour are predictable. The major influences on courtship, breeding, flocking and migration are the changing seasons. On the sea-shore or estuary, the tide is a considerable factor in knowing what is likely to be seen and where to position yourself. For example, waders may be scattered far and wide at low tide, but will be driven close inshore to favoured resting places at high tide. One can arrive ahead of time and wait; keeping below the bird's skyline, if possible in the shelter of rocks or dunes with the sun behind you. An incoming tide will also encourage seaducks, grebes and divers to follow sand-eels closer to the shore. Another winter activity is roosting; thrushes, finches, Starlings and many other species will gather at dusk, forming large flocks to spend the night together. Geese and Rooks follow regular flight lines between roosts and feeding areas. In summer a woodland clearing, especially near water, would be a good sitting place. (We are not the only creatures to enjoy sunshine and shelter from the wind!) A tree at one's back may be enough cover; stillness matters more than camouflage; though one should avoid conspicuious colours at all times. Woodland birds are often curious, and will sometimes peer at one closely through the leaves. They can be attracted by imitating alarm 'clicks' or what the Americans call 'Pishing'.

The golden rule at all times is to keep a low profile and to let the birds get used to you as a harmless presence.

John Busby

Half an hour later, when passing by, I'll swear Charlie gave me a wink: beside him, neatly side by side on the grass, were the two smoked haddies. How in his capacious crop he had contrived to single them out from the rest must forever remain a mystery. For shortly afterwards Charlie, who by now was flapping his wings to such good effect that he could more or less fly from one end of the lawn to the other, was taken down to the beach for his daily splash and dozen. There was a stiff nor'easter blowing. Charlie, standing on tiptoe and flapping vigorously, was suddenly airborne and very soon out of sight. It was an excellent way of launching Gannets. But one of Charlie's less venturesome

Shunter's pole

The early morning express from Newton Abbot to Penzance, hauled by a famous GWR locomotive *Chepstow Castle*, came to a halt halfway across Brunel's Royal Albert Bridge over the Tamar. A large swan in the middle of the track refused to be intimidated by the locomotive or its hissing steam or shrill whistle. After taking in the view in a more leisurely manner than normal, passengers began poking their heads out of the window – and saw a shunter walk over from the Saltash end complete with pole to encourage the bird to clear the line.

David St John Thomas

successors, left on the beach to recapture his love of the sea, thought better of it. Glancing back as I was walking down the road to find somebody, I found the Gannet instead plodding along behind me!

These are the lucky ones, sound in wind and limb, needing only a little care and replenishing to get them on the wing again. For every one of these, however, there are all too many others severely injured, badly oiled, exhausted beyond recovery, for which one can do nothing but put them speedily out of their misery. Earlier on we used to clean up many lightly oiled birds and, as soon as they seemed better, let them go. Then, despite orders to the contrary – for they were no longer 'normal' birds – I started ringing them. Almost invariably the rings or their corpses were returned from bays or beaches farther along the coast. In my opinion a pelagic bird that ought to be out of sight of shore, if, being oiled, it comes to land and lets you pick it up, that bird is doomed whatever you may do.

And so with broken wings (not a leg, which *can* be mended or done without if need be) in birds whose very existence depends on wing efficiency, neither can they be dealt with confidently. We say therefore that if there is a reasonable chance of a sick bird regaining its rightful place, it shall have it: if not the sooner it is destroyed the better. One should not be ruled by sentiment. Some of the birds brought in, especially gulls that in gusty dawns have fallen foul of telegraph wires, have a wing almost severed but otherwise seem to be in pretty good fettle. You could if you like snip through the shred of skin with a pair of scissors and have a tame gull following you around for the next twenty years may be, for big gulls are long-lived fellows. But *I* would not and yet . . . there was Hector.

Eric Ennion's illustration of Hector

Eric Ennion

Gannets on Grassholm Island

Hector was a Herring Gull, the subject of a most interesting experiment before he had reached the age of consent. He was still in the egg when put to hatch in a Kittiwake's nest, where he acted as stooge for a set of important behaviour observations. Herring Gull chicks in the ordinary way soon leave the nest, each to find a little hideout for itself in the rocks or herbage not far away, whence they run back at meal times, the nest from now on becoming a dining-room rather than a dormitory. It would seem to be safer for these speckled downy chicks to be dispersed in this way rather than to have all one's eggs in one basket. Kittiwake chicks on the other hand seldom leave the nest until they can fly. Wandering abut the dizzy sites that cliff-breeding Kittiwakes select would be suicidal.

But Hector was not to know this. He was very properly rescued before he went overboard and the experimenters accepted the responsibility of bringing him up by hand. As a result he came to look on human beings as his rightful providers and playmates and was not in the least interested in gulls. So much for the Call of the Wild! The time came when Hector's foster-parents had to go and Hector was dumped on Monks' House: we were only too pleased to accept him but Hector had other ideas. By then he could fly and saw no point whatever in staying in one place. One human being was very much like another: if you went up and begged, somebody before long was sure to throw you something: and gulls are nothing if not omnivorous. Here

143

Baldhead

In personal intercourse with the Great Tit Baldhead I am sometimes outwitted. His favourite food is nuts and last autumn I bought some indoors in a paper bag, giving him one which he ate on the rungs under a chair. Knowing he would tear open the bag to help himself to another, I wrapped it in a double-folded tea cloth, rolling this round the bag and turning both ends under securely in a way that seemed impossible for a small bird to undo. I placed this on a side-table. I had my back to Baldhead while wrapping the bag and he could not possibly have seen what I was doing from where he was, under the chair seat. He soon flew to my hand for more nuts, but I gave him cheese – his second choice of food. He threw this away with an impatient toss and looked up at me expectantly. Again I offered him cheese. He made a curious sort of grimace with his beak half-opened, refused to take the cheese and flew round the room, looking for but unable to find the paper bag. I left the room for a few minutes; on my return he flew out of the fanlight window with the haste habitual to him after theft. Several nuts were rolling on the side-table. He had pulled the cloth undone and torn open the paper bag, helping himself to a nut. I have never before wrapped food in this cloth or in any other kind of cloth, nor had I ever put bird food on that side-table, which was used for painting materials, so he had no reason to suspect the cloth contained the paper bag, which was solidly covered with a double layer of cloth.

Len Howard

was the mentality of the beach dog – except that Hector was more intelligent. He discovered that if you selected human beings in blue guernseys, or in oilskins and sou'westers, instead of little tiddly bits of bread, you got WHOLE FISH! Hector knew which side his bread was buttered and he joined the fishing fleet. But at times he came back.

I would meet him on the rocks, head on one side, holding just that far aloof until he was satisfied that your intention really was to knock him a dozen limpets off and not to catch him. For Hector, in his teens, had been caught and brought or sent or fetched back so many times to the observatory that he had got a little tired of it. A game of family cricket on the sands would be upset by the arrival of a big brown gull, landing on the pitch and running up with loud persistent begging-calls and suppliant movements of the head. Until his fame was spread abroad sufficiently by the local press, the result was either a telephone call or Hector himself being bundled out of a towel or the boot of a car on to Monks' House lawn – whence he promptly took wing and flew back to his picnics again. We have heard nothing of him lately. Perhaps he fell foul of some trigger-happy wildfowler or perhaps he has at last found comfort in the company of his kind.

Another engaging patient was Lucy the Barn Owl. She was picked up on the dunes with some idiot's shot wound suppurating in one wing. She would lie quietly on her back on the lab table, nibbling my finger as, night and morning, I painted her wound with iodine. It got better; but I was loth to let her go until I was satisfied that she could fly well enough to keep herself alive. As no bird could achieve that without room to practise she had to have the freedom of the lab. During the day she dozed on the top of a bookcase in the darkest corner. In the gloaming I would go in quietly and find her on the back of a chair. Towards the end, when perhaps she had forgotten being caught for treatment, she would sometimes take the mouse I offered from my fingers, but usually I stole in and out, leaving my offering there. I did not want her natural instincts blunted by familiarity. I wanted to restore her to the night from whence she came.

And this we did, by a two-stage operation through the kindness of a friend who had a large indoor piggery. He was over-run with mice. He built a wooden hutch up in the rafters, wired-in the doors and windows, and we transferred Lucy there. After a few weeks he removed the wire and she was seen no more. She had in fact escaped before on one occasion and had been at large for two whole days. Two miserable rainy days at that; and on the morning of the third I saw a very bedraggled Barn Owl on one of the posts of the Heligoland trap. She flew away when I approached her, along a line of fenceposts by a ditch, on one of which she settled. I drew near and off she went again. It looked as if we might be doing this for the rest of the morning (for I felt sure she was not yet fit to go) when suddenly a bunch of Rooks caught sight of her, joined in the chase and knocked

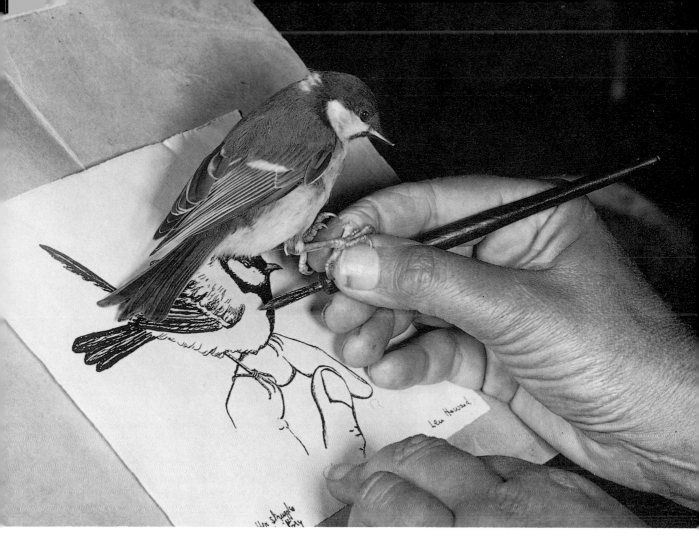

Len Howard drawing one of her house guests

her for six into the bottom of the ditch. I retrieved an exceed-ingly wet, and I hope a contrite, Lucy and carried her back to a sparrow breakfast in the lab.

Perhaps the most rewarding of all, orphans for the child-ren's ward, were four baby Shelducks brought in on a foggy day from 3 miles down the coast. We rushed straight back with them hoping against hope that we might find the pa-rents with the remainder of the family. If only people would't pick them up! They are seldom really 'lost' at that young age. Go away and give the hen a chance to collect her chicks, and the chances are that all will be well when you creep back: if not, there is still time to play the good Samaritan. But now a sea-fret rolling in reduced our vision to a radius of 30yd at most. We listened and walked on a bit and listened again. We let the little ducklings pierce the fret with their shrill piping. Again we listened – not a sound. Too long had elapsed. The duck and drake had cut their losses and gone off with the rest of the brood – but where? It was impossible to say. We went home and prepared the first of many, many saucerfuls of raw mince and oatmeal and chopped lettuce swimming in milk. A hotwater bottle under an old flannel cot blanket did duty for the brooding duck.

OPERATION FREEDOM

In early October a small boy arrived at my house carefully carrying a baby House Martin. He had found it by the wayside, and it was clear to me that it was, at the very least, a week off flying.

I thought ruefully of the type of feeding that young House Martins get in the wild – those ceaseless pellets of flies that are delivered by the energetic parents. My heart sank as I felt the small boy's eyes fixed on me. What was I going to say? It was on the tip of my tongue to tell him that to think of rearing the bird was hopeless, and that it ought to be put out of its misery; but the boy was very small, and very young – not more than eight – and very, very anxious.

I temporised by telling him that I would see what I could do if he left the bird with me, and he departed fairly happily. I looked at the little scrap of blue-black and white feathers, and then examined it more carefully. Much to my surprise I could find no injury. Then it made a rather feeble attempt to open its beak for food. From that moment I was lost!

I thought of the stock of mealworms I always have in the house, and wondered if very small ones would be accepted; and, if they were accepted, whether they would be suitable food. I also wondered whether my theory that quality of food makes up for frequency of feeds would prove right in this very special case. I collected some tiny mealworms and a pair of fine forceps. To my very great pleasure the mealworms were eagerly taken. I gave the little martin about five of them, and I then put it in a cardboard box lined with lint and covered it up. I waited about an hour or so and then gave it another feed – this time of chopped earth-worm. It was certainly more perky and sat on my finger to be fed as though it had been doing this all its life.

The first night passed off without mishap; and so, on a diet of mealworms, chopped earth-worms and my own special soft food mixture – given at intervals of about one and a half hours – this most unusual foster-child thrived amazingly. It grew rapidly, and its wings developed well, so that in a few days it could flutter quite vigorously. I used to give it flying exercises after each meal, by taking it on my finger and raising and lowering my hand so that when the air caught its little wings the bird was induced to flap them.

My House Martin was with me for nine days – except for a break of one day when I had to go to London – and on this occasion a kind friend took it over for me.

When I judged from its behaviour that it had the full use of its wings, and therefore had the chance of survival, I had to consider the question of how and where to let it go free. Its own brothers and sisters had already gone, and in my district colonies of House Martins are few and far between. I rang up my friend, John Clegg, curator of the famous Haslemere Museum, and asked for his help. He told me that fortunately there was a late colony of House Martins actually at the museum. The young birds were still being fed on the wing. He suggested that the next day I should take my little friend over there and try to liberate it among the others as they were flying about. However, early the following day John Clegg rang me up to say that his House Martins had only that very morning decided to go off!

He told me, however, that he was expecting that afternoon a party of naturalists from Alton. This party was paying a visit to the museum, and he would, as usual, be doing the honours. He suggested that if I brought over the young House Martin I might like to show it to his visiting party, tell them the story of how it was rescued, and see whether someone there might know of a late colony into which it could be introduced. I accepted this invitation with gratitude, and duly took my little bird over to Haslemere.

The naturalists from Alton were certainly interested to see it and hear the story of how it came to be there; and when I explained the plight I was in regarding its future, one member of the party very kindly offered to take it over to a place near his home where he thought there were still some House Martins about. I gave him a supply of mealworms, said goodbye to my foster-child, and returned home. All this happened on a Sunday. On the succeeding Tuesday I learned from the man who had taken charge of the House Martin that 'Operation Freedom' had succeeded completely. He had taken the bird to the place where he had seen a whole lot of young still flying around with their parents; he had cast our young hopeful into the air, and away it had flown to join the others – a very happy ending to a most interesting experience.

Maxwell Knight

The credit for rearing three out of those four ducklings to maturity belongs entirely to my wife. We heard long afterwards that they are very difficult to rear: with the hours she spent in coddling them and countering their waywardness I can believe it. As they grew older they needed any amount of greenstuff. They fell upon seeding lettuces out of the garden like a plague of locusts. Two were drakes, one and the last to fly was a nimble little duck. She was found dead some months afterwards 30 miles north of Monks' House; one of the drakes was also picked up exhausted and presumably died; the third, so far as we know, lived. We could give them food and lodging but could not impart the wariness and *savoir faire* they would have learned from the old pair.

Baby Eiders, the most active and exhausting little beggars ever hatched, are another problem altogether. Shelduck broods remain apart and supervised strictly by their own parents until nearly half-grown, when they may amalgamate: until then it would be almost impossible under natural conditions to introduce a stray duckling; as indeed with any other wild birds' broods unless one can contrive some subterfuge by night. But it *is* possible with Eiders. Partly, perhaps, because of Eider ducklings' exceeding wilfulness and their capacity for getting lost; partly, and arising from these losses, because of the high proportion of bereaved mammas in the right physiological state, it is fairly easy to add stray ducklings to an already miscellaneous crèche if you know the way to do it. Those who have enjoyed *King Solomon's Ring* – and who has not? – will remember the way Konrad Lorenz got himself tied up with the fixations of Greylag goslings and baby Mallards. This is mere trifling compared with the fixations developed by baby Eiders. Pick up one of these dusky 'lost' ducklings and it is yours for life . . . and the chances are that it *wasn't* lost, but playing truant. It and its penetrating 'peeep' (which becomes maddening after an hour or so) will follow you through thick and thin. So when visitors on the beach get tired of them, or, on the point of leaving, begin wondering what to do, they bring them in, transferring to us the duckling, the fixation and the 'peeep'.

The technique is to wait until low tide when the ducks with their mixed broods come bobbing among the wrack in the reef pools. Take the duckling in your hand and, creeping as close as you dare to the dabbling broods, *bowl it out overarm as far as you can* towards them. Then turn tail and run. Success hangs by a hair: if, as the duckling hits the water and bobs up again, it sees the ducks, it scuttles across the pool towards them and you have won. If not, if it first sees your flying form disappearing over the rocks, it follows you. Ten minutes later, when you have settled down comfortably with a book, louder and louder through the open common-room window grows that persistent 'peeep' as the duckling struggles manfully up the shore. If you cannot persuade anyone with a better turn of speed to do it for

Injured birds
People frequently bring me birds they have picked up; some are badly injured, but more often they are suffering from a minor injury with shock and they would have recovered soon if left on a safe perch close to where found. The fright of unaccustomed human handling and being taken away from its home, although kindly meant, often results in its death. Sometimes, too, the bird brought me is merely an immature fledgling, which always is better left in a hedge or bush close to where it is found. If taken away from its parents it has little chance of survival for it is deprived of its natural food. People sometimes have told me they tried to revive the injured bird by giving it brandy, but this is very bad for birds. Water should be given as soon as possible and a little later some milk, bread dipped in milk and cheese, grated or broken into very small fragments. The bird may not be able to eat for a time, but the food can be left within its reach and then the quieter it is, the more chance it will have of recovery. The wild bird does not understand caresses, so there should be no petting and stroking of feathers. This may only aggravate the bird's fright. Alcohol is considered very bad for human beings in cases of head injuries, and it should be remembered that the same applies to birds, whatever their injury, but especially this should not be given to them when stunned.
Len Howard

Paddling Passerines

Can all birds swim? A question posed by Peter Davis after an astonishing encounter with a Sand Martin in July of this year.

We took a 60ft mist-net along to Frensham Ponds in the hope that the Swifts might be flying low. While we were erecting the net at the water's edge I spotted a small dark triangle moving quite rapidly through the water some 20-25yd from the shore. It came in obliquely towards the bank – possibly because the only dry land it could see was a small willow in a patch of phragmites. Its progress was excellent, very determined and without any sign of flagging or floundering. We watched fascinated.

Eventually it reached the phragmites and disappeared so we waded out and collected it from its perch low down in the reeds. It was a Sand Martin. Amazingly its head and upper back were completely dry; the rest was sodden. We rolled it up in a handkerchief to absorb most of the surplus water. Then we took it along to the ▶

you, there is no option but to pick the duckling up and go back for a repeat, praying that *'third* time lucky' will not come true in this case. A three-day-old Eider duckling will bring a grown man to his knees any day of the week.

Other ducks, enfeebled by disease or wounded by shot, have been brought in at various times, Wigeon, Scoter, Goldeneye, and an RSPCA Inspector once carried in a swan as an out-patient. Another swan, a wild Whooper this time, took off from Monks' House Pool one winter's evening for a fly-around. It struck the 'grid', involving both itself and a sector of north-east Northumberland in a blackout dark as Egypt's night. And we have had waders too; an exhausted Knot for which we contrived a miniature mud-flat on a large teatray in the lab, well stocked with sandhoppers; a Redshank that ate half a dozen 8–10in lobworms at a sitting and asked for more; a Lapwing with an oddly twisted wing, which we undid but never found out how he came by it; and an Oystercatcher that stayed with us longer than them all. He was soon christened 'Squeakie' by Jessie the Scots housekeeper, below whose window he skirled his morning pipes.

He had been pricked no doubt by one of the gangs of shore-shooters that infest the north-east coast – I have no quarrel with the genuine wildfowler, having shot a good deal myself; but there is no excuse for indiscriminate shooting at anything that gets up, gull, tern, wader, pipit, even Swallows, protected or not, so long as these 'sportsmen' empty their pockets and cartridge-belts before they pack up. That can never be wildfowling in its intended sense. However that may be, Squeakie presumably dropped injured among the rocks where, one evening, he was caught by a dog: not *retrieved*, unless that dog had an incredibly hard mouth, for when he was brought in, one red eye looking up at me was about the only sign of life. The rest felt like pulp. I put him on a bit of sacking in a box, expecting to find him dead next morning. But he wasn't. If anything he was a little better and accepted a sip or two of water; and later, a small shelled limpet. I examined him carefully all over, as I thought, and finding no wound and no bones broken, decided that he should be given a sporting chance.

Before long Squeakie was hobbling round like a rheumaticky old man, shelling limpets for himself while I held them steady for him. He remained thin in spite of an excellent appetite. It was not until some time afterwards that I found I had missed a fractured scapula, the result perhaps of the original stray shot. A bird's scapula is impossible to splint and it was improbable that he would ever fly again. But by then, of course, it was too late to apply the rule. Squeakie had been taken on the strength. He survived for eighteen months until a fox nipped into his enclosure one wild night and that was that. Perhaps after all the strongest argument against keeping pets is that sooner or later you are bound to part with them.

Small birds with broken wings are not infrequent patients.

If I can see that the wing *is* broken there is but one sensible cure: a *sprained* wing can recover. But it will not do so in a cage, the bird must have free range and should not be encouraged to become too tame. You cannot always help it. A cock Redstart with a sprained wing, picked up in a field, insisted that I should carry him round on my finger in the evenings to hunt for spiders on the walls and window-frames. He lived in the study, darting into his own recess in the bottom of the bookcase when anyone else came in. We had to pin a PLEASE SHUT notice on the door. One of our daily chores was to collect a bundle of the hollow stems of hogweed from the roadsides: they are full of earwigs and woodlice and of the chrysalids of the small caterpillars that make 'tents' in the umbels in July. When the stems were split the insects scattered and dashed across the floor. The Redstart flickered to and fro and this exercise did more than anything else to restore the use of his wing.

At first the little white marks of his droppings lay on the carpet under the chairs where he had been perching on their lower rails. Presently they appeared below the chair-arms and the edges of my desk; then below the tall chair-backs and finally the curtain rails. The window was left open at the top. I had said all along that he could, and would, go once he had made that. And he did, remaining about the garden for a week or so until, when a wave of autumn passage Redstarts came through, he went with them. In the same year, 1957, one of a brood of Redstarts we had ringed in Alnwick Park that summer was recovered in Spain. We wondered whether 'our' Redstart ever got as far as that.

Shortly afterwards a paper bag was handed in containing a 'lark' that had been picked up on a stubble. It was a Lapland Bunting, also with a wing sprain. We gave him the liberty of the lab – another PLEASE SHUT notice on the door – and strewed its wide windowsill with fresh green chickweed and canary seed and gave him a shallow pan of water for his bath. He accepted my presence philosophically whenever I went to work there but, as the days went on, although I had seen him flutter, I had never seen him fly. Then, while sitting at the table, suddenly from behind me came the clear flight-call of a Lapland Bunting, and I turned to find him hovering in the middle of the room. He was taken back to join his boon companions on the stubble the next day.

And that is the case book to date of one who would not keep birds as pets.

reserve's information centre where the ranger dug out a stove so that we could complete the drying operation. But would it fly?

I took it, perched on my finger, back to the heather and launched it gingerly into the air. It flopped down 6ft away. We let it rest for a while before trying again. I raised my hand high above my head and let it fall rapidly. The bird flapped its wings but clung tightly to my finger. Repeating the exercise several times, the wing flapping became gradually stronger until, at the sixth attempt, it took off. It covered 50yds, not making much height before we lost sight of it behind trees. With the opportunity to preen its feathers into some sort of order I think it would have had a good chance of surviving.

I suppose it was a lucky Sand Martin. The water was absolutely flat calm – even the slightest ripple on the surface would almost certainly have proved its undoing. Whether it would have survived without the aid of the ranger's stove is also questionable!

Peter Davis

Sleepy Times and Nightwork

Birds spend about as much of their days asleep as we do, averaging about eight hours. And, like us, they indulge in a certain amount of idle loafing. Doubtless if they wanted to rationalise the idleness they would, again like us, say it was necessary 'thinking time' . . .

Species not only differ in the amount of time spent sleeping, but in the way they sleep. Sitting, standing (on one leg or two), many birds sleep with the bill tucked snugly under the scapulars. The Avocet, Pintail and Mallard all prefer this position. Another popular posture is with the bill resting on the back or drooping onto the breast feathers. The Stork, Cormorant and many birds of prey are good examples. In addition there are a few species, including the Ostrich, which sleep with neck outstretched and head resting on the ground.

If you see a bird in one of these postures you can be fairly sure that it is sleeping. But not always! Herring Gulls, for instance, will suddenly break off in the middle of a territorial dispute and take up sleep postures. However they are not *really* sleeping. Their eyes are wide open and they are clearly keeping an eye on each other. They are 'pseudo-sleeping'.

Perhaps eye closure might be a better indicator of sleep? The problem is that birds rarely close their eyes for more than a few seconds. If you watch one of those snoozing pigeons more closely, it appears to be rhythmically blinking its eyes. Experiments have shown that such rhythmic blinking is diagnostic of sleep in birds. Blinking birds are slower to respond to stimuli and have the characteristic brain patterns of sleeping animals. In fact very few birds sleep without blinking at all.

John Hawkins/Hosking

Roosting Red-legged Partridges . . .

There is obviously more to sleeping than just getting your head down. And birds go to a great deal of trouble to find the right place to use as a bedroom. The main requirement is that the roost place should offer protection from predators and shelter from the elements. Obviously winter is the time when they most need roost sites. Many birds roost in thick cover, gathering together in evergreen jungles, as for instance a rhododendron thicket. Some have learnt to take advantage of centrally heated roost places like street lamps or greenhouses. Those which roost on perches have a special adaptation which ensures that they do not fall off while

Eric & David Hosking

. . . and Pied Wagtails

they are asleep; the more they relax the tighter do their toes grip the perch. A muscular locking device makes the toes curl up as the tarsal joint is flexed. In addition, they have non-slip surfaces on their feet . . .

At night people feel, all self-respecting birds should be tucked up in bed asleep. In fact, birds sleep at odd times throughout the day and night. Whether they are active by day or by night is related to their feeding habits rather than their sleeping habits. In summer they will spend more time feeding than roosting, though if food is plentiful they may go earlier to bed. Wading birds, which feed when the tidal mud-flats are uncovered, work to a tidal rhythm, feeding when the tide is out, whether it is day or night-time.

During the breeding season, birds generally roost in their territories but, afterwards, it is typical of those which feed together that they roost together. The finches and Starlings, which kept themselves to themselves, will now be gathering in multi-family groups to search for food, though Chaffinches will part and all-male parties will forage together. It makes sense for them to sleep together as well. Sparrows, never very territorial at the best of times, search the country in loose-knit gangs. In late autumn, House Martin families will still be going home to their nests at night, though when they have flown these same sanctuaries may serve for sparrow roosts. Swallows gather in enormous numbers on tele-

Open house

One January a keen birdwatcher was in her bedroom in the afternoon and heard a queer tapping noise. At first she took no notice. When the noise was repeated several times she went to the window and opened it. To her utter surprise two Long-tailed Tits (of all birds!) flew in. They circled the room once or twice and then settled on the edge of a lampshade. After a short interval another Long-tailed Tit flew in, and this was followed a little later by two more. The later arrivals behaved exactly as the first ones had done; and moreover, the birds stayed there all night, and appeared to be quite unafraid.

Maxwell Knight

Early morning call

There is a general impression that a bird sleeps with its head tucked beneath the feathers of its wing. The Golden Eagle does not, during the daylight hours at all events, sleep in this position. During several years my wife and I have watched eagles during many days in hides built only a few yards from the eyries. As the mother eagle gradually falls asleep on her nest, her proud eyes close and her head sinks forward until it is resting upon her breast. The eaglet sleeps like a dog. It lies stretched on it side, its head pillowed on the hard branches of the eyrie. The Golden Eagle is a heavy sleeper. One summer night my wife took an all-night watch in the hiding post, and before sunrise, when the eagle was sound asleep, a wandering Blackbird unexpectedly alighted on the rowan tree beside the eyrie and began to sing. The strong liquid notes aroused the eagle with a start. She knew the Ring Ouzel's song but this Blackbird was a stranger. She glared at the singer. He continued to sing undismayed and when he had flown away the eagle closed her eyes and resumed her interrupted sleep.

Seton Gordon

phone wires but go to roost in places like reed-beds, where they funnel down at dusk to cling tight to the vertical stems. Hole-nesters tend to roost in holes, most tits in solitary splendour; Starlings make a noisy exception. Treecreepers sleep alone, hollowing out an egg-shaped burrow in the soft bark of the Californian redwood and pressing themselves tightly in, beaks pointing to the sky and feathers well fluffed. Many birds find a hole or crevice in a tree-trunk or an old building. Blue Tits may find a way into a street lamp, where they have the added benefit of central heating. Pied Wagtails, relatively unsociable in the breeding season, assemble after it and roost gregariously in great numbers, in city-centre trees or in horticultural glasshouses, comfortably warm.

The main advantage of a communal roost is that in cuddling together the birds conserve energy. Wrens may carry that logic to excess, cramming themselves into nestboxes in astonishing numbers. Severe winters hit them hard, so it makes sense for them to join together in beating the cold. Small birds like Wrens have a lot of surface area in relation to their volume. Surface area directly affects heat loss. That is why, each day, they must eat a greater proportion of their bodyweight than larger birds. Hummingbirds do not even try to keep warm at night; they chill to a state of torpor.

I once watched as a steady stream of twenty Wrens made their unobtrusive way into a tit box at dusk. One of my correspondents wrote of thirty-five descending on her nestbox. Even that is nowhere near the record. There was a tit box in Norfolk just 4½x5½x5¾in (11.4x14x14.6cm), which served as a dormitory for no less than sixty-one Wrens. Each bird occupied 2⅓cu in (38cu cm) of space.

Starlings assembling at a staging post before flying off to roost

Eric Hosking

F. Polking/FLPA

Starlings coming in to roost by the light of the moon

Apparently the last arrivals were so desperate to get into the warm that they grouped themselves together and barged in the entrance hole like a rugby scrum. Only one of these birds died; presumably this was the effect of cramped quarters on a bird which was already in poor condition. It is not likely that suffocation was the cause of death; at night bird metabolism slows down and there is a reduced requirement for oxygen.

Birds which roost in the open go to a great deal of trouble to find shelter. Blackbirds will choose thick foliage on the lee side of a building if they have the choice. They also take a lot of trouble to keep warm. Provided they are well fed, they are able to manage this. Fluffing out their contour feathers increases the insulating layer of warm air against their skin, in the manner of a string vest. Their heads are turned so that the bill is tucked away among the feathers on the back, not, incidentally, under the wing. Pigeons prefer to lean forwards, hunching their heads but not tucking them back. Most passerines look headless and rounded when they rest.

Carrion Crows enjoy reputations as solitary birds but in

Martin magic

One evening in July I visited the lake hide at Adel Dam Nature Reserve. About twenty House Martins were flitting over the water. Suddenly, one of them left the others and headed straight for the hide. To my amazement it landed on the open window frame 2in from my left hand.

It was a very young bird, not long out of the nest, and looked very tired. For the next ten minutes we just sat there, looking at each other.

Eventually it flew off to catch some food. I followed its flight through my binoculars and then it returned to the same spot on the hide. These actions were repeated another five times with a short rest in between each flight.

What happened in the next few minutes will be etched on my mind forever. The martin suddenly fluttered off the ledge and landed on my left shoulder; it then walked across the back of my neck and settled on my right shoulder, closed its eyes, tucked its head in its wing and went to sleep. By now all the other martins had disappeared and it was almost after dark. Before leaving the hide, I very gently lifted the bird off my shoulder and placed it on the arm rest below the window. It opened its eyes briefly and then settled down to sleep once more. It certainly was an unbelievable night to remember.

Brian Hewitt

fact roost communally in quite large numbers outside the breeding season. That is true of all the crow family, including Jays, Magpies and Ravens. There may be a hundred or so together; there may be thousands. They settle, call and circle again with noisy excitement before finally settling down for the night, high above the ground, in their chosen piece of woodland.

Swifts may roost on the wing, though at breeding time they will settle on the nest. Observation by radar has shown that they fly high into the sky and settle into a rhythmic pattern in which they beat their wings for a few seconds, then rest for about the same time.

Though Starlings are solitary birds during the early part of the breeding season, their family parties soon join together into those familiar raiding and swooping gangs which forage wherever food is to be found. It is no surprise that they gather for roosting in uncountable numbers.

Towards sunset, the foraging garden parties of Starlings fly off to join others. Following well-defined flight paths, perhaps covering as much as 30 miles, the groups coalesce into enormous flocks: a rush-hour in reverse, with countless thousands making their purposeful way to the chosen rest-place. Reed-beds, rhododendron thickets, woods, ship-yards, city centres all serve their purpose. The build-up begins in mid-June, but reaches a peak much later in the year, after our home-bred birds are joined by a great access of immigrants from the Continent.

When the birds reach the vicinity of the roosting area there will often be a spectaular flying display. Dense clouds of Starlings fill the sky, sweeping back and forth, changing patterns and densities on a mighty scale. It seems that these displays help to locate the roost site and also act like a navigation mark to assist the incoming parties in making a correct landfall. High winds or rain cut short the performance, but even in these conditions the incoming flocks mark the spot long enough to guide in the next squadron, then funnel down to roost leaving the newcomers to take over the signalling. On a good night the swooshing, rocketing and funnelling of massed swarms of Starlings in these aerial firework displays is one of the most exciting natural events to be seen anywhere, at any time.

As the seemingly endless stream of black rockets funnels down, each individual flies in to land at its own bedside. Whether it is to grasp the stem of a reed or the twig of an elm or a ledge of the Bank of England, each has its chosen perch. As in all small birds, a Starling's hind toe is opposed to the others and the flexor tendons are so arranged that when the bird relaxes, its grip is tightened, a comfortable arrangement which ensures that the bird does not fall out of bed the moment it goes to sleep. But before sleep it joins its fellows in singing the evening chorus, a volume of sustained twittering which rises even above the noise level of city traffic. Suddenly the singing will stop, almost as though some sound-man had pulled out a plug; then just as sud-

Room for many more Starlings yet

denly start again. Like the aerial evolutions, which involve mass changes of course seeming to invite multiple collisions, these instant effects are more apparent than real. In fact we are back to the old familiar pattern. When one changes course, they all change course. And they follow suit so quickly that the action appears, or sounds, instantaneous. The truth can be demonstrated by looking at a piece of film showing the 'instant' manoeuvre, then re-running it as a slow-motion 'action replay'. It is easy to spot the way an individual changes course, to be followed first by those nearest it and in turn by the rest of the flock as the message is passed on within a fraction of a second.

Starling roosting habits are all very well, tidy, cosy and resourceful, unless you have to live in their shadow. The sheer weight of numbers breaks branches, the sheer quantity of droppings kills trees and fouls buildings with a barely tolerable mess. The smell becomes revolting. But it's an ill wind that blows no good. Cast your eye along those thickly encrusted ledges, and here and there the odd nitrogen-loving elderberry will be thrusting out of a crevice, imported as a seed in a Starling stomach and voided into the night to take root and enjoy a guano-rich environment.

Sleeping birds may be divided into three groups, those which share our habit and roost during the hours of darkness, those which work the night-shift and sleep by day

155

Roost in peace

What begannet all was the love of a bank lark named Albert Ross for a gull whose tastes were too eggs-pensive for his poultry wages. She was his starling, his swan and only love.

Aviary night this chick had a quail of a time at the local casino and, with a few wings driving heron, she swiftly frittered away his little nest-egg. With no money left, she threatened to auk out of his life and never return. Desperate to keep his dove, our little bank lark cooked the rooks at work, though he knew it was ill-eagle. He thrushed home that night, but the bird had flown.

The next jay, a surprise chick was made on the accounts and Albert was arrested for robin the bank. The life of a gaolbird was hard and in his lonely shell, the bank lark became very bittern. His heart filled with regret and driven beyond the linnet, he simply lost the quill to live, and in a few beak's time was as dead as a dodo.

S. Wade

and those whose rest is determined by the time of the tides. In wintertime waders work the tidal mud- and sand-flats during the period of low water and roost when the flood-tide forces them away. This means that they have two feeding and two sleeping sessions each twenty-four hour period. If there is no moonlight, then they will need to forage in the dark at night-time.

Like the shorebirds, waterfowl also feed to a tidal rhythm, although the activities of wildfowlers may persuade them to become largely nocturnal . . .

Among seabirds there are diurnal and nocturnal species. There are a few, too, which appear to be diurnal or nocturnal at will. The Manx Shearwater at its nesting island is nocturnal, and yet it is often seen flying at sea in bright sunshine. The shearwater lays her single white, polished egg at the extremity of a burrow in the peat of some island. There she sleeps away the long hours of the summer day, and an observer might walk over the colony, consisting perhaps of hundreds of birds, without hearing or seeing a sign of life. But almost on the stroke of midnight the colony awakes. The birds on the nests bestir themselves, and their mates, which have passed the daylight hours out at sea, begin to arrive. For an hour or more an indescribable medley of sound is heard – grunts, squeaks, moans, also sounds recalling the crowing of cock Pheasants and the hooting of owls, to the deep accompaniment of the roar of the Atlantic surge. The darkness cloaks the birds, but from time to time one sees, against the afterglow on the northern horizon, the dark form of a shearwater appearing like some gigantic Swift as it passes at great speed on long narrow wings. Before the first thrush has awakened, the last of the shearwaters' cries have died away.

The Storm Petrel, Mother Carey's chicken, is perhaps the

WREN FAMILY

Watching a family of Wrens being guided to the roost is a delightful experience. As the sun nears the horizon and the long shadows slant across the wood the male is heard calling and, when we draw near, the squeaks of the fledglings are heard here and there. Often before we realise what is toward, the little party has drifted away and we may then be hard put to rediscover the birds before they have disappeared into the dormitory. If the male is leading he moves towards the roost with staccato flights, calling and singing. He indicates the chosen recess by singing outside, and, perhaps, creeping in and out as he did earlier in the year when showing his nests to prospecting females. When the female leads, as she does less often than her mate, she may attract the family's attention by flying repeatedly from where they are assembling to the roosting place. I have seen a Wren fly eleven times across a road before she succeeded in inducing the young to follow; and when they did so they crossed, not at the place indicated, but farther on where overhanging trees shortened the journey. When the roosting nest or niche is attained the mother may sing the dainty whisper or 'swallow' song as she puts the chicks to bed and after they are ensconced. If they are disturbed she will return and lead them to another dormitory, and yet another, if they are again alarmed, but a point is reached – probably due to the increase of darkness – when she departs and leaves them to fend for themselves. This is true of the male also.

E. A. Armstrong

most truly nocturnal of all British seabirds. It is no larger than a Swallow, and indeed in its flight closely resembles one. As to its heralding bad weather, it is true that it does not fly abroad in daylight during fine sunny weather. Yet I have seen it flitting over the sea on a dark midsummer day, when no bad weather followed. Except for a short time in the summer, the Storm Petrel sleeps on the sea. When the young petrel chick is a week old, it is deserted by day by its parents. It is fed during the hours of darkness. By daylight its parents are sleeping on the sea perhaps a dozen miles, perhaps a great deal further, from their nesting island.

It is a remarkable thing that so small and delicate a bird should be able to sleep at all on the Atlantic during the winter months. Scarcely a winter passes but a number are found exhausted, sometimes dying, far from the sea. Their plight is due, not so much to want of food as to want of sleep. Picture their sleeping place out on the Atlantic, hundreds of miles from land. A gale has, perhaps, been blowing for days, even weeks. Immense waves, white crested and menacing hurry past. These breaking waves must render sleep impossible, except for a few seconds at a time. The small petrel, exhausted and longing for sleep, is aroused a fraction of a second before the wall of breaking water is upon it. It must struggle up into the air to escape being engulfed and this seemingly endless task of saving its fragile life continues, day and night, in stormy winters, for weeks at a time. The wonder is that any Storm Petrels survive.

Seabirds remain at sea, however hard their life is. They have the same mistrust of land as a land bird has of the sea. Watch the flights of Gannets returning from a fishing excursion in the Minch to their home on St Kilda. The Outer Hebrides rise between them and their goal. A few minutes' flight would take them across these islands and out on to the open sea beyond, yet, rather than trust themselves over the land, they fly along the east coast of the Outer Hebrides until they reach the entrance to the Sound of Harris. At any hour of daylight, from May until October, parties of Gannets from north and south may be seen converging on the entrance to the Sound of Harris and passing west low over its friendly waters to the open Atlantic where, 50 miles on the western horizon, St Kilda rises, faint and ethereal.

There is no sounder sleeper than the Gannet. Tireless of wing, so that it thinks nothing of a hundred miles' flight to fish for its nestling, it sleeps after a heavy fishing so soundly that on occasions it can be caught on the water. Its ochre head is deeply hidden beneath its feathers; it is deaf, even to the approaching of a passing steamer, until the vessel is almost upon it. A Hebridean fisherman told me that on one occasion he had seen a Gannet disgorge no fewer than seven mackerel before it was able to rise from the water. Presumably it even then retained a fish or two in its capacious crop!

Owls are the most obvious example of birds which work at night and sleep by day. Barn Owls tend to roost in the privacy of tree-holes, or, for that matter, barns, but Tawnies

B. S. Turner/FLPA

Storm Petrel at night

Surprise visitor

Imagine my alarm when, on entering our tiny bathroom, I noticed the curtains twitch. Cautiously I lifted them back and, to my great surprise, I came face to face with a handsome Blue Tit. It fluttered around me as I opened the window and then swooped out to land in a tree opposite, glad to be free.

Nothing unusual about a bird in the house, you might think! But as our windows had been tightly shut against the icy weather, this bird had found an unusual route into our house.

Behind our external guttering is a hole which leads inside the brickwork to the bathroom pipes. These emerge in the space beneath the bath. By chance, we'd dislodged the panel along the side of the bath in order to remove some old tiles and the Blue Tit had squeezed through the narrow gap. Luckily he seemed none the worse for his adventure.

A. Daphne Gallagher

often retire to a dense growth of ivy. Owls that roost in the open are often bedevilled by persistent mobbing attacks from smaller birds. If a foraging Great Tit unexpectedly comes across a Tawny or Long-eared Owl, it will keep its distance and exhibit alarm movements of the wings and tail, at the same time uttering very characteristic calls. As likely as not, these will attract a host of other small birds, and they will all mob the owl together. Mobbing is the common response of birds to certain predators that pose some degree of threat – for example, mammalian hunters such as cats, foxes and snakes from which birds with their ability to fly have more than a sporting chance of escape, providing they are not caught unawares. Presumably this behaviour has survival value to the mobbers by drawing everyone's attention to the whereabouts of the killer. The participants make themselves conspicuous with wing and tail cocking movements, and their alarm calls are usually raucous and repetitive with a wide frequency range to offer as many directional clues to all birds within earshot.

This situation contrasts strongly with the response by small birds to very dangerous aerial predators, such as Peregrines or Sparrowhawks; these elicit alarm reactions of quite a different sort, such as fleeing to the nearest cover and freezing. The calls given are usually thin and high-pitched, and are drawn out with no real beginning or ending, so that it is difficult to locate the whereabouts of the caller; in fact, they have a ventriloquil quality. Alarm is thus signal-led to all within hearing distance without the signaller betraying his own location, an obvious advantage if the enemy is fast and can fly! It is perhaps curious that owls are neither treated with indifference nor as other birds of prey, the fact

Tawny Owl roosting in daytime

Roger Hosking/Hosking

that they, together with crows and Jays for example, are mobbed, indicates that owls must be treated warily by small birds, and rightly, as pellet analysis shows. We can hazard a guess that although resting owls pose little threat to birds in general, some owls are diurnal and more dangerous than others, so that birds cannot afford to take chances. Yet, in fact, owls are not as potentially dangerous to other birds as hawks. When owls are around, and have been discovered, the action which best ensures survival of the local birds seems to lie in exposing the enemy by means of mass displaying. After all, surprise is a predator's chief ally, and to small birds an exposed predator is a 'paper tiger'.

Experiments have shown that owls are recognised by their characteristic rounded shape, and that in Song Sparrows at least, the response to owls is inborn, that is to say no learning is involved. In Chaffinches, Hawfinches, Reed Buntings, and Yellowhammers, the mobbing response does not appear until they are several weeks old, but then occurs automatically as a result of a nervous maturation or growth process, without needing any experience of owls. Furthermore, when stylised owl shapes are placed in aviaries the amount of mobbing tends to wane with each presentation. In the artificial conditions of captivity, successive introductions may even result in a long-term reduction of the mobbing response, so that the model, or even a stuffed owl, eventually becomes accepted as part and parcel of the surroundings. Under natural circumstances one suspects that this would not happen, although a short-term waning of the mobbing response probably does occur, or else owls would be unmercifully harassed throughout their 'sleeping life'. Although owls will occasionally attempt to escape from a troop of 'clacking' and 'chinking' birds, they are more likely to do nothing. The mobbers then lose interest. Experiments have shown that once birds have 'mobbed' in one place, they will either avoid the area or exhibit alarm reactions, perhaps months after, at the spot where the owl was encountered. An owl's roost, once discovered might therefore tend to be

Owls

Owls move in a buoyant manner, as if lighter than air; they seem to want ballast.

A neighbour of mine, who is said to have a nice ear, remarks that the owls about this village hoot in three different keys, in G flat, in B flat and in A flat. He heard two hooting at each other, one in A flat and the other in B flat.

Gilbert White *The Natural History of Selbourne*

159

Eric Hosking

*A Barn Owl returns to her nest in a
Suffolk barn with a vole for her young*

Five young Barn Owls

avoided by birds which have taken part in the mobbing, although should the owl change its sleeping place it will probably have to put up with further mobbing by the local bird population.

Owls are pre-eminently birds of twilight and darkness, and when the dwindling light of day sends most birds flighting swiftly to their roosts the majority of owls are galvanising themselves into action in their daytime hideaways, with yawns, blinks and wing stretches. While other birds are passing away the time as gently throbbing balls of feathers, the nocturnal owl must earn its living, finding enough food to survive, and defending its territory against both space-hungry neighbours and wandering owls only too willing to stake a claim where the hunting is good. There may, too, be the business of wooing a mate, or of meeting the almost insatiable demands of fluffy owlets. All these activities may be carried out under cover of the night sky when the woods, pastures or wetlands may be, at best, only glazed by the silvery glow of the full moon. More often than not, even this aid to navigation and prey-finding will be dimmed by clouds, or the moon will be competing elsewhere with the sun.

There are, of course, owls that hunt by the light of day. The majority of owls, however, are strictly nocturnal or crepuscular, and this fact alone has caused both poets and naturalists to marvel at their habits. Most of us would be lost if we had to live in relative darkness; when the light of the sun wanes we have to flood our homes, offices, and city streets with artificial light, and though it in no way matches the intensity or quality of sunlight, it does relieve us of total dependence upon the sun and variations of light due to weather and season. Because light to us is almost synonymous with life we assume too readily that there can be no other world but our strongly illuminated one, and that animals which live 'outside' our world are eccentric or possess strange supernormal powers. And yet the world as

SAFE SHELTER

Where to find safe shelter for the night is the first great problem the young fledgling has to face. One morning I watched a young Great Tit spend a long time trying to widen a narrow hole in a tree. He managed to get out a few bits of rotten wood, but his beak was not yet strong enough for the job and he could not widen the hole sufficiently for turning round inside it; a bird will not roost back to the opening. There was only one possible solution for the young tit, he tried entering the hole backwards. It was amusing to watch his efforts, for steering the tip of his long tail into the opening proved very difficult and he went through many antics, always with his head turned round to keep an eye on the troublesome tail, before he successfully got the tip into the hole. Then he slowly squeezed the rest of his body backwards along the narrow, level crevice. It was obviously a tight fit and his head came too near the entrance for safety as a roost, but he stayed there for some minutes then came out and went in search of a better one, which later was found and he slept in it at night. He had worked very hard for his bed.

Len Howard

Barn Owl brings a field mouse to its young

perceived by animals depends upon the sense organs they have and the use they make of them.

One of the most appealing features of owls is their big eyes. Their forward position on the face, together with their ability to blink with the upper (not the lower, as in other birds) eyelids, gives them an uncanny, primate-like appearance. This frontal position is no accident and has great survival value.

Owls are by no means unique in also using the *parallax* method in judging distances. This involves their bobbing and pivoting in a most attractive manner in order to get several viewpoints of an object, and to observe the relative movement of things within the visual field of vision as the head shifts around. It is easy to understand the value of this method of judging distances if we cover up one eye; the world then suddenly goes flat, like a photograph, but depth of vision is restored if we move our viewpoint around.

One suspects that many people, in attempting to attribute supernatural powers to night owls, forget that eyes are *light receptors*, and that the generously proportioned ones of owls are no exception. With poetic licence, Joel Peters has immortalised a popular misconception in his lines from 'The Birds of Wisdom':

> Embodied silence, velvet soft, the owl slips through the night,
> With Wisdom's eyes, Athena's bird turns darkness into light.

Even with 'Wisdom's eyes', nocturnal owls cannot see in the dark, and are as blind as we would be in absolute darkness. However, total darkness is rare in nature and confined to places like deep cave systems where only bats, Oilbirds, some fish and a host of invertebrate animals have penetrated. The truth of the matter is that owls are particularly well equipped to make use of whatever light is available, and can detect and approach objects in conditions of illumination that we would subjectively think of as pitch blackness. An owl flying in to the kill has to make allowance for the fact that its talons are following a different trajectory from that of its head; they are hanging below the body and correspondingly displaced from the line that joins the head and the prey. When there is sufficient light for a Barn Owl to see its prey, the bird launches itself into the air and makes for the rodent in one decisive glide; but just before striking the wings are raised, the head thrown back, and the feet, with the razor-sharp talons outstretched, are projected forwards. When striking in total darkness the behaviour of the owl differs, as has been demonstrated with the aid of infrared photography. When the mouse first rustles some leaves, the owl turns its head towards the prey and, once orientated like this, it must hear one more sound before striking. If it does receive another sound clue, the flight towards the mouse is not a quick sure glide, but the bird flaps vigorously with the feet swinging underneath the body like a pen-

In search of prey

About an hour before sunset they sally forth in search of prey, and hunt all round the hedges of meadows and small enclosures for mice, which seem to be their only food. In this irregular country we can stand on an eminence and see them beat the fields over like a setting-dog, and often drop down into the grass or corn.

Gilbert White *The Natural History of Selborne*

dulum. When it has arrived over the prey, again the head is thrown back and the feet swept forwards into the same path as the head was taking for a moment before. So when Barn Owls are flying 'blind', it is the head which is flying on a collision course with the prey, and not until the last moment are the weapons substituted for the sound-detectors.

Another characteristic of the majority of owls, and one which has frightened people out of their wits after dark, is the ability of these birds to appear and disappear like apparitions. Whereas most birds ride the air on whirring noisy

LUMINOUS BARN OWLS

Some eighty years ago the 'transactions of the Norfolk Naturalists' Society' carried an extraordinary account of what was almost certainly a pair of luminous Barn Owls. They were seen on a misty February afternoon floating like will-o'-the-wisps above a patch of marshy ground. One 'emerged from a covert about 200yd distant, flying backwards and forwards across the field, at times approaching within 50yd of where I was standing . . . it literally lighted up the branches of the trees as it flew past.'

The owls – if that is what they were – had probably picked up phosphorescence from roosting in the crumbling 'touchwood' of a tree smitten with honey fungus. Yet they were an eerie enough sight to convince one astonished Norfolk naturalist that the birds had the power to generate their own illumination.

Barn Owls have always hovered between the light and the dark. They have been viewed with admiration and superstitious nervousness in about equal measure. Of all our birds of prey they have lived on the closest terms with human beings, and yet are still surrounded by mystery and folk mythology. The Latin name, *Strix*, was the Roman word for witch, and there are stories of owls being burned for witchcraft in the Middle Ages. Their screeching call is an almost universal omen of bad luck, and dead birds are sometimes nailed on barn doors to frighten off evil intruders – of all sorts and substances.

At the same time they were respected by farmers for their prowess at keeping down rats and mice, and increasingly over the past two centuries, their pale vigil kept over the winter pastures has seemed like a reassurance. They are village familiars; white witches, if witches at all.

Of all the Barn Owls I have watched – fewer each year, sadly – I cannot recall ever seeing one more than a few hundred yards from a village or human settlement. They haunt the roughest, oldest edges of the parish landscape – the green lanes and stackyards and hedgebanks – and with those open, inquisitive faces that look as if they are mounted directly on to the wings, seem like guardian spirits, patrollers of the bounds.

In the Cornish churchyard of St Filii de Eglosros, one first day of spring, I saw a Barn Owl cross paths with a tramp, headed east with a full backpack. In Dorset, another peered inscrutably out of a hole in an old lime kiln. In East Anglia, during the sixties and early seventies, they were constant evening companions, dipping along the lerges in front of the car. This March, in north Norfolk, I watched one in mid-afternoon, endlessly quartering a patch of rough fenny grassland that bordered a village green.

But no Barn Owl can ever match the first. Our childhood owls nested in a barn just 30yd from the A41, and their hunting range corresponded almost exactly with the territory of our local gang: over the old brick piles that were all that remained of a Victorian mansion, up the ivy-clad wall that lined the council estate, across the steep field we used for tobogganing, then down, if we were lucky, through the bosky edges of our back gardens. The memory of it beating past the poplar trees – burnished gold wings flickering against lime-green leaves in the evening light – is one of the few images of childhood I can recall with absolute clarity.

Those home owls vanished just before the barn was demolished and the whole area was given over to a housing estate. Now they are almost extinct right across the Chilterns. In the country as a whole the population is only a third of what it was fifty years ago. The Barn Owl has been under enormous stress during this period from pesticides, unscrupulous wings, owls make their way in and out of the shadows in utter silence. Even a 6lb (2.7kg) Eagle Owl flies with hardly a whisper on its 5ft (1.5m) wing span. It is not difficult to appreciate the survival value for owls of silent flight. First, to a hunter that surprises its victims by pouncing out of the darkness, noisy whistling wings would shatter the silence of the night and give the prey warning of impending attack. Although many nocturnal rodents have miserable sight, their powers of hearing adequately make up for it. Secondly, as owls use sound clues to detect and to home in on their prey, swishing wings would hardly aid their powers of dis-

gamekeepers, loss of nesting trees. As many as 5,000 may be killed every year on the roads. But none of these factors, taken either separately or together, seemed sufficient to explain such a continuing, remorseless decline.

Now Colin Shawyer seems at last to have solved the riddle. Putting an immense body of field records through sophisticated computer analysis, he has shown beyond any reasonable doubt that the Barn Owls' decline in Britain is a result of a deteriorating climate and the loss of hunting (not nesting) habitat. Taken together these factors severely limit the small mammals on which the Barn Owl depends. Even if the adult birds survive a hard winter, they can find it impossible to raise young in our increasingly cool, wet springs. One of Colin Shawyer's most inspired and convincing programmes was to correlate nesting sites with rainfall. It turns out that in the dry east of England, Barn Owls nest chiefly in trees. In the high rainfall areas of the west and north they nest almost exclusively in buildings, despite an abundance of suitable natural sites. What they are after is a roof over their heads, something to keep the rain off their easily waterlogged fledglings.

But the overriding impression of this report is of Barn Owls as human familiars, haunting the margins of our own society. They will nest in almost any kind of man-made structure – chapels, mine shafts, even motorway bridges – provided they are not too sanitised and tidied. They hunt along the margins, too, in those left-over patches that are neither wholly cultivated nor wholly wooded: the boundary hedges, the streamside roughs, the muddles and back-lots, all those places that are today so ruthlessly gobbled up.

Ten years ago, I wrote in the conclusion of a book called *The Common Ground*, that we might do worse than reintroduce the ancient idea of a tithe – an offering of a tenth of the land to ensure the continued fertility of the earth. Most of our fellow creatures depend more or less on this marginal fraction, and to the Barn Owl it is critical. The owl's sad decline is a reflection of our own greed, and its return to our parishes would be the surest indication that we have mended some of our ways.

Richard Mabey

Eric Hosking

Young Tawny Owls are adventurous...

Help at hand

One evening last summer a baby owl fell out of a large cedar tree near our house. We were wondering what to do when it started to climb very slowly back up the tree. We rushed off to get a camera before it had disappeared – and in that moment a cat appeared from nowhere and started to go after it. We couldn't reach the cat and waited in horror for the next few moments until, believe it or not, a huge owl (mother/father?) suddenly appeared, ignored us, and with one great sweep of its wings knocked the cat for six to the ground! With that it flew silently back to another tree and the baby got home safely. The parent owl had evidently been watching the whole time and took action as soon as it was necessary. The cat was not injured but beat a very hasty retreat.

Mrs G. Winnett

---

crimination; in other words, they would deafen themselves to the squeaks and rustles of their prey.

Owls achieve their noiseless flight in two ways. They are endowed with generously proportioned wings, so that their weight is spread over, and supported by, relatively large surface areas when they are flying. Although their portly shape might lead one to the conclusion that they are heavy, their loose plumage, in fact, covers comparatively small bodies. A Barn Owl weighing 505g (1oz is equivalent to 26g) has a wing area of about 1.680sq cm (ie about 1lb supported on an area equivalent to three foolscap sheets of paper), which means that the wing loading is only about 1gm for every 3.4sq cm. By comparison, the Common Crow of North America has a similar weight to that of the Barn Owl but has a wing loading of 1g/2.4sq cm. The higher the wing loading the more difficult it is for the bird to support itself in the air and the more noise the hard-working wings are likely to make (consider the fuss a heavy, round-winged Pheasant makes as it explodes from the undergrowth!). Owls with their low wing loadings glide easily and can fly leisurely through woodlands, or quarter the ground at comparatively low speeds. Low wing loading leads to buoyant flight, and this has an even greater survival value for Short-eared Owls of open spaces, which can actually outclimb a swift-flying Peregrine Falcon. Incidentally, the migratory owls, like the Short-eared and Long-eared, have relatively longer wings than sedentary species, and this no doubt helps them in their long journeys. Also, forest-inhabiting owls like their raptor counterparts, have comparatively short rounded wings to aid manoeuvrability, an important asset in habitats criss-crossed by twigs and branches.

The second adaptation towards achieving quiet flight concerns the structure of the feathers, particularly of the long primary pinions. In most birds whose lives are not dominated by the need for silence, the pinions are usually stiff and resilient, and cut through the air like a knife. Those of typically nocturnal owls, by contrast, are finely fringed at their edges and have a velvet pile on their surface. The fine combs are obviously concerned with minimising the noise that wings normally make when they beat through the air, presumably by damping down the movement of air rushing around the surface of the aerofoils. The damping may use up some energy, but this is well spent. The more strictly diurnal Hawk, Pygmy and Fishing Owls have hard plumage and, not surprisingly, make more noise on the wing.

The popularity of the owl then stems from its design for coping with, and hunting in, the darkness. Enormous frontal eyes stare out from cheek-like facial discs, and they have wide, almost bulbous, heads like ours for accommodating the widely spaced and highly developed ears; both are part of the owl's equipment for homing in on elusive and alert prey. The tools of a killer, although of mesmeric quality, to us are never particularly endearing. The owl, however, misleads us because the tools of his trade are neatly concealed

John Hawkins/Hosking

Tawny Owls hunt in noiseless flight

– as near as birds will ever produce to the wolf in sheep's clothing. Soft, billowing plumage fills the body out into a cuddly, round shape, hiding cruel, savage talons and a de-curved predatory beak which, incidentally, pokes out just where we would expect a nose to be! Add to this a seemingly elastic neck and cute ear tufts, and here is a bird which is a caricature of man. Athene's bird might not be able to work the miracle of turning night into day, but the truth in the case of owls turns out to be no less remarkable.

Seabirds

Martin B. Withers/FLPA

Gannet with young

In Britain we have well over a dozen different species of gull, some of them obscure enough to delight any rarity-hunting birdwatcher. But one of them has the distinction of being the best known of all seabirds. One of the hardy annuals in broadcasting jokes, at least among the public, has been, that the BBC possesses but one gramophone record of 'the seagull's' voice, trotted out on any occasion when the atmosphere of the sea is required. In fact there are umpteen recordings of gull calls, but the typical alarm cry of the Herring Gull serves better than any other sound to create an instant mind-picture of the sea, or more strictly the sea coast. Quite apart from its evocative call, the gull's white plumage and strong, graceful flight mark it out as one of the very few birds which almost everyone can identify, however meagre their interest in the subject.

The Herring Gull, and its smaller cousin the Black-headed Gull, are the two commonest species (the Common Gull is separate and not particularly common). These are the ones most often seen in the seaside towns and, nowadays, many other towns and cities.

They are easily distinguished apart. The Herring Gull has grey upper-wing surfaces with black tips terminated by a white spot, flesh-coloured legs and feet, and a yellow bill with a striking red spot. The Black-headed Gull has a chocolate-brown head(!) in the breeding season, and its bill and legs are red. In winter the head loses the all-over chocolate, but retains a black flash behind the eye. The juveniles of both species are a dusky mottled brown or grey, and perhaps at this stage it's best to opt gracefully out of writing about gull identification, because the variety of plumages in both adult and juvenile is not something to go into lightly. Apart from the Black-backed Gulls, the Herring and Black-headed are far and away the most likely everyday gulls. A very crude division would have the Herring as the typical gull of coast and estuary, whereas the Black-headed is a bird of inland waters. But there is considerable overlap.

Both species have increased their numbers enormously within this century. Herring Gulls have always been abundant, but are at present undergoing an explosive increase. They breed all round the coast of the British Isles, and even in some inland areas, mainly in Ireland, where they colonise

A mixed nesting colony of Guillemots and Kittiwakes

lakes and bogs. In Cornwall they have taken to china-clay pits.

These birds are scavengers by trade, and they have benefitted hugely by exploiting the waste products of man. Not so very long ago they patrolled beaches for tideline casualties, then they tidied the offal and waste from the fishing grounds and shore-based fishing communities, but their breakthrough came with the growth of rubbish dumps and sewage farms, and even the handouts of holiday tourists and retired, lonely, seaside residents.

Black-headed Gulls nest in colonies inland as well as on the coast: on sand dunes and slacks, marshes and saltings, freshwater marshes and rushy loch-sides. The nest is a scruffy structure of any available vegetation, sometimes nothing much at all, just a scraped saucer-shape on the ground. Once these gulls were much esteemed for food, and a nesting colony on a property was regarded as a valuable asset. Reeds and rushes were cut away in the autumn to prepare a welcome ground for the returning birds in the spring.

Herring Gulls nest on the rooftops of seaside towns

Brian Hawkes

Puffins line up for take-off on their fishing trips

Young birds were collected in great numbers, the gentry assembling to see the sport, and subsequently to enjoy the feasting, patronised by bishops and nobility. Thomas Bewick tells of gulls fetching five shillings a dozen, and of £60 worth being collected in a few days – a princely sum in the first part of the nineteenth century.

Herring Gulls have been exploited more for their eggs than their meat, and still are to a certain extent. Like the Black-headed Gulls, they nest mainly in colonies, but on coastal sites, cliff-top ledges and the grassy slopes of small islands.

In the early spring the birds congregate at courting grounds, where pairs stand about and unpaired birds trumpet their suitability. The males lower their heads, beak on throat, and croon. They snatch at bits of grass, and just as impulsively drop them again. Other males, accepting the challenge, behave in similar fashion. They approach each other, then back away, trying their weight. Several males may group together, and status and rank slowly emerge.

There may even be fights and a few lost feathers. The females may not appear to be involved, but in due course birds make attachments, marked by formal promenades, where they bow and circle each other, bow again and finally sit face-to-face, in what looks very much like an olde-tyme-dance performance. Over a period of time the pair-bond is formed and consummated, with much excitement and noise, billing and begging. The large nest is comfortably built by both sexes of whatever vegetable material is avail-

COUNTING GUILLEMOTS

Guillemots on a ledge can present the enquiring ornithologist with a problem. It may be easy to count the individuals, but how many pairs are breeding? You have the same sort of hopeless feeling when inspecting a bowl full of walnuts and trying to decide how many shells contain rotten kernels.

The trouble with Guillemots is that they are adept at hiding their single egg and, at a later stage, the chick, from prying eyes of potential predators – hence also from prying ornithologists. They huddle together, making it impossible to pick out mated pairs and the confusion is made worse by a variable number of apparently non-breeding birds. Experts have, therefore, given up trying to count Guillemot *pairs*, and have decided to make the best of a bad job by taking several counts of *individuals* at the same, carefully delimited site.

Last summer I had to count Guillemots and other seabirds at various colonies in Orkney. These counts were to establish a standard against which future populations could be measured. The day I remember best was, for Orkney, a scorcher: the temperature had soared into the upper fifties, and local people were stripping right down to their anoraks. Furthermore, the wind had dropped away to a murmuring Force 5. The count site that afternoon was on Marwick Head, a beautiful west-coast sea-cliff reserve, recently acquired by the RSPB. I settled into an almost-safe, Jones-size niche at the top of the 300ft high cliff, the biggest of my count sites, with about 1,500 Guillemots – a fine array of birds on ledges, more ledges and yet more ledges.

I was in the eight or perhaps the nine hundreds, when I started wondering how a Guillemot, rushing in from the sea on whirring wings, could recognise its home at Niche No 27a, Ledge 14, Cliff Section 3/21/05b, let alone land successfully with a large fish in its bill. That bird there, for example, landed so neatly before sidling up to another with the air of one who had spent too long at sea with the lads. The home bird looked up from hours of slaving over a hot egg, and delivered a series of sharp pecks which the errant fish-bringer accepted with a few resigned shrugs before settling down to another session of domestic responsibility. Now where was I? Oh well, back to the start: one Guillemot, two, three . . .

Things went better the second time; no mind-wandering but intense concentration, so that something like a warm wet fish behind the right ear was something of a surprise. A large black labrador was licking my neck, then with zealous affection it leapt down for a game on the edge of the cliff. I'd already lost my composure and my woolly hat, and now the precipitate arrival of the dog threatend to hurl Jones and telescope into salty oblivion 300ft below. The labrador suddenly seemed to realise this – it leapt back on to the cliff-top. I gathered my scattered wits and equipment, and began once again: one Guillemot, two three . . .

I was getting on remarkably well: no dogs, no people, and well over a thousand birds tallied. The heady scent of the flowers of cliff-clinging plants wafted over me, but I continued manfully until somewhere in the twelve – or was it thirteen – hundreds, I was racked by an enormous, pollen-induced sneeze. Amazed Fulmars leapt off ledges all around, and when the smoke cleared, I found I'd bumped the telescope and it was now set for counting migrating Swifts at 10,000ft. There was nothing else for it: one Guillemot, two, three . . .

This was definitely the last attempt. If it failed, I was all set to resign before taking up something comparatively simple, like brain surgery or nuclear physics. Luckily for the Royal College of Brain Surgeons, the last count was duly completed, but if you think it's easy to count Guillemots . . .

Peter Hope-Jones

able – grass, seaweed, heather – and is made complete with three, sometimes four, speckled olive eggs.

These nests are mainly built on cliff ledges and island slopes, but over the last sixty years or so there has been what at first sight is a striking departure from this norm. Herring Gulls (and to a lesser extent, Kittiwakes, and Lesser Black-backs) took to nesting on the roofs and amongst the chimney-tops of buildings. Although the first records date back to 1910, the phenomenon really became established in

A crowded Guillemot nesting colony – note the bridled form top right

David T. Grewcock/FLPA

Cormorant at nest with chicks

Tony Soper

the twenties, in the south-west, spreading by the thirties to the south-east, and subsequently to the east coast and to Wales and Scotland. When 'Operation Seafarer' counted the seabirds of the British Isles in 1969–70, there were about 1,300 gull's nests on buildings. And although this number represents an insignificant proportion of the Herring Gull population – most of them still nesting on traditional sites – the venture has had a considerable impact on some people·

Being colonised by Herring Gulls is something of a traumatic experience. The birds can be aggressive in defence of the nest territory, and if your front drive happens to come within those bounds then they will divebomb you without mercy. In Newquay, Cornwall, where the habit has been long established, people have actually lost blood in these battles. So they can be awkward neighbours. And of course many people regard their natural processes as dirty habits especially when the droppings fall on their newly washed status symbol. In Brixham car park it is well established, incidentally, that blue cars are bespattered more than those of other colours. Genteel resorts like Torquay have for years been perplexed by the problem. Anxious to rid the town of muck-producing birds, the council has toyed with solutions ranging all the way from egg-collecting to shooting, none of which can possibly work; they resolutely avoid the real cause of the 'problem' which is, of course, the availability of easy feeding at rubbish tips, augmented by fish offal and the handouts of sympathetic visitors and gull-loving residents.

The spectacle of ignorance fighting the gulls of the world is not enlightening. The most amusing 'solution' was the suggestion that boys should be paid to collect the seagulls' eggs. Quite apart from the fact that not a few boys would inevitably have ended at the bottom of the cliffs, the removal of a gull's egg simply stimulates the female to lay another. The female gull will, rather like the domestic hen, continue to lay until she sees the right number of eggs in the nest

Tony Soper

Perhaps a careless choice of nest site for this Shag on the Farne Islands

before she goes broody. In fact the eggs are very good to eat, and if the proposal had been to institute a form of farming it would have made some sense.

When the eggs hatch, the nestlings only remain within the nest's confines for three or four days. On the traditional breeding grounds they then find their way to the nearest cover, the shade of bracken or a rock crevice. But up on the rooftops we have the curious spectacle of young birds on the eaves, circumnavigating the chimney pots and strutting in the gutter, waiting for the periodic arrival of the parents with food for regurgitation. As time goes by they play with any bits of twig or pieces of slate which lie about, and they run up and down the roof-slopes, flapping their wings and preparing for take-off. There is no doubt that they make a lot of noise and a lot of mess. Nor is there any doubt that in their role as scavengers they tidy up a lot of mess. And they bring colour and interest to a lot of lonely lives. Even in central London, these enterprising birds have established a stronghold in, of all places, the Regent's Park Zoo. There they have taken over an artificial 'cliff' conveniently placed alongside the seabird aviary, so they have the stimulus of an existing 'colony' of gulls and other seabirds. Doubtless they will breed on the rooftops of the metropolis, and after all from the bird's point of view the ledges and slopes of those buildings are only another version of the more usual cliff-slopes. What really attracts them in the first place is the food; there's no shortage of nest sites.

They are not choosy in their attitude to food. Scavenging is their main preoccupation, but they will hunt mice, small birds and rabbits, hawk for flying insects and, when they get the chance, steal from man. Leave a fishbox unattended for a few minutes on a quay and the gulls will move in, just as freely as they'll take your sandwiches. One is said to have entered a restaurant and flown off with a fillet of cod, which it promptly found too heavy and dropped on to the street below. That was a mistake, but at other times gulls

---

Gull stopped play

I was playing golf one day in January, when to my amazement a Herring Gull swooped down, picked up a ball on the green and flew off with it. It then proceeded to drop the ball from a height, trying to interrupt it before it landed. It did this several times before dropping the ball into a bush where it was irretrievably lost.

This sort of behaviour is well known in large gulls. The bird follows the ball down to pick it up immediately after it hits the ground. A hard object which might be food such as a shellfish, is usually dealt with in this way, and the unbroken golf-ball stimulates the bird to repeated attempts to 'open' it.

John Grover

Razorbill in flight

John Barlee/FLPA

will drop cockles or hermit crabs deliberately from a height on to pavements or promenades, in order to break the shell and get at the juicy meat within.

Another piece of gull behaviour is often seen on places like playing-fields and water meadows, when rain has left them soaked. The gulls find a sopping patch and mark time on it, trampling up and down, encouraging creatures like worms to come to the surface. For the job the gull foot, rather like a duck's paddle, is very well designed. Much the same thing happens on the sea-shore, Black-headed Gulls in particular specialising in 'stationary puddling' in shallow pools, picking off the small marine worms and molluscs which are swirled to the surface. Perhaps gulls hunt cockles this way, too. You may try it for yourself easily enough, next time you are on a sandy beach at low water of spring tides. Pat the sand with your palms to make a quicksand. This is quite an effective way of discovering what shellfish are just under the surface.

By comparison with its size, the British Isles provide a home base for an astonishing number of the world's seabirds. Just what it is that makes our islands so special that nearly three-quarters of the *world* population of Razorbills nests on them? Most good seabird islands have precipitous cliffs, providing natural nature reserves with little need for fencing. They are further guarded by treacherous and almost always rough seas – or so it seems to those trying to land to observe the seabirds. Some of the cliffs and stacks are gigantic and magnificent, rising 1,000ft or more from the sea. But for seabirds it is important that the rock is of the right type, with strata and fractures producing a habitable terrain. Caves provide sites for Black Guillemots, smaller crevices places for the Razorbills and Puffins to lay their eggs. Boulder screes house more Razorbills and Puffins, with petrels and Manx Shearwaters for good measure. The cliff ledges, which need to be more or less horizontal to be of use (hence the importance of how the rock fractures), provide a home for Gannets, Guillemots, Kittiwakes and Fulmars.

Most Razorbill colonies are relatively small, and often interspersed among other auks. Because the nest is hidden, observation and counting is difficult, but the Razorbill is perhaps the most handsome of our seabirds. The plumage is immaculately contrasting black and white, the black offset by elegant white trim on the beak and in a fine white line of tiny feathers running from beak to eye – suggested by some to be a sighting device when hunting underwater.

Structurally, the Razorbill and the other auks are part way, as it were, to penguins. They lead a split existence, partly in the air, partly on land, and partly on or under the water, but their major adaptations are for swimming. Their wings are reduced in size and stiffened – approaching penguin flippers – which gives poor flight but excellent underwater propulsion. The head and body are streamlined, the eyes deep-set, for underwater movement, with the extended webbed feet serving like control fins on a submarine. The body is purpose-built for deep diving, with an immensely strong ribcage. The ribs are fused, through projecting spurs, to each other and to a rigid backbone and breastbone, forming a rigid box protecting the vital organs from the crushing pressure of the sea.

A recent census suggested that the Guillemot population exceeded the half-million mark in Britain and Ireland, and they seem to be holding their own in the modern environment, despite their all-too-often tragedies when caught up in oil spills. A glance at photographs of the seabird stacks of St Kilda or the Farne Islands confirms this, with Guillemots packed tight on the tops and ledges, standing upright and looking much like a month's uncollected deliveries of milk bottles. Each new arrival, trying to find a space to land, causes noisy confusion as he blunders among his fellows.

The Guillemot has one of the simplest of all nests: it just lays its single egg on a ledge, with no nest foundation, not even a few sprays of seaweed for decoration. The egg that allows such simplicity is a masterpiece of evolutionary design. It is large – 4–5in (10cm) long – and tapered sharply like a pear. If knocked accidentally (as often happens in such crowded conditions) it rolls in a tight circle but stays on the ledge. In similar circumstances, the normally shaped Razorbill egg would have as much chance of survival as a breakfast egg rolling off the kitchen table: so Razorbills tend to be crevice nesters.

There are other differences, too. Razorbills, like Puffins, bring fish to their young in beakfuls, often of ten or more but sometimes up to fifty sand-eels or small fry. The Guillemot usually comes home with a single much larger, fish for its youngster. In the crowded circumstances of colony life, even feeding must be circumspect. To exclude neighbours' greedy offspring, the Guillemot extends its wings like an umbrella, surrounding its chick, and then transfers the fish head first, so that it can be easily swallowed. When the chick is very young, not all the fish may get in at first attempt, and replete Guillemot chicks are a common sight with several inches of fish tail dangling from their mouths. Digestion is astonishingly rapid, however, and a couple of hours later the chick is clamouring for more.

Some Guillemots, particularly in the north, show a peculiar white ring round the eye, with a bar stretching back, looking like a pair of spectacles. They were once known as a separate species, the Bridled Guillemot, and just what the function of this plumage variety is, nobody knows; nor why it becomes more frequent as you travel north.

Guillemot and Razorbill chicks leave the nesting cliffs before they are full fledged: usually they are about two-thirds grown. They have plenty of warm down, covered by a layer of water-repellent body feathers so that they can swim safely. The 'wings' are mere bristly stubs at this stage. Their early departure from the nest is amazing: they jump off into the sea, which may be several hundred feet below!

E. A. James/FLPA

The Razorbill's contrasting black and white plumage

Puffin

Despite their inability to fly, feathers and fat combined apparently have a sufficient cushioning effect to allow them to bounce off any projections on the way down without harm. The operation is often made more hazardous by taking place at night, but at least this allows the chicks a better chance of escaping marauding gulls. Once off the cliff, the chick swims with its parents – often in a group with other families – out to the open sea to complete its development away from the gull menace ever-present on the cliffs.

Much scarcer than its larger relative, the Black Guillemot is particularly a bird of the islands of the north-west. It is jet black, save for bold white wing patches and bright vermilion feet – so bright as to be visible underwater even at long range. The Black Guillemot is a cave nester, usually in colonies of only a few pairs. Strangely, unlike its auk cousins, it lays two eggs and often manages to rear both young. Off-duty birds occasionally roost in buoys, emerging in a black cascade when their roost is rocked by the wake of a passing vessel. The solemn note of the bell-buoy is then joined by their improbable whistling tinkle of a call. Another improbable feature is its change to winter plumage. The other auks become generally greyer, but the Black Guillemot emerges almost as the photographic negative of itself in summer: the body white with contrasting mainly black wings.

The Puffin, perhaps more than any other bird of sea or land, has the ability to arouse the enthusiasm and fascination of man. Often described as 'like little men in evening dress', perhaps it is the upright stance of the Puffin, and its busybody enthusiasm to observe and participate in all the social functions of its neighbourhood, that most endears it to us. For all its handsome charm and its popularity, the Puffin is most difficult to study. Its coming and goings about the colony are notoriously fickle, despite the spectacle when a whole large colony decides to indulge in an evening 'flypast'.

Puffins outside nest burrow – compare the winter and summer plumage

J. Watkins/FLPA

David Hosking

Puffin with a fine billful of sand eels

The Puffin is one of the most sociable of birds, and it would not be difficult to interpret many of its yawning and preening and sleeping poses, and the visiting of neighbours, pattering and parading about, in the light of our own human attitudes and habits. Brawls between neighbouring males are perhaps rather more common than they are at the tavern corners with us, but possibly less serious. Usually the Puffin is quite a friendly fellow in his many gregarious hours, and a group standing and sitting about on a cliff-edge or an outcrop of rock of a fine evening in summer is most strongly reminiscent of a crowd of happy human beings by the sea-side. Even to the end of the season, in late July, the Puffins continue their bill-rubbing and sociable assemblies and visiting. Another activity which goes on throughout the summer is the gathering of nesting material. Bits of grass and feathers from the land and odd straws picked up at sea are carried into the burrow long before (and after) the egg is laid. Some Puffins can be seen vigorously tearing up the withered stems and roots of last year's grasses on the cliff-edge, and carrying these to build quite a substantial lining to the burrow, but as often as not some of this material will be dropped along the passage to the burrow quite indiscriminately. So that nest-making seems to be no serious affair, but merely another outlet for superabundant energy.

All this activity on land is conducted during the hours of

daylight. There is no movement at night, every Puffin being then at sea or in its burrow.

The Puffin lays its single egg usually at the end of a burrow dug in the soil eigther by itself or some other burrowing bird or rabbit. The egg is white with a faint zone of lilac freckling around the big end. Early in April the old burrows are cleared out, enlarged, and improved, the Puffin working with its powerful bill as a pick, and shovelling the loose material back out of the burrow with its strong webbed feet, which have very sharp claws.

Examination of the Puffin at egg-laying time – end of April and early May – has proved that it has not one, but two, brood spots, suggesting that at one time during its evolution it used to brood two eggs. These brood spots are placed one each side of the body just forward of the 'thigh', so that the Puffin holds its egg well against one side of its breast, almost under its wing. This is impossible to observe in a burrow-nesting species, but it can easily be studied in the Razorbill (nesting in the open) which has two brood spots similarly placed.

David Grewcock/FLPA

A pair of Bass Island Gannets in mating display

TENEMENT DWELLERS

Our superb seabird colonies provide some of the greatest summer spectacles for birdwatchers in Europe. It is the combination of sight, sound and smell – the exposure – that makes the experience. No film, however well made, can ever match the thrill of peering over the edge of several hundred feet of rocky ledges, through milling streams of auks, Kittiwakes and Fulmars to the boiling sea below.

Within the apparent chaos is extreme organisation and great efficiency. Each species occupies the part of the cliff that suits its precise nesting requirements. Indeed very few locations can meet the needs of all our seabirds.

Terns and Black-headed Gulls need flat, open areas – low islands, sand dunes, beaches – where they make scrapes on the bare ground or under vegetation. Shags often find sites for their large, untidy nests on rocky shores, Guillemots, Razorbills and Kittiwakes need crevices or ledges on vertical faces for their eggs, and can form large colonies only on sutstantial cliffs.

The Guillemot lays its egg, which is pointed to keep it from rolling, on a bare ledge, and the Razorbill makes use of a crevice. Kittiwakes build their nests out of seaweed and guano on a ledge or the snag of a cliff.

Such sites are provided only by certain geological formations, although sometimes man-made structures will fill the bill for Kittiwakes (Dunbar Castle and the warehouses at South Shields harbour fine colonies).

The grassy ledges at the top of a cliff may make good nesting sites for Fulmars. These birds are a recent addition to most colonies, having increased in numbers over the past hundred years by exploiting the abundance of offal provided by the fishing industry. In the last century their only breeding place was on the remote islands of St Kilda, which remain a stronghold, but now there are more than a quarter of a million pairs of Fulmars breeding all along the British shores.

Gannets build nests either on ledges on the cliff face or in serried ranks along the top, and in some cases can cover a whole island. While some colonies, such as Bass Rock, are very ancient, new colonies are also being founded every few years.

Gannets use nesting material picked up from the sea, and the recent introduction of zero-buoyancy plastic netting has caused dreadful problems. The birds become entangled in the netting they have brought to the nest, and since the material does not decompose, it is becoming an increasingly serious problem. The nests at Bempton Cliffs in Yorkshire have to be cleaned up every year by local birdwatchers with the help of coastguards and cliff-rescue teams.

Kittiwake chicks stand tight in their nests and therefore avoid falling over the edge. But the chicks of other gulls wander and are not

The newly born chick is covered with a sooty down and is quite active immediately. It quickly learns to walk. It is fed on small fishes brought by both parents. Sand-eels and the fry of herring, mackerel, and pollack are numerous in inshore waters from mid-June onwards. When the high tide fills the bays and creeks with the deep-blue Atlantic water the abundant shoals of these rapidly growing young fish are brought up close to the cliffs and you may see their orderly regiments gleaming silver and green as they swim in columns close to the red rocks of the island. So twice each day the 'table' is spread for the Puffins to gather food, and it is during the two high-water periods in each day during June and July that the adults are busiest in gathering food for their chick. As this grows the parents are able to bring in still larger catches of larger fry to match the appetite of the voracious young bird.

It is popularly supposed that the Puffin holds its catch of fish nicely in its bill with the heads all one side and the tails the other. This is, however, just a pleasant fancy, for in fact the fish are carried irregularly. I cannot say how the Puffin

David T. Grewcock/FLPA

Fulmar at its nest on the Farne Islands

at all bright about heights. Their nests therefore tend to be sited on shallow-sloping parts of the cliff or on top of it. The man-made equivalents are the roofs of large buildings, which are used by Herring and Lesser Black-backed Gulls.

Several species nest in burrows in or on top of cliffs. These include the Puffin and the nocturnal Manx Shearwater, which may take over rabbit burrows; they will also nest in boulder-scree areas, along with Storm Petrels – tiny, nocturnal seabirds, about the size and shape of House Martins.

In the far north, the scarce Arctic and Great Skuas may breed on top of cliffs. The skuas not only steal from other seabirds flying in with food, but also take many eggs and chicks.

When watching a colony, don't approach too close. If you scare incubating or brooding birds away from their charges, predatory gulls may swoop in for a quick meal. The loss of a chick or egg is a tragedy for a seabird. Most species can only raise a single chick each year and are seldom able to lay a replacement.

A ledgeful of tightly packed Guillemots, for example, will contain numerous pairs each maintaining a tiny territory. This may be defended for weeks, often months, before the single precious egg is laid. Indeed, if they are breeding successfully, the same birds are likely to remain paired and to occupy exactly the same few square inches of rock for years.

In a Kittiwake colony, the experienced breeders take the central places. They often retain the same mate from year to year, and they occupy their sites earlier, lay eggs earlier, have larger clutches and heavier eggs and rear more and healthier youngsters to fledging. Young Kittiwakes leave the ledges in July to wander for three years over the North Atlantic before returning to the breeding colonies. An individual can live twenty years or more and attempt to breed fifteen or more times.

Many seabirds can live even longer than this, and it may be that quite a number of the Fulmars nesting this year were eggs when George VI was on the throne.

A species such as the Fulmar, which lays a single egg, obviously has a low potential annual productivity. Other layers of single eggs – Guillemot, Razorbill, Puffin, Gannet, Manx Shearwater, Storm Petrel – also have quite a long pre-breeding period, between four and seven years, but because they are long-lived, their lifetime productivity can be good. Indeed, with the excellent supply of food – chiefly sand-eels – which has been available off our coasts for the past ten or twenty years, some populations are showing an annual increase of 4–6 per cent.

Chris Mead

J. Watkins/FLPA

Manx Shearwater searching for its nest burrow at night

manages to catch and hold so many fish at one time, working as it does under the water, but perhaps its tongue and slightly serrated bill assist in this operation. I have counted as many as twenty-three small fish dropped from the beak of a single Puffin which I disturbed.

These fish are devoured raw by the chick, who thus passes far more waste than that other burrow nester, the shearwater. The burrow would become thoroughly insanitary within if the young Puffin did not soon learn to walk down the passage, turn round, and squirt its waste with some force into the open. This semicircle of grey-white guano at the entrance to a burrow is a sure advertisement of the youngster within.

The young Puffin grows fat rapidly. The feathers appear under the long straggling down in the third week, and in six weeeks from the time of hatching it is ready for the unpleasant but salutary event which then occurs. The adults stop feeding it; it is deserted suddenly and completely.

How long does the chick remain deserted? That I discovered by placing match sticks upright in the mouths of marked burrows containing Puffin chicks. The last visit of the adult was thus ascertained by the pushing inwards of the match sticks. By this means I found that desertion of the chick occurs on or about the fortieth day of its existence. The abandoned chick may then remain several days (up to a week) alone and fasting. Its unanswered hunger call – a feeble 'chip-chip-chip' – gradually ceases. It walks almost to the entrance of the burrow and squats there, well inside and retiring fully within on the slightest alarm. It will not venture out until the force which it has so far resisted – the force which we can call hunger, or thirst, for lack of a better understanding of its nature – at last moves it to take the seaward plunge.

To observe the behaviour at sea it was only necessary to take some of those young birds which had fallen at night into the garden. When dropped into the sea these youngsters would paddle with their feet, their wings half open upon the surface of the water. They would dive swiftly, swimming rapidly under water with easy, distinct strokes of their wings. They did not appear to use their feet when swimming thus, as far as I could see, but only used them in coming up to and swimming upon the surface. The average length of time spent under water was twenty-one seconds, the extremes nine and twenty-seven, while the intervals of resting on the surface were much shorter, averaging less than ten seconds. They seemed a little bewildered at first, and often swam near the shore as if they meant to land, but they soon appeared to get their bearings and make off straight to sea, proceeding by a series of dives with increasingly longer intervals of swimming upon the surface.

The desire to get far out into the ocean is very strong. Each morning in late July and August the night's contingent of young Puffins may be seen floating down with the currents in the sounds about the islands, but by the evening they have scattered and swum far out of sight offshore.

Until it has learned to fly with ease the fledgling escapes the gulls, which frequently swoop at it, by diving, and no doubt in the more hospitable underwater world soon obtains small fish with which to break its recent fast.

Puffins have little to fear from birdwatchers, who have a special fondness for them, but they need to keep a wary eye open for predators like the Great Skua, or bonxie. Seton Gordon came across this fearsome creature while searching for northern birds in wildest Scotland . . .

The voyager from Aberdeen or Leith to the Shetland Islands perhaps notices, while yet that island group is invisible, that a strange bird joins the seagulls following the steamer. The newcomer is a large, dark brown bird, with an area of white on either wing, and its flight is undistinguished, and apparently aimless, until a seagull swoops down and picks up a scrap of meat which has been dropped overboard by the cook. The Great Skua – for this is the name of the dark brown bird – which has been idly following the ship then shoots forward, like a racing car which is suddenly accelerated by its driver, overtakes the gull, and very soon forces it to drop or disgorge its prize.

There is something remarkable in the sudden speeding up of the Great Skua's flight and the impression is given of most formidable power in reserve. The Great Skua, or bonxie, as it is almost universally named in Shetland, is so powerful that even the Great Black-backed Gull is afraid of it. A light-keeper of the Out Skerries light told me that he had watched one day a bonxie deliberately murdering a Great Black-back on the rocks below the lighthouse, and I heard of a Great Skua which, on seeing a Great Black-backed Gull snatch a herring from the deck of a drifter in Lerwick Sound, swooped down, killed the Great Black-backed Gull with a single blow, swallowed the herring, then flew unperturbed away, as though slaying Great Black-backs was an everyday affair.

Martin B. Withers/FLPA

Portrait of 'a little man in evening dress' – the Puffin

W. Wisniewski/FLPA

Great Skua or bonxie

On the water below the great cliffs of Noss I saw another bird tragedy. East of Lerwick, chief port of Shetland, is Bressay Isle, and east of Bressay is the grassy isle of Noss, inhabited only by a shepherd. On its east face Noss is a sheer precipice, and the cliffs, 600ft high, appear even higher when viewed from the sea immediately below them.

It was on a July morning that my friend and I left Lerwick in a small open motor boat, and passed out through the Sound to the open sea to the north. In Lerwick harbour the scene was an animated one. Hundreds of herring drifters were moored to the quays, and to one another. Boats from Yarmouth and Lowestoft rubbed shoulders with Scottish craft from Peterhead, Fraserburgh and ports of the Moray Firth. Out in the Sound were anchored fishing craft from Holland and Norway, and there were fish-carriers from Germany and the Balkan States. At intervals, between misty showers, the sky over the sea was a deep blue.

We steered north through the entrance to the Sound, where many Fulmars were resting on the deep blue water or flying gracefully above the sea, and felt the lift of the north-easterly swell which broke white against Beosetter Holm and Score Head. Soon we had left Bressay astern and were sailing along the north coast of Noss. As we approached the great cliffs on the east side of that island we saw many birds ahead of us, and it was here that I realised first the reprehensible habits of the bonxie.

On the sea beneath the great precipice of Noss a bonxie was deliberately murdering a Kittiwake. Like a winged stoat, the Great Skua had attached itself to the victim's back and was eating away the flesh at the back of the neck while the Kittiwake flapped its wings despairingly, and attempted to rise from the water and throw off the deadly grip of its implacable enemy. We rescued the Kittiwake, but too late to save its life.

Martin B. Withers/FLPA

A fine shot of the Fulmar's tubenose bill

But not all seabird watching is quite so bloodthirsty. Edmund Selous wrote of the pleasures of leaning over the cliff-edge to watch the activity of seabird cities . . .

Oh, is there anything in life more piquant than to lie on the summit of a beetling cliff, and watch the breeding seafowl on the ledges below? In the Shetlands, at least, it is possible to do this in perfect safety, for the strata of the rock have often been tilted up to such an extent that, whilst the precipice formed by their broken edges is of the most fearful description, their slope, even on the landward side, is so steep that when one has climbed it, and flung oneself full length at the top, one's head looks down – as mine does now – as from a slanting wall, against which one's body leans. To fall over, one would first have to fall upwards, and the knowledge of this gives a feeling of security, without which one could hardly observe or take notes. The one danger lies in becoming abstracted and forgetting where one is. Those steep, green banks – for the rock, except in smooth, unclimbable patches, is covered with lush grass –

Marin B. Withers/FLPA

Shag with one newly-hatched chick – one to go

have no appearance of an edge, and I have often shuddered, whilst plodding mechanically upwards, to find myself but just awakened from a reverie, within a yard or so of their soft-curled, lap-like crests. But I think my 'subliminal', in such cases, was always pretty well on the watch, or – to adopt a more prosaic and now quite obsolete explanation – the reverie was not a very deep one.

At any rate, here I am safe, and, looking down again from my old 'coign of vantage' of two years before, the same wonderful and never forgotton – never-to-be-forgotten – sight presents itself. Here are the Guillemots, the same individual birds, standing – each in the old place, perhaps, if the truth were known – in long, gleaming rows and little salient clusters, equally conspicuous by their compact shape and vividly contrasted colouring; whilst both above and below them, on nests which look like some natural, tufted growth of the sheer, jagged rock, and which touch, or almost touch, one another, sit hundreds and hundreds of Kittiwakes, the soft bluey-grey and downier white of whose plumage, with their more yielding and accommodating outlines, make them as a tone and tinting of the rock itself, and delight with grace, as the others do with boldness. Seen from a distance all except the white is lost, and then they have the effect of snow, covering large surfaces of the hard, perpendicular rock. Nearer, they look like little nodules or bosses of snow projecting from a flatter and less pure ex-

Eric & David Hosking

The Fulmar – a master of flight

panse of it. An innumerable cry goes up, a vociferous, shrieking chorus, the sharp and ear-piercing treble to the deep, sombrous bass of the waves. The actual note is supposed to be imitated in the name of the bird, but to my own ear it much more resembles – to a degree, indeed, approaching exactitude – the words 'It's getting late!' uttered with a great emphasis on the 'late', – and repeated over and over again in a shrill, harsh, and discordant shriek. The effect – though this is far from being really the case – is as though the whole of the birds were shrieking out this remark at the same time. There is a constant clang and scream, an eternal harsh music – harmony in discord – through and above which, dominating it as an organ does lesser instruments – or like 'that deep and dreadful organ-pipe, the thunder' – there rolls, at intervals, one of the most extraordinary voices, surely, that ever issued from the throat of a bird: a rolling, rumbling volume of sound, so rough and deep, yet so full, grand, and sonorous, that it seemed as though the very cliffs were speaking – ending sometimes in something like a gruff laugh, or, as some will have it, a bark.

This marvellous note is the nuptial one of the Guillemot, or rather, it is that, swelled and multiplied by the echoes to which it gives rise, and which roll and mutter along the face of the precipice, and mingle with the dash of the waves. The effect is most striking when heard at a little distance, and especially across the chasm that divides one precipice from another. Under these circumstances it is less the actual cry itself than what, by such help, it becomes, that impresses one.

A seabird which has become common all round our coasts within the last few decades is the Fulmar, the nearest thing we have to an albatross. James Fisher made this 'his' bird, and he writes with transparent pleasure of its life. Although we tend to think romantically of seabirds patrolling the endless waves of the open sea, the fact is they spend a great part of the year close to their breeding sites . . .

On a still morning in early November some Fulmars come back to their ocean-facing cliff. In ones and twos they fly silently up and down the rock-face, occasionally gliding over the cliff-top and making an overland excursion of a few yards. A group of twenty settles on the calm sea a hundred yards from the cliff-foot; they growl and cackle. From time to time a Fulmar leaves the water-group and flies up to the cliff-face, to tour up and down. In the evening the wind gets up, and with it the sea; next morning the Fulmars have gone. A week later it is calm again, and they are back; this time one settles on a ledge for a few minutes. All through December the number of visitors increases, though all disappear whenever the weather is stormy; many now land on ledges, and visit each other, display and cackle on them; on a fine day the cliff is decorated with Fulmars alone, Fulmars in twos, and Fulmars (commonly) in threes. And so the situation continues; not long after Christmas, on a fine day when the temperature is nevertheless well

John Hawkins/Hosking

Fulmar nesting on Islay's sea-cliffs

John Hawkins/Hosking

Fulmars nesting on old buildings

Eric Hosking

A real bird island – Grassholm with its Gannet colony showing up white

below freezing-point, an observer may see some hundreds of Fulmars on the cliffs, perhaps as many as half or two-thirds of (and sometimes actually more than) the population at the peak of the previous breeding season.

The Fulmars continue to visit the cliff and occupy it in fine weather throughout February and March, with some further increase of number. In April the numbers increase more rapidly, and the amount of display and visiting becomes very great. By the end of April the population is at its highest, and all nest sites have been claimed; the cliff is alive with busy birds.

At the beginning of May the non-breeders begin to drop out of the population. On (but never before) 5 May the first egg is laid, and most of the birds lay their eggs between 20 and 29 May; a few delay laying until about 7 June or even later.

During May and June the birds of the pair share in the incubation of their egg. Some lose their egg, lay no replacement, hang about the colony for a week or a fortnight 'incubating' an empty nest, and then begin to moult their flight feathers (primaries) and tail and go away to sea. The population of adult Fulmars in occupation of the colony thus continues to drop. The first young hatch on about 24 June, though as late as 31 July some eggs may still be found. The young is tended continually by one or both parents until it is about a fortnight old. As time goes on it is left alone for longer and longer periods. The population of adults visible at any one visit to the colony continues to decline; after mid-July it is quite usual to find more young on the ledges than adults occupying nest sites or flying around. Adults that lose their young soon go into moult, go to sea, and do not return in that season.

The young begin to be entirely deserted by their parents in the middle of August, and themselves begin to fly from the ledges in the last ten days of that month. Young continue to fly in early September, most leaving the ledges in the first week of that month. Some are occasionally still on the ledges in mid-September, the latest date being 22 September. Though the adults have nearly all disappeared by the end of August, and though hardly any are found still tending young in September, a few may outstay the young on the ledges; on large British colonies what were believed to be adults have been seen until 1 October, and at St Kilda until 8 October. But a young or an adult Fulmar at a British colony after mid-September is quite unusual. Such is a general description of the cycle of the year at a largish British Fulmar colony.

Fulmars often nest on man-made sites, in Norfolk the boys of Gresham's School created nest-ledges for them on a cliff which offered no natural ledges. Other seabirds occasionally use artificial nest sites, but perhaps Kittiwakes are the most enthusiastic customers. They patronise windowsills, old jetties and seaside piers, and plaster their nests of flotsam, jetsam and seaweed to these unlikely sites . . .

As the nest is plate-sized, often with only air beneath it, the Kittiwake chicks are amongst the best behaved of young birds: one false step in the excitement of greeting a parent returning with food would be one too many. Kittiwakes call their name, and are deservedly popular, seeming from the safety of such inaccessible nests, not to mind birdwatchers who are fascinated by the noisy comings and goings.

Islands are often natural fenceless nature reserves. They can be the undisturbed home of countless thousands of seabirds, where the birds (as for centuries past) get on with their lives unmolested by man and in harmonic balance with their natural surroundings. And for small land birds, islands can be salvation. Many a tired migrant blown off-course by unfavourable winds or grounded by heavy rain or cloud, owes its survival to them.

Flight

Eric Hosking

White-fronted Geese flying in typical V-formation

Perhaps the most significant factor in our enjoyment of birds is their power of flight. There is more than a touch of envy in that enjoyment. How splendid it would be if we could climb effortlessly into the sky like a lark, to view the country round about! How convenient to take off for a season in the sun, when days shorten and the nights are chill! Birds seem able always to go where the living is good. Reality is less rosy, of course, but flight appears no less wonderful. It has given birds the chance to diversify and conquer the world. Arctic Terns pole-hop from the top of the globe to the bottom, enjoying a life of almost perpetual daylight. From the polar regions to the seemingly barren deserts, from the highest Himalayan peaks to the heart of the jungle and into the sea itself, from the caverns within the earth to the industrial wastelands and city centres, there are birds taking advantage of opportunites and looking for new ones. In sober truth, birds are not quite everywhere; they do not penetrate far underground or far below the surface of the sea but they explore caves and dive underwater about as far as we do ourselves – yet one more way in which bird behaviour parallels our own achievements.

Birds come in all shapes and sizes and follow many different life-styles. Most hunt by day, only a few by night. Some are vegetarian, some are carnivores, some eat anything they can get hold of, including other birds. Some walk after their food, some hop, some fly, some swim or dive for it. Each is specially equipped for its job. One way or another, anything which grows gets eaten. Fruits, nuts, seeds, leaves, living creatures or decaying matter, all are grist to someone's mill. But the major facility which allows them to flourish is their power of flight.

A flying bird has two problems, to keep up and to move forward, the latter normally needing the greater effort. When air passes over an object cambered in cross-section like a wing, a reaction is set up giving a force mainly upward (lift) and slightly backward (drag). Further force is needed if the winged object is both to keep up and to move forward, and this is supplied in aircraft by propellers and in birds by flapping the wings. Men in gliders and slow-soaring birds like vultures can, however, get the needed force from upcurrents, especially those caused by wind against steep slopes

190

Eric & David Hosking

A pack of Knots above their estuary feeding grounds

or by hot air rising from rocks or sand heated by the sun. In hot countries glider pilots seeking upcurrents often find themselves in company with eagles and vultures doing the same. Such soarers have wings that are extremely large in proportion to the body of such a shape that they fall through the air as slowly as possible. They move forward by losing height relative to the air, falling gently forward as it were, which they can afford to do when the air is rising at least as fast as they are sinking through it. To give a big lift a broad wing is needed, which means that the drag is also great, and the bird moves forward slowly, but that is how it seeks its prey, gliding at a height and scanning the ground below. Vultures, it may be added, are more efficient than human gliders because, in an emergence when air currents are failing, they can flap their wings to help them out.

A quite different type of gliding or sailing is found in albatrosses and to some extent in gulls, which have long narrow wings. In a narrow wing the drag is reduced, hence the bird can fly faster. The lift is also reduced, but since more lift is given when air flows faster past the wing, the bird can stay up so long as it is travelling fast. At sea in a strong wind, the air is moving more slowly close to the sea than higher up. An Albatross makes use of this by flying downwind in a long glide, losing height as slowly as possible; then, when it is near the surface of the sea, it turns and rises steeply into the wind, which brings it into an increasingly faster stream of air, hence its airspeed remains high though its speed relative to the sea is low. Provided that the wind is strong enough to give a big reduction in the speed of the air close to the water, an albatross can

Whooper Swans

Eric & David Hosking

191

maintain itself in this way without flapping. That is why albatrosses are found chiefly in regions of strong winds, notably the roaring forties, and the only one found in the doldrums, the Galapagos Albatross, often flaps its wings, which look broader than those of the other species.

Both the slow-soaring vultures and the fast-sailing albatrosses fly for long periods without beating their wings. At the other extreme, various birds beat their wings almost continuously when flying and rarely if ever glide. The swift is intermediate, as it usually beats the wings a few times in rapid succession, then glides for a few seconds, and then flaps again. Its narrow wings enable it to glide fast, but it cannot go far without losing height, so that each glide lasts

A migratory flight of Barnacle Geese

Arthur Christiansen/FLPA

only a short time. Many kinds of birds glide with the wings held rather above the horizontal, but in Swifts, as in certain petrels, the wings may be held a little below the horizontal, a position which gives greater speed and manoevrability but less stability. But stability is far less important in birds than aircraft, since when the need arises a bird can react much more quickly than a pilot.

Swifts, like most other birds, use upcurrents when they are available. On a windy day in a town they often utilise the rising gusts caused by the wind beating against walls, and they gently lift a wing to clear a roof, like a shearwater clearing a wave at sea. Swifts also hunt for food in the upcurrent on the windward side of a belt of trees, as already

THE MYSTERY OF BIRD MIGRATION

We have here more than enough to excite our wonder, and indeed are brought face to face with perhaps the greatest mystery which the whole animal kingdom presents – a mystery which attracted the attention of the earliest writers, and can in its chief point be no more explained by the modern man of science than by the simple-minded savage or the poet or prophet of antiquity. Some facts are almost universally known and have been the theme of comment in all ages and all lands. The hawk that stretches her wings towards the south is as familiar to the latest Nile-boat traveller or dweller on the Bosphorus as of old to the author of the book of Job. The autumnal thronging of myriads of waterfowl by the rivers of Asia is witnessed by the modern sportsman as it was of old by Homer. Anacreon welcomed the returning Swallow in numbers which his imitators of the colder north, to whom the associations connected with it are doubly strong, have tried in vain to excel. The Indian of the fur countries, in forming his rude calendar, names the recurring moons after the birds of passage whose arrival is coincident with their changes. But there is no need to multiply instances. The flow and ebb of the feathered tide has been sung by poets and discussed by philosophers, has given rise to proverbs and entered into popular superstitions, and yet we must say of it still that our 'ignorance is immense'.

Alfred Newton
Dictionary of Birds 1896

ON THIS DAY

18 APRIL 1939

By the spring of 1939 it was widely recognised that the outbreak of war could not be far away. Day after day, The Times carried news of measures being taken to meet an emergency

NATIONAL SERVICE FOR PIGEONS

'WIRELESS' DUTIES WITH RAF

A REGISTER OF BIRDS

A register of carrier pigeons for use in wartime is being compiled by the Air Ministry. The pigeons would be carried in RAF machines and used to convey messages if an aeroplane's wireless apparatus were put out of action. Since the War the RAF has maintained a pigeon service, and at Calshot and two centres overseas it breeds and trains carrier pigeons of its own.

During the crisis last September the Air Ministry received offers of pigeons from thousands of fanciers. All the offers were filed, and on this basis a national register is being prepared. Owners of pigeons seem keen to place them at the Government's disposal, and it is expected that about 500,000 of the birds will be available to play a part in national defence. That part might well be vitally important. With a moderate tail wind a good bird will fly at 1,600 yds a minute over 300 miles, and in highly favourable conditions speeds of over a mile a minute have been reached. The highest speed claimed for a carrier pigeon is a mile and a half a minute over 300 miles.

mentioned, and at times they rise in the updraught of an approaching thunderstorm. With a following wind on migration they may travel by drifting in circles, which again indicates the use of upcurrents. Under all these conditions, however, they alternate short glides with rapid wing-beats. They are not sustained gliders.

It is unfortunate that the same word 'wing' is applied to both bird and aircraft, since a bird's wing gives propulsion as well as lift, and so is equivalent in function to both the wing and the propeller of a flying machine. In flapping, the chief part is played by the outermost feathers, the primaries, as these are furthest from the body and so exert the greatest force as the wing moves downward. They are attached to the bones of the wrist and hand, which for greater strength are fused together, not separate as in man. Lift is provided chiefly by the inner feathers, the secondaries, which are closer to the body and are attached to the forearm. A songbird or pigeon has what might be termed a general-purpose flapping wing, the upper arm (humerus), forearm (ulna and radius) and hand (carpus) are of similar length, while the secondaries (giving lift) and the primaries (giving forward propulsion) occupy areas of equal size on the outstretched wing. In birds of this type propulsion comes from the downstroke, while in level flight the upstroke is effectively wasted, being merely a way of getting the primaries back into position for the next downstroke. On the upstroke the wing is partly folded at the wrist (carpal angle) and is turned edgeways on with the primaries partly open, little resistance is offered to the air and the wing moves up more or less of itself. Consequently the muscles used on the downstroke, the pectoralis major, are much larger than those used to raise the wing, the pectoralis minor, being in the ratio of nine to one in various songbirds. These flight muscles are attached to the keel of the breast-bone.

The details of the upstroke vary in different species, especially in the extent to which the wing is folded at the wrist, which is great in songbirds but less in long-winged birds such as gulls. Also the wing is raised more strongly at the moment of taking off than in level flight, and this is the time when the pectoralis minor muscles are chiefly used. A rising pigeon gives a rapid backward and upward flick of the wing-tip at the end of the upstroke, which produces an upward and forward force, but the bird can maintain this effort for only a few seconds at a time and in level flight the upstroke is not powered.

A powered upstroke also occurs in hummingbirds when they are hovering. The body is nearly vertical, so that the bird makes two sidestrokes rather than an upstroke and a downstroke. Both strokes are powered, the action being like that of a paddle, and the wings are winnowed at up to seventy-five times a second, a frequency within the range of our hearing, hence the hum. On the upstroke the wing remains fully extended with the primary feathers locked together, so that the action is quite different from that in most other birds, which bend the wing at the carpal angle and open the primaries. The hummingbird's wing consists almost entirely of the primary feathers, which are supported on the relatively large carpal bones, while the middle arm is short and the upper arm bone is extremely short and squat, which helps in the rapid rotation of the wing in winnowing. The wing has a shallow camber, which reduces the drag, and also helps when the wing is turned over on the upstroke. The pectoralis minor muscles used on the upstroke are nearly half the size of the pectoralis major, proportionately much larger than in any other type of bird, and the short narrow wing is effectively all propeller, giving amazing control. Thus a hummingbird can hover in front of a flower to suck nectar, keeping its position so accurately that it seems hung on a wire, and can then shoot off sideways too rapidly for the eye to follow it. Hummingbirds are also capable of extended flight, since one species regularly migrates across the Gulf of Mexico on a nonstop flight of at least 600 miles. The wing action in such continuous flight has not been studied.

The Swift has a long, narrow, swept-back wing with a shallow camber, clearly designed for high speed. It is much the smallest 'racing model' among birds, and since air resistance becomes proportionately more important the smaller the bird, a Swift is more finely designed for high speed than any other species. Its flickering wing-beats look peculiar and suggest that it may have an unusual wing action. This is probably so, for though the long recurved wings are similar in shape to those of a falcon, in structure they closely resemble those of a hummingbird. Thus as in a hummingbird, the long primary feathers make up most of the wing, with a short area of secondaries close to the body, while the carpal bones are relatively large and the upper arm bone is short and squat. As in a hummingbird, also, the primaries of the Swift are stiff and grip tightly together, so that they cannot be separated by the bird, and when the wing is fully extended, the outermost primaries are bent slightly backward and the inner ones are bent slightly forward by the tension. The breastbone has a remarkably deep keel for the attachment of the powerful flight muscles, which are dark red in colour indicating an efficient blood supply.

The power of flight allows birds to make themselves scarce when danger threatens. But far and away the most valuable facility it offers is the power to travel to more attractive feeding areas. When this activity involves a regular journey between seasonal breeding and wintering grounds it becomes migration. The habit of migration has been encouraged by the periodic changes in the extent of polar ice. When the polar ice-cap melts, new land slowly becomes exposed and birds quickly learn to follow the summer northwards, to the very edge of the ice . . .

The swift melting of the snows uncovers the wild fruits which the early winter preserved in its refrigerating grasp Billions of insects hatch out to enjoy the long hours of sun-

Arthur Christiansen/FLPA

Swifts in flight

Greylag Goose

Arthur Christiansen/FLPA

SHEARWATERS

We have watched the shearwaters swimming away, reluctant to rise from the smooth sea, their twin screws threshing the water with a beautiful easy motion. The tarsus is specially flattened for the purpose, presenting at each forward stroke a knife-edge to the water, and so reducing resistance. The thin toes, joined by semi-transparent webbing, collapse like a closed umbrella at this forward impulse of the feet, but at the backward stroke they open wide to lever the bird forward.

As the boat rides down on the sluggish birds the nearer ones half-open their wings and dive. I eagerly lean forward to watch their progress in the translucent depth. No doubt they will screw along tolerably well with their feet? But not a bit of it. The feet are not used – they are invisible, doubtless lying parallel with the tail; they are most out of the way there. Instead, each bird simply flies through the water. They have turned their wings into the paddles of the penguin, and are beating the water with a forward hooking motion. But, most interesting of all, the wings are not properly spread so that each quill feather shows. In so dense a medium that would be difficult, would present too great an area of resistance for the strong but slender flexed wing muscles. There are no air currents to help here. No, the wing is opened only as far as the wrist or carpal joint, the 'fingers' with the primaries remain closed to make a strong solid fin or flipper with which to beat a way through the water. Each beat drives the bird forwards and downwards, so that progress is by a series of jerks with the tail as rudder. And though the bird is said to feed largely when hovering in the air just above the surface of the sea you can imagine that it is not difficult for it to find a breakfast of small fishes under the surface too.

Only a few have dived, the rest turn their heads to meet the slight air from the north, and begin fluttering over the water. A slow-motion film would reveal fully what the eye can only just catch – the pounding of the surface of the water with the wing-tips, and the swift paddling with the feet. The birds run taxiing across the water, beating it noisily for some 30yd before they are able to get safely away on the wing.

The movement is contagious. It spreads through the assembly; the clatter of wings and feet is like the roar of a mountain stream in flood. The magic carpet slowly rolls upward from the sunset-tinged sea.

Once on the wing the shearwater is all grace as it glides, careening from side to side, now skimming the water for 50yd with one wing-tip, then rising to about 10ft above the surface, beating its wings once or twice or thrice to gain a fresh momentum, then skimming the sea for a similar distance with the other wing down.

There is here none of the swift simultaneous uprising and flight of other birds, such as notably the Teal. Your shearwater will not be easily hurried. The flock has risen slowly, and from end to end has taken a whole minute to establish itself on the wing. Now it whirls around us in a great circle, a living wheel of which our red sail is the hub. A spring of Teal would have dashed about us, simultaneously manoeuvring at a speed that might deceive us into supposing that theirs is a flight synchronised by some mysterious form of thought transference. But if the leisurely shearwater assembly is but a slow-motion film of the flying Teal, then we have the secret of so-called simultaneous flight-movement unravelled. It is after all only the old game of follow the leader. Those in front set the course and the long winding flock follows. I soon saw that some of the leaders dropped behind, or that more thrustful birds came forward and took up positions as pilots. In general the decision of the leading bird was followed by the rest, with exceptions to prove the rule – as when one bird ahead of the rest by several yards veered to the right, but those behind him led the flock in a glide to the left. Again, the assembly divided into several groups, and when we sailed back home it was then in three or four parts and, thus divided, had settled on the water again.

On another evening, with a fresh wind blowing from the south, we sailed again through the shearwater assembly. The sea was fairly rough and the broken water and the strong wind enabled the birds to rise from the surface without any taxiing. They were busily feeding on small crustacea floating near the surface, and to obtain these they were at times making short dives of two or three feet. Their sluggishness of the calm evenings was gone. They were lively and graceful, hovering at times like Kestrels, and dipping and diving as Kittiwakes do.

Later, like the Kittiwakes, they feed in this hovering, dipping manner on the shoals of sand-eels and small fry which fill the inshore sea on the tides of summer.

Ronald Lockley

light, and there is abundant food for the short period during which the migrants are able to nest and rear their young. Then winter swiftly returns and the birds fly south again.

It is generally true that the farther north a migratory bird breeds, the farther south it winters. Competition for breeding places and food drove the bird to migrate in the first place; and in flying south it passed over the central and equatorial areas already occupied by less mobile species, to winter far south in conditions similar to those of its breeding grounds. Familiar examples are the Golden Plover and the tern; while the British-breeding Swallow is an example of migration between two temperate areas: Britain and South Africa. There are, of course, many degrees of migration between, from seasonal movements within the British Isles, or within Europe and north Africa, down to the limited movements of more resident birds, and some birds do not migrate at all.

In Spitzbergen and Greenland and on Scottish mountains, Ptarmigan are resident, even through the severest winter. On Skokholm the Raven and some Rock Pipits and a few Great Black-backed and Herring Gulls are also sedentary throughout the year. Plainly they are dominant species and get enough food to live satisfactorily without migrating.

But if food and competition for nesting sites are the main incentives to the migration of less dominant and hardy species, this explanation only tells us why birds migrate. It does not tell us *how* birds are able to migrate, or what guides the bird on migration.

How does the young petrel or shearwater or Puffin, deserted by its parents, find its way to the wintering ground of its species alone?

How does the young warbler, living alone after its parents have started another brood or gone into moult, find its way unaided to its winter quarters in Africa? Most young birds move south before their parents, with the exception of the young Cuckoo which leaves the country some time in August and September, the adult Cuckoos having departed in July.

There is a plausible fable, still regarded as true in the minds of the average person one questions on the subject, that the old birds lead the way on migration. But as far back as Temminck there were ornithologists who knew otherwise. Temminck says that 'the young birds migrate apart from the old ones.' While Gätke of Heligoland wrote that he agreed with Temminck, but that 'the last ten to fifteen years have amply taught me what an almost hopeless task it is at first sight to oppose an opinion which has remained uncontested for centuries.'

You cannot live long on a small island without being aware that the young bird needs no adult to guide it along the traditional migration route, and that it actually initiates the first move southwards in the autumn. In fact it is safe to say that, always excepting the exceptional bird the Cuckoo and seabirds, the old fully adult breeding bird is the last to

An ancient ringing record

Before the start of 'modern' ringing, with each ring bearing not only a return address but also an individual identifying number, there were a number of experimental markings of birds. These ranged from threads tied to a Swallows' legs and coloured with water soluble dye to see whether it was washed off over the winter (it had not and so it was correctly concluded that they did not hibernate in the mud of ponds), to silver collars placed around the necks of herons and Cranes brought down unharmed by falconers' birds. Another example has recently come to light through David Smee, an Essex member of the BTO, who discovered the following passage in a local history book *Wherstead Territorial and Manorial* by F. Barnham Zincke published in 1893:

Some forty years ago one of the late Archdeacon Berner's keepers shot on Wolverstone ooze a heron with a brass plate on its leg which gave information that it had come from a certain heronry in Lincolnshire. The brass plate he returned to the gentleman who owned the heronry who replied that he was not surprised that one of his herons should be shot on the Orwell for not long previously one had been shot on the Danube not far from Vienna.

This Suffolk record, from about 1853, would not ▶

surprise current heron ringers too much as British herons regularly move to this extent. However, the record of a Lincolnshire bird in central Europe has never been repeated and, to the end of 1976, British-bred herons have only been reported from Holland (3), Belgium (7), France (45), Spain (8), Portugal (1) and Morocco (1). One wonders, but will never know, whether the Viennese record was genuine and if so, was it an aberrant individual or an indication that the movement of herons in the mid-nineteenth century were different from those we know today.

BTO News

leave the nesting area in the autumn just as it is the first to return to it in the spring.

Thus, as early as June, and until the end of July, considerable flocks of young Starlings in the conspicuously drab grey-brown plumage arrive on the Welsh island of Skokholm. The adults do not arrive until three months later. Young Willow Warblers in bright-yellow dress are to be seen from the end of June to the end of August, at which time the paler adults are caught in our migratory bird-traps. And juvenile White Wagtails precede the adults in autumn.

Young Wheatears and young Meadow Pipits, with a sprinkling of young Rock Pipits, are on the move then, though it is not easy to distinguish the true migrants from the island-bred youngsters. The adult Wheatears and pipits remain until after the majority of young birds of these species have moved on during August and September.

From these few observations it is clear that the young bird in migrating is acting as blindly, or shall we say – to cover up our ignorance – as instinctively, as the brainless caterpillar that lays a silk thread across a leaf and waits for the thread to dry and shrink and roll up the leaf so that it has a shelter in which to pupate; or as instinctively as the wasp which paralyses the living grub by stinging the nervous ganglia, and then places two such living but helpless grubs in a cell along with her egg. The egg and the living food are sealed up in a chamber of salivated dust or pulp and the wasp goes away to die.

There is no satisfactory answer to this problem of how the young bird migrates without an experienced leader. We only recognise that it does and that therefore it is an inherited ability, unreasoned and as natural as the act of a baby sucking at the breast. It is as automatically begun or 'released' by certain stimuli. In the case of birds the annual moult is an important factor. Most adult birds are in perfect plumage during migration: most young birds are in their first full plumage which they retain until midwinter. Adults (of land-birds) usually moult after nesting at their breeding grounds and are thus unable to migrate until their new plumage is acquired. But seabirds – whose habits are so different from land-birds – usually moult in their wintering grounds, eg petrels and shearwaters, Gannets and Puffins desert their young and go off to moult at sea in the autumn. Guillemots and Razorbills take their young with them to sea.

When I visited the bird observatory at Heligoland in autumn I was shown newly caught Redstarts in cages with perches electrically sensitised so that any activity of the bird was recorded on a tape which registered both the time and amount of the activity. In this way it was found that during the migratory season the Redstarts were restless and beat their wings for a certain number of hours at night. This illustrated vividly the powerful and automatic nature of the impulse to migrate. Other workers have successfully induced birds to sing and migrate at the wrong time of year by artificially stimulating them with light, food, and exercise.

The general principles of migration have been well understood since the earliest historical times. Yet, in some cases, as with Swallows for instance, enlightenment and belief in the astonishing truth came slowly . . .

Before migration, the Swallows join in mass gatherings. For a while after they have left the nest, the young birds roost in it at night, but in the early autumn they gather together to form communal roosts where enormous numbers twitter and chat before sleeping. At the edge of a lake or large pond, or alongside the higher reaches of an estuary, where the tall *Phragmites* reed grows, they flock at sunset and find an unoccupied stem to grasp for the night. The intensity of the singing is remarkable, and there's a general atmosphere of bonhomie. These gatherings are a prelude to long-distance migration, but until relatively recently the generally held belief of science was that the birds were preparing to emulate bats and hibernate for the winter. But instead of finding caves and secret holes like bats, the Swallows were said to be preparing to work their way down the reed stems into the water, and to snuggle into the soft mud under its surface, there to sleep away the winter. And while it is easy now to smile at this ignorance, it was never difficult to make a good case for the theory. Aristotle firmly believed that birds hibernated in holes in the ground, and gives it as fact that naked Swallows had been found in a comatose state, waiting only for the spring sun to warm them and clothe them with a new suit of feathers. Much later, in 1555, Olans Magnus, the king of Norway, writing about Swallows at their autumn reed-bed gatherings, said that 'They join bill to bill, wing to wing, and foot to foot, and after a most sweet singing fall down to pools and lakes, whence in the spring they receive a new resurrection.' As further proof of their watery hibernation, he told of fishermen bringing up torpid Swallows in their nets. In 1703 'A Person of Learning' vouchsafed that in fact the Swallows migrated – to the moon.

Ronald Thompson/FLPA

Powerful downbeat of the Swallow's flight

HERON DROPS IN ON HERMES

Men of the Royal Navy's Commando ship HMS *Hermes* are used to handling a variety of flying machines but mainly the helicopters used for transporting the Royal Marines Commandos. A surprise arrival on board *Hermes* during August when the ship was 500 miles east of Puerto Rico in the Caribbean came in the form of a Great Blue Heron *Ardea herodias*. This bird closely resembles our own Grey Heron *Ardea cinerea* which, together with *A. cocoi* of South America, comprise a super species. After spending two enjoyable days on the quarter deck feeding on pilchards the heron took its leave.

BTO News

J. C. Holland/BTO News

And yet another belief was that to assist their passage across the oceans each Swallow carried a liferaft in the shape of a little stick on which to take the occasional rest.

Late in the eighteenth century, in Gilbert White's time, naturalists were still not sure about the facts. One of the puzzling aspects of the case was that, while the great majority of the Swallows had disappeared from view by mid-October, nevertheless there were frequent sightings of both House Martins and Swallows well into November, and even December. How could these birds possibly build up the fat reserves required for a great journey of several thousands of miles? And, indeed, it seems highly likely that the greater part of these birds from third broods, hatching so late in the year, must perish on the journey. White felt that they might live in holes in the sea-cliffs, emerging in warm weather to hunt, in much the same way as bats. But nevertheless he felt sure that most Swallows migrated, while only a few remained, hidden, for the winter. The truth is that a very few Swallows do stay for the winter, though they certainly do not hibernate naked in muddy ponds, but face hard times and probable starvation. The number which overwinter successfully must be very small. Shortage of food compels the overwhelming majority to leave our shores in October.

The departure flight is triggered by shortening days with reduced light intensity and a fall in temperature.

Martins and Swallows massing on wires ready for their autumn migration

Many small migrants leave at night and we must watch for them feeding avidly to put on weight, laying down reserves of fat that fuel their migratory flights. Willow Warblers and Blackcaps will feast on elderberries and wild privet in coastal scrub, or gorge themselves on our garden honeysuckle, the berries supplying the sugary food they need to reach Africa south of the Sahara.

On coastal grasslands and marshes Yellow Wagtails feed amongst cattle and gather each evening to roost in reeds, while Wheatears flit ahead of the birdwatcher walking along the shingle. Africa will be host to some 70 million Yellow Wagtails, 120 million Wheatears and 900 million Willow Warblers from the north in the autumn!

Whereas Wheatears are in ones and twos, Sand Martins, House Martins and Swallows gather in much larger flocks. Sand Martins have suffered a drastic decline in recent years due to the African drought, and the flocks heading south will face difficult problems of survival in their wintering quarters, even if they survive their flight across the Mediterranean and the Sahara. They fly through Britain to the south-east, to reduce the sea crossing to France, then move south along the Biscay coast and on through Spain, a more westerly route than the one taken to return in spring. The routes taken are well documented by ringing recoveries, suggesting that our Sand Martins go to West Africa at first then move east along the southern edge of the Sahara as winter progresses.

Swallows are quite different, penetrating much further south to spend the winter in South Africa, even further south than those from the Continent of Europe. However many times we remarked on it, it still seems barely possible that the Swallows from the garden shed can fly to the far end of Africa, spend the winter there and then return to the very same shed next spring, using information programmed into each little head!

The bigger birds on the wires, where Swallows and martins line up before the off, are Turtle Doves. These small, delicate doves that purred from the hedgerows all summer long, now feed greedily in the fields to make themselves ready for the dangerous flight to the far side of the Sahara, where the land is less able to support them with each passing year of drought and degradation.

The Swallows may break ranks and fly up in a panic, circling tightly and calling endlessly in response to their greatest enemy – the Hobby. The Hobby is itself a summer visitor, that might one moment be dashing headlong into a group of martins and, the next, be seen lazily coasting towards the nearest headland to make the shortest possible sea crossing. Hobbies are only at all frequent in the south of Britain, but another migrant bird of prey breeds in the north – the Osprey.

Ospreys from Scotland or Scandinavia stop off at reservoirs and lakes, or by coastal marshes. They may be seen almost anywhere in Britain in autumn, sometimes hanging around for a few weeks before resuming their southward

Eric Hosking

Sand Martins preparing themselves for flight

Heady problems

Letters reporting recoveries are often inadequately addressed and get re-routed to the BTO in peculiar ways. A recent letter from Senegal, reporting a ringed Sandwich Tern, finally reached Beech Grove via the Tower Hamlets Inter-Agency Group for Alcoholic Services and Problems. An accompanying note suggested that the re-routing was not inappropriate since both organisations had clients with navigational problems!

The Osprey's immensely powerful wings . . .

Eric Hosking

journey. Ospreys have a broad-front migration, rather than being concentrated along narrow routes. Those from Scotland and Norway move to the extreme west of Africa, those from Sweden cross Denmark and France to winter further east, and those from Finland cross the eastern end of the Mediterranean to spend the winter in East Africa.

As well as the several species of wader that only move through our islands on passage, a few breed here and leave for the south each autumn. The Common Sandpiper is often seen on the shore as well as inland, but the Little Ringed Plover likes fresh water and is likely to be seen near shallow pools if it is spotted near the coast.

Flickering by offshore, the fast-flying, white shapes of Little Terns show that seabirds are moving too. The Terns will be heading for West Africa, but they can fly by day and feed on the way, even resting on the sea if they get tired. Compared with the tiny warblers, perhaps theirs is a much easier life.

For all of them, the north no longer has any attraction. Even at the expense of thousands of miles flown over seas, mountains and deserts, they will ultimately benefit from the extra food and warmth to be found in the south, and must respond to the inbuilt urge to be on their way before it is too late.

Yet as the summer visitors and the passage migrants leave

our shores fresh waves of visitors arrive to spend the winter with us . . .

The first Brambling or the first Fieldfare is a sign of the winter to come, just as much as the first Swallow is a sign of spring. With our natural preference to look forward to the long, warm days of summer, the symbols of the winter to come have claimed less of a place in our hearts than the eagerly awaited summer visitors. For the birdwatcher, however, the loss of the warblers, the Swallows and the terns is compensated by the arrival of hundreds of thousands of new, exciting birds from the north and east that seek a mild winter refuge in our islands.

There is something indefinable about the wild swans that makes them specially thrilling, be they Whoopers from Iceland or northern Scandinavia, or the smaller Bewick's from the far north of Siberia. It is always exciting to see a party of swans, wary and alert, and to confirm that they do have yellow-based bills, so must be one of these romantic visitors. They arrive in family parties, like geese, an added interest to the student of breeding biology who wishes to monitor their productivity from year to year.

Eric Hosking

. . . in effortless migratory flight

THE RINGING SCHEME

Eric Hosking

A ringed Marsh Sandpiper

Almost since the inception of the BTO, it has organised the National Bird Ringing Scheme. The essence of ringing is a uniquely numbered metal ring with a return address. The ring fits loosely round the bird's leg and there are sixteen sizes to fit each size of bird. Most of the rings issued by the BTO carry the address Brit Museum, London SW7. All letters reporting ringed birds are forwarded from there to the BTO at Tring.

The scale of ringing has increased over the years and currently about 2,000 ringers mark approximately three-quarters of a million birds each year. About 13,000 of these are subsequently reported to us but many thousands more are caught again at the site of ringing and provide much valuable information. Ringers are licensed through the BTO acting under the Wildlife and Countryside Act 1981. All have to undergo an extensive period of training before they become fully qualified.

Birds are caught for ringing in a wide variety of ways. Many, for example, are ringed as chicks before they are able to fly. This and a variety of traps were the most common techniques until the advent in the late fifties of mist-nets, set vertically to catch birds in flight. This technique has been largely responsible for the scale and value of the scheme at present.

BTO News

THE CARING, SHARING SWAN

Bewick's Swans are renowned for returning every year to their favourite wintering grounds in Britain and the Netherlands; in the spring, they once more undertake the arduous return journey to their breeding grounds in Arctic Russia. Most famous of all was Lancelot, who returned without fail every winter for twenty-three years to the Wildfowl Trust at Slimbridge, until 1986.

Bewick's apparently mate for life, but in the breeding grounds, young single birds and older birds who have lost their partners probably court and pair again. This creates a problem, though – there is a good chance that the male and female will favour different wintering grounds. So when winter comes, who decides where the pair will eventually end up?

Eileen Rees of the Wildfowl Trust has studied records of the overwintering Bewick's Swans at Slimbridge to determine who wears the trousers in the Bewick's Swans' household.

Each bird is identified by the unique pattern of black and yellow on its beak and is given a name; and each year the time of arrival and departure of the swans is recorded, along with any changes of partners from previous years.

Rees found that a male was more likely to return to his wintering grounds after pairing or re-pairing with a female on the breeding grounds. Swans encourage their mates to fly with them, using pre-flight display which includes pumping the head and neck and making a special contact call. As a result, females are more likely to shift their arrival time at the wintering grounds to coincide with their mate's. Females which go it alone are less likely to achieve a dominant position in the social hierarchy, and to obtain the best feeding and roosting sites. Lancelot returned to Slimbridge at the same time of year with three different mates during his life, demonstrating that the winter holiday is the male's decision. But come the spring, the tables are turned, and it appears to be the female who decides to return to Arctic Russia to breed.

The shift of responsibility within the pair may, perhaps, be affected by day-length – the males decide to migrate south as the days get shorter and the females migrate north again as the days become longer. What is not known yet is whether the females return to their favourite nesting sites. The long-term stability of Bewick's Swans' relationships seems to thrive on the sharing of these important decisions.

Andrew Kitchener

Geese have a special aura about them, charismatic birds from wild parts of the world finding our estuaries, marshes and pastures rich sources of food during the dark days of winter. Brent Geese come mainly from Siberia, though the pale-bellied race flies to Ireland from the Canadian Arctic. Barnacles from Greenland make landfall on Islay and other western isles off Scotland and Ireland while all those from Svalbard (Spitsbergen), head for the Solway Firth. The Pink-footed Geese that spend the winter in Scotland and north-west England come from Iceland, the land of ice and fire, to live most of their lives on our green and brown fields.

Wigeon breed in Britain in very small numbers but the thousands that winter on our coasts and floods come from a vast area of northern Europe and Asia and fly prodigious distances to reach such ideal wintering sites as the Ouse Washes and the East Anglian coasts. Many other ducks, like Teal, Shoveler and Pintail, also undertake enormous journeys, the equal of many of the summer visitors which reach us from Africa.

British and Irish estuaries have a special place in the world of birds: the warm seas that surround us keep our islands frost-free for much of the winter when continental coasts may be iced-up for weeks on end. Naturally, we receive wading birds from the north and east in vast numbers. The Knot breeds in the extreme north of Siberia, in east Greenland and in the Canadian Arctic, and either spends the winter in Britain or passes through in autumn and spring en route to and from Africa. Because Knots breed in the twenty-four hour long summer days of the high Arctic where the minimum length of time is needed to finish the cycle from eggs to fledged young, most of their life is spent here rather than where they nest. They migrate very quickly – some ringed in Britain have been found in west Africa within two weeks.

Grey Plovers visit our shores, not in the dense packs of the Knots but more loosely scattered, mixed in with Godwits, Dunlins and Curlews. As the tide rises the birds gather on the tops of beaches to roost, in the same positions each year. The Jack Snipe, a thinly spread visitor from Scandinavia, crouches in wet vegetation, out of sight until practically trodden on.

Out on the beach the gulls mostly come from far away – the Black-headed Gulls mainly from the Baltic countries – and with them may be the odd exciting rarity such as a Glaucous Gull, beautiful in adult grey and white, or eyecatching in pale, creamy immature plumage.

Near the shore, in the shelter of bushes, hedgerows or out on the fields, a variety of new arrivals feed greedily to replace the energy used up in the nocturnal flight across the sea. Fieldfares and Redwings search for berries, while tiny Goldcrests give the thick scrub a minute examination. Many are totally exhausted and, if the weather turned bad during their crossing, many more will have perished at sea.

Bramblings join flocks of other finches and sparrows in the fields before moving inland; Snow Buntings, already moving in a flurry along the shore will stay on the beach all winter. Few birds are more evocative of chill winter days than these 'snowflakes'.

A really good find comes our way once in a while like a splendid Great Grey Shrike perched high at the very top of a bush or tree, on the look-out for small birds, small mammals or big insects. It is a reminder that winter brings its own special rewards, as good in their way as the much-loved migrants of summer.

Genesis

After forty days Noah opened the trap-door that he had made in the ark, and released a Raven to see whether the water had subsided, but the bird continued flying to and fro until the water on the earth had dried up. Noah waited for seven days, and then he released a dove from the ark to see whether the water on the earth had subsided further. But the dove found no place where she could settle, and so she came back to him in the ark, because there was water over the whole surface of the earth. Noah stretched out his hand, caught her and took her into the ark. He waited another seven days and again released the dove from the ark. She came back to him towards evening with a newly plucked olive leaf in her beak. Then Noah knew for certain that the water on the earth had subsided still further.

ACKNOWLEDGEMENTS

I should like to record my gratitude to Eric and David Hosking, the Frank Lane Picture Agency and to Brian Hawkes for their splendid photographs. Also the editors of the RSPB's *Birds* magazine, BBC *Wildlife*, *British Birds* and the British Trust for Ornithology's *BTO News*. For kind permission to quote from their works, I acknowledge also:

E. A. Armstrong, *The Wren*, Collins (1955), 156

Ursula Brighouse, 'On Safari', *Devon Birds*, 108-9

Jeffery Boswall, 'A Comic Turn', *BTO News*, 44

John Burton, 'Field Outings', *Bird Notes*, 17-26

John Busby, *Drawing Birds*, RSPB (1986), 140-1

Bruce Campbell, *Birdwatcher at Large*, 20

William Condry, 'Autumn Tide', *Birds*, 48-51

Joy Crawshaw, 'Kestrels in the Cathedral', *Birds*, 80-1

Peter Davis, 'Gardening for Birds', *BTO News*, 94-6

Peter Davis, 'Paddling Passerines', *BTO News*, 148

Eric Ennion, *The House on the Shore*, Routledge & Kegan Paul (1960), 137-49

Grey of Fallodon, *The Charm of Birds*, Hodder & Stoughton (1927), 124-37

James Fisher, *The Fulmar*, Collins (1952), 186-9

Jim Flegg, *The Observer Island Britain*, Macdonald (1982), 176-8, 189

David Glue, 'To Feed or Not to Feed', *BTO News*, 124

Peter Goodfellow, 'Twitching in Norfolk', *Devon Birds*, 42-3

Derek Goodwin, 'For Ever or a Day', *Birds*, 60-4

Seton Gordon, *In Search of Northern Birds*; RSPB in association with Eyre & Spottiswoode (1941), 152, 156-7, 183-4

Mike Harris, 'In Memoriam', *BTO News*

Peter Hope-Jones, 'Counting Guillemots', *Birds*, 172

Len Howard, *Birds as Individuals*, Collins (1952), 87, 89, 128, 160

Rob Hume, 'Festive Food', *Birds*, 102-4

Rob Hume, 'Migrants', Birds, 201-5

H. G. Hurrell, 'Bird Stowaways', *Devon Birds*, 174

Julian Huxley, *Birdwatching and Bird Behaviour*, 51

John Jones, 'The Big Day', *Devon Birds*, 34-8

Clare Kipps, *Sold for a Farthing*, Frederick Muller, 129

Andrew Kitchener, 'The Caring Swan', *BBC Wildlife*, 204

Maxwell Knight, *Bird Gardening*, Routledge & Kegan Paul (1954), 129-37, 146

David Lack, *Swifts in a Tower*, Methuen (1956), 190-8

Dennis Lendrem, 'In the Wink of an Eye', *Birds*, 150

R. M. Lockley, *Letters from Skokholm*, J & M Dent (1947), 179-83, 195-8

R. M. Lockley, *Shearwaters*, Dent (1942), 196

Richard Mabey, 'Luminous Owls', *BBC Wildlife*, 164-5

H. J. Massingham, *An Englishman's Year*, 58

Chris Mead, *Robins*, Whitter Books (1984), 61, 68, 94, 134

Chris Mead, 'Goldeneye', *BBC Wildlife*, 93

Chris Mead, 'Tenement Dwellers', *BBC Wildlife*, 180

Col R. Meinertzhagen, *Pirates & Predators*, Oliver & Boyd (1959), 100

Richard Millington, *A Twitcher's Diary*, Blandford (1981), 36-37

Edmund Selous, *The Birdwatcher in The Shetland's*, Dent (1905), 184-86

David Sexton, 'Operation Sea-Eagle', *Birds*, 185

Eric Simms, 'Country Cousins', *Birds*, 26-30

Dorothy Underhill, 'Rather a Lot to Swallow', *Devon Birds*, 70

Brian Unwin, 'Football Birding', *Sunderland Journal*, 45-8

Tom Wall, 'Orange Blue Tit', *BTO News*, 110

Dave Webb, 'The Big Day', *Birds*, 38-42

Diane Williams, 'Festive Fare', *Birds*, 122-3

Kenneth Williamson, 'Habitat is Everywhere', *BTO News*, 16

Douglas Willis, 'Classroom Ornithology', *Birds Magazine* Summer 79, 13-16

Pip & Eve Willson, 'Hazards of Feeding', *BTO News*, 107